Franz Schubert;

and

his times

"However beautiful and varied the harvest Time may have in store for us, it will not bring us another Schubert."—
ROBERT SCHUMANN.

Franz Schubert
By Leopold Kupelwieser

Franz Schubert;

and his times,

by

Karl Kobald

TRANSLATED FROM THE GERMAN BY

BEATRICE MARSHALL

KENNIKAT PRESS
Port Washington, N. Y./London

FRANZ SCHUBERT

First published in 1928
Reissued in 1970 by Kennikat Press
Library of Congress Catalog Card No: 70-102840
SBN 8046-0756-7

Manufactured by Taylor Publishing Company   Dallas, Texas

Preface

MANY books have been devoted to Schubert's life and
works. Among the most exhaustive are the biographies
of Kreissle von Hellborn, Walter Dahn, and the great
work of reference, " Schubert, die Dokumente seines Leben und
Schaffen," by that admirable and praiseworthy Schubert student
and inquirer, Otto Erich Deutsch. The present book is a *résumé*
of other writings on the subject by the same author, and is meant
to be a supplementary contribution towards the solution of the
insoluble Schubert problem. It does not boast an array of new
biographical material such as has been sufficiently exploited in other
works, but its object is, by means of picturing the *milieu* in which he
lived, to throw new light on a figure which more than any other is
representative of Viennese art and culture.

Schubert, reflected in the mirror of his time, is the theme of this
book, which should be accepted as a book essentially characteristic
of Austria's domestic life—in short, a Viennese Schubert book.
May it promote in ever-widening circles a love and appreciation of
his work, and a more intimate knowledge of the wealth of beauty
and melody with which the Master's genius has enriched the world
in the sense of a memorable utterance of Nietzsche's :

" Franz Schubert, a lesser artist maybe than some other great
masters, but of them all, endowed with the most abounding heritage
of music. He expended it with a generous heart and a lavish hand,
so that musicians for a hundred years to come will nourish themselves on his thoughts and ideas."

Contents

The Illustrations

NOTE

The translations of the poems on pages 91,
100, 118, 258 *and* 276, *were made by*

ETHEL TALBOT SCHEFFAUER

The Vienna of "Biedermeier" *

AN eminent English man of letters, Sir William Henry Hadow, Vice-Chancellor of the University of Sheffield and editor of the great "Oxford History of Music," has said that if he were asked to name the three greatest artistic periods of the world's history, he would place first—Periclean Athens, second Elizabethan England, and third, without any hesitation, the Vienna of the second half of the eighteenth and the first quarter of the nineteenth century. Those who are in agreement with this opinion may go further and add that in some respects the highest point of this golden Viennese age was reached in what is known as the *Biedermeier* period, when Vienna harboured a galaxy of genius in every branch of art, in poetry, painting, the drama and music, the like of which is only met with in the most brilliant flowering epochs of human culture. It was the Vienna of Beethoven, Schubert, Raimund and Grillparzer ; the days when the youthful Grillparzer gathered the first ripe fruit in the garden of the tragic muse, when the art of the people blossomed forth in the *Vorstadt* in the fairy plays of Raimund and the dances of Lanner and Strauss. It was the time when the poets Bauernfeld, Lenau, Stifter, Nestroy, the painters Schwind, Waldmüller, Dannhauser and Führich were young, when the small Burgtheater under Schreyvogel's management rose, from an artistic point of view, to the first rank among German theatres, and it was the time of the Karntnertortheater's dazzling glory. Those days, too, were the last years of Beethoven, when the master, deaf and disabled from playing any part in society, withdrew more and more into himself, and, escaping from the sordid cares and the suffering of this mortal life, took refuge in the

---

* Biedermeier was originally a comic figure whose verses, *Biedermeier-lieder*, first appeared in the *Fliegende Blatter*. His name, used to denote an honest, ingenuous kind of Philistine, became proverbial. It was given to a period—*Biedermeierzeit*—when people with simple tastes cultivated music and art inexpensively. . . . To-day it is associated with *Biedermeierstil, i.e.*, Chippendale furniture, polished floors, decorations of true lovers' knots and garlands of roses, and dresses with full skirts and flounces.—*Translator*.

sublime temples of the imagination, where reigned an atmosphere
of divine joyousness and beauty. Above all, it was the Viennese
Schubert time. The soul of this period is revealed to us in old
pictures and prints, its fragrance lingers on in antique interiors,
in faded letters and diaries. In its poetry we hear its echo,
and most wonderfully of all it comes to us in music. That
old far-off Wien, with its green glacis and bastions, seems like a
symphony of vibrating stones. The artists, the poets, the actors,
the painters, all seem in some way or other connected with the
music and to have drawn the inspiration for their best creations
from music's inexhaustible fount. Music was task-mistress and
queen to Grillparzer, who, in the sad history of the poor " Spielmann," had written the finest of all Austrian narratives :

> " Mit der strahlinden Herrscherkrone
> Mit dem lieblich tönnenden Munde
> Und dem Wahnsinn sprühenden Blick
> Schwingend das zarte Plektron.

Lenau and the fiddle were inseparable companions. With the
spirit of melancholy the instrument accompanied him through life.
The feverish passion which throbbed in his blood and nerves found
expression on the strings in uncontrolled frenzies of wildest
fantasy. When this youth, wandering over the Hungarian steppes,
came to a village inn and played with irresistible *élan* the march of
the rebel Rakoci, the peasants and gypsies flocked round the
young poet, kissed the hem of his coat, carried him on their
shoulders and fêted him as if he had been a gypsy potentate. His
loveliest poems—" Die Werbung," " Heideschenke," and " Die
drei Zigeuner "—gushed forth from his soul, as did the music of
his fiery fantasias from the fiddle. Already on the threshold of
madness, he fiddled in wild abandon his own Dance of Death.

" When I look around me," said Beethoven to Bettina Brentano,
the Sybil of the German Romantic movement, " I can't help
sighing. For what I see is against all my cherished religion, and I
must despise the world which has no conception of the truth that
music is a higher revelation than all the wisdom of all the philosophers. She is the wine that inspires ever anew, and I am the
Bacchus who taps this glorious nectar for men and makes them
spiritually drunk."

The musical soul of the city, in its most Viennese form, sounds from the works of Franz Schubert. He was the musical genius of that time ; his life and work reflect, as in a dream, the grace, the charm, the poetry and romance which were woven then into the town's very vitals. Schubert's music signifies the embodiment of the *genius loci* of the antique Biedermeieren Vienna. Its joys and sorrows, laughter and tears, love and suffering, breathe through his music.

The old, beloved, immortal WIEN, whose immortal singer Schubert was, greets us in his melodies.

We learn from study of the history of art that the greatest artists owe even their most individual characteristics to the influence of their *milieu*, that their life, development and creations stand in close relation to their contemporaries, that their work, in fact, mirrors the world in which they lived, and which has helped to form their thought and mentality. Thus to understand Schubert the man and the artist means getting a clear grasp of the time in which he lived and worked. To fathom the secret of his life and great creative work means to penetrate into the *milieu* in which his existence was passed, into the heart of the character of ancient Vienna, and into the art and culture of the Wiener *Biedermeier* period.

Those were the years when the intoxicating *finale* of the Napoleonic era, the Congress of Vienna, that settled the most important questions for the future of Europe to the sound of music in a whirl of festivities, dances and theatricals, had died away. After a period which had lasted a quarter of a century of terrific struggle, which had nearly exhausted the strength of the Hapsburg Empire and its capital, peace was at last signed. The stormy wave of the French Revolution, with its exalted ideas of freedom, had subsided, casting up a few pearls, but more slime and wreckage, on the shores of the Danube metropolis.

Metternich's reactionary—but, in his own estimation, God-sent policy had come off victor in the conflict against the Revolution. The idea of a centralised State in Middle Europe, threatened by the Corsican, was politically and dynastically saved. The Viennese population was sick and tired of the ravages of war-time, and longed for the return of a patriarchal *régime* which would ensure peace and plenty and a revival of trade. The outgoing epoch had through the genius of Napoleon Bonaparte in politics been martial and heroic, and in art was represented by the Titan, Beethoven.

Now was to follow a time of peace and spiritual intercourse at home, a development of citizenship combined with romanticism. If the object of Metternich's reactionary policy had been the suppression of the ideas which Europe had revolutionised, so the conception of freedom of humanity, the dæmonic power of creative genius, took flight into the spacious domain of art.

Vienna now experienced a second blossoming period of culture. It resembled a spring aftermath of that ancient Austrian art which had its first spring in the time of Gothic architecture and the poesie of a Walter von der Vogelweide. One can see its glories in the architecture of the St. Stephankirche in Vienna, in the St. Wolfganger altar-piece of Michael Pacher, in endless monuments, pictures and carvings. It shone forth in the high summer of the Baroque period in the building of magnificent monasteries and noble palaces, in an abundance of artistic pillared temples and mausoleums, in the brilliance of fantastic coloured frescoes, in gay operas, in the music of Glück, Haydn and Mozart.

It was like the swan song of an ancient culture, a culture which subconsciously felt that a great epoch in the world's history was slowly dying, and so fell back on itself to form a new and increasingly artistic method of life by the cultivation of local powers and in the deepening and refining of the individual personality.

At that time, the more political thought threatened to asphyxiate in materialism the more the town, struggling nobly towards the highest, turned for distraction to the arts, the theatre, painting, music, literature. Vienna, already known of old as the centre of the world in music, became the most zealous cultivator of the fine arts in Europe. Let us contemplate next the blossoming period of the Viennese theatre. Let us mount the car of Thespis and enter the Viennese Temple of Thalia. Here the new ideas of humanity, the beauty and harmony of new creative thoughts and feelings had kindled on the far horizon the light of a great and wonderful mystery. It is true that the promotion of the Burgtheater to the rank of Court and national theatre was the Kaiser Josef II's embodiment of an ideal of giving happiness to the people. Not in Austria, hitherto, or in Vienna during the classical era, had German literature produced any remarkable figure, nor had the theatre played any leading *rôle*. The task Kaiser Josef set himself was to raise the play to a high level of excellence. He found in Sonnenfels the man who by word and deed could work for the fulfilment of his lofty ideals. The pantaloon was banished from the Kärntnertortheater; a limit was set to French productions and Italian opera. German pieces and German translations of foreign masterpieces were frequently given. The court stage became, according to the Kaiser's desire, a German national theatre. The great Schröder came to Vienna. Shakespeare and German classics were performed, and Mozart was introduced on the stage. The new direction taken by the Burgtheater was during the Biedermeier time, which coincided with the entry on the scene and activity of Josef Schreyvogel, who first came into prominence as an antique art dealer and editor of a much-read and improving Sunday paper, a mine of " erudition, philosophy and views on art and life." He obtained a post at the Court, and, through the influence of two artist friends, the distinguished Chevalier Moritz, Count Dietrichstein, and the musical Ignaz Mosel, was appointed manager of the Burg-theater as dramaturgist with the title of *Hofsecretär.*

Schreyvogel had several officials over him, and was never called Director or Intendant, but he was actually the organiser and leading spirit of the Burgtheater movement. To his indefatigable energy, to his genius and his leading position in German dramatic art, the Burgtheater owed its world-wide historic reputation as the most famous of German stages. " He was," as Bauernfeld wrote, " a serious man of sterling character, with knowledge, judgment and taste. In business, rectitude itself; dependable, impartial, and his nature foreign to all intrigue."

The repertory was his foremost achievement. He gathered it together with caution and discrimination, not without coming into fierce conflict with the Censor, and even with the Court Chamberlain. If sometimes he was a little too domineering and outspoken, the well-meaning, good-natured *Theaterhofrat* Mosel acted as conciliatory mediator and made peace. As dramaturgist, in the distribution of parts he was equally fair and discerning. He never showed favouritism, and talent was his only criterion. He conducted the rehearsal of new pieces himself, aiming always at a harmonious *ensemble* according to the author's style and ideas, without insisting too strongly on detail, though here and there he would suggest a *nuance.* He would discuss leading parts with the artists, and was not sparing with æsthetic and historical hints. In the case of finished actors, he left the individualising of a character to their own discretion, as anything like interference or fault-finding or a school-masterish tone would naturally have been resented, and with justice, by those who were conscious of their artistic powers. But beginners, on the contrary, had to be drilled in elocution, mimicry, walk and carriage. Neither were the pupils to be suddenly plunged into new and difficult parts for which they were not yet equal, but gradually trained to test their capabilities and exercise their powers in smaller *rôles*. Schreyvogel adopted this method with the young Fichtner, whom he took over in the year 1824 from the Theater-an-der-Wien. He constantly associated with him, allowed him to visit the theatre daily, made him take notice of the acting of others, especially of the consummately elegant Korn, in whose footsteps the novice was advised to follow. It was a long time before he entrusted him with an important part. Fichtner rose quickly from *rôle* to *rôle*, but when he had become a perfected master he never made any disguise of what he owed to the coaching of his older colleague.

None of the great names in German literature were missing from the repertory of the Burgtheater. After prolonged battles with the Censor authorities, Schreyvogel engineered the first perform-ances of Schiller's " Wallenstein " and " Tell." Schiller hence-forth took a commanding place in the Burgtheater programmes. The most distinguished foreign authors were also represented, especially Shakespeare, whose works Schreyvogel adapted for the German stage. Calderon and Moreto were included in the reper-tory. Schreyvogel's greatest service was the discovery and bringing out of Grillparzer. In the year 1816, as Bauernfeld relates, he became acquainted with the shy young Grillparzer, who confided to him the scheme of his " Ahnfrau," and showed him the first act. Schreyvogel warmly encouraged the young author, and he talked over with him the *dénouement* of the tragedy, and in these discussions the critic was able to infuse into the poet many of his own ideas. A few weeks later the piece was produced.

" The actors," Grillparzer wrote, " are delighted with their parts. When I appeared at the rehearsals I was hailed as a young demi-god, in spite of my threadbare, shabby overcoat. Thanks to the efforts of the Court actress, Madame Schröder, and the actor Lange, who appeared as guests in the principal parts, the play was more brilliantly performed here than it has ever been anywhere

Franz Grillparzer
Pencil drawing by Goebel, 1823
(Dr. August Heymann's Collection)

else on the German stage. . . ." It was first given at the Theater-
an-der-Wien. Not till later was it included in the Burgtheater
repertory with Heurteur as the hero and Sophie Schröder as the
heroine. "I was presented by the Beneficiare (Madame Schröder)
with three free seats in the upper circle," the poet relates with
regard to the first night of the play. "I occupied these with my
mother and my small brother of 12 years old. Although the
performance was first-rate, it made a most revolting impression on
me . . . it was like a hideous nightmare. I made a resolution
there and then never again to be present at the performance of
any other of my pieces, a resolution to which I have held to this
day. The conduct of my family on the occasion was not a little
extraordinary. I myself unconsciously recited the whole play
while it was going on in a whisper. My mother, with her back
to the stage, regarded me with dismay and exclaimed : ' For God's
sake, Franz, be quiet, are you mad ? ' My brother was on his
knees, praying fervently that the play might be a success." For
the third performance the theatre was sold out. The piece took
Vienna by storm. The whole town talked of nothing but the
"Ahnfrau," and the discovery of the young dramatist was the chief
topic of conversation for a long time to come.

The first performance at the Burgtheater of "Sappho" on
April 21st, 1818, caused even greater excitement and the wildest
enthusiasm. "' Sappho,' " Schreyvogel wrote at the time in his
diary, "is a grand success, especially in the first three acts, and has
been received with extraordinary applause. At the end there was
no stemming it, and the author was called for. The young man's
fortune is made." And Gressinger wrote to Böttiger : ". . . In
case you didn't get my letter, I must write again to inform you of
the wonderful reception given to Grillparzer's ' Sappho ' at the
Imperial Burgtheater. It brought down the house. At the end
of the third act, which ends in such an interesting manner, the
clapping and calls for the author lasted during the whole interval,
so that one couldn't hear the music. What a marvellous effect is
gained with little scenery and only a few characters. The author,
partly from modesty and partly because he is a clerk in the Civil
Service, would not appear before the curtain. Schröder as
Sappho and Korn as Phaon acted to perfection."

"Dear young friend," Sophie Schröder is said to have asked the
author, " where have you learnt to probe so deeply into a woman's

heart ? Few parts that I have played have touched me so nearly as your Sappho."

Vienna acquired in Grillparzer her greatest dramatist. An Augustan age for Austrian poesie was thus inaugurated, and new life poured into the dried-up receptive faculties of *blasé* playgoers. The young poet became the sensation of the town.

"Great personages busy themselves," Schreyvogel remarked, "with the author of ' Sappho.' Here are Metternich and Stadion summoning him to an interview, and some trade magnates talk of founding a company for him."

The authoress, Karoline Pichler, whose salon at the time was the rendezvous of the most celebrated representatives of the arts and sciences, invited him to one of her reunions, and Schreyvogel presented his young *protégé*.

"Never shall I forget," she records in true Biedermeier language, "the evening and the favourable impression that his appearance made. Grillparzer cannot be called handsome, but he has a slight figure, above the average height, beautiful blue eyes which give his pale features an intellectual cast, and a mass of ash-blond curls. One would notice with admiration such an exterior even if one did not know the name of its owner, and his possession of a highly-cultivated mind and noble nature. Everyone at our little gathering in the garden that evening was equally impressed, and the young poet must have felt himself here in congenial company, for he came afterwards to see us more and more frequently during the winter. . . ." And again she writes : " Grillparzer from the first seems to have felt at home with us. He came as our guest to dinner nearly every Tuesday and Wednesday and often on Sundays, and stayed sometimes the whole afternoon and evening playing duets with my daughter. He played the piano very well, and improvised with talent and taste. His gifted mind, his simplicity and frankness won our hearts, and the attraction seemed to be mutual, for he responded warmly to our friendly overtures. He told us about his young days, confided to us his plans, and many of his little poems had their origin in his visits to our house. For example, ' Das Gespräch in der Bildergalerie ' and the beautiful ' Frühlingsgesspräch ' which soon after came out in the ' Aglaja.' "

Grillparzer's works give us insight into the artistic receptivity of the Viennese in those days. They were not greatly moved by the tragic end to " King Lear; " Kleist's " Prince of Homburg "

left them cold, but in the tragedy of Grillparzer they found themselves in their element.   Here was their own flesh and blood, here
the landscape of their native soil, here lived and breathed the same
spirit that lived in them.   Whether or no Sappho and Hero,
Medea, Kreusa, Melitta, or Esther were classical names, the
figures called by these names belonged to their own sphere, were
to them dear and sympathetic because they had sprung from the
Viennese earth, the Viennese life.   Something of the colour and
melody of the old Baroque theatricality, its sensuousness and
careless art, tinge Grillparzer's works, and his genius was drawn
towards the romanticism which in Catholic Vienna found an
echo in the Spanish dramatists.   What Grillparzer owed to
Schreyvogel, under whose direction "Das Goldene Flies,"
"König Ottakars Glück und Ende," "Ein treuer Diener seines
Herrn" were produced at the Burgtheater, we are told in his
own words, on the death of Schreyvogel in 1832 : " Now he
is gone there is no one left in Vienna with whom I can converse
on artistic questions."   And the two other successful Burgtheater writers, Bauernfeld and Zedlitz, also held Schreyvogel in
grateful memory.   The latter not only knew how to win new
authors to help raise the standard of the Burgtheater repertory to
dazzling heights, but he was to the actors an inspiring leader,
educator and adviser.   Always on the look-out to engage the best
talent of the German stage, he created a magnificent *ensemble* for
the Burgtheater, and laid the foundation of that brilliant series of
illustrations of the *ensemble* art which, almost to the present day,
have been the chief ornament and characteristic of this unique
stage.   In the exercise of the talent which he valued at its true
worth, and which placed him in the category of the patriarchal
heroes, he won for Vienna the highly gifted Wilhelmi, the
tragedienne Sophie Müller, and the gently powerful Costenobles.
He formed the fiery Ludwig Löwe and the graceful Fichtner,
whom he brought from another theatre to adorn the Imperial
stage.   He made of Sophie Schröder the leading actress of Germany.
Those were striking individualists who contributed their best
powers to enhance the glory of the drama.   The Burgtheater
became the most famous centre of culture in Vienna ; it was the
meeting place of all that was most talented and brilliant in the
society of the town.   All who by day met in business, in salons,
or on the *Bastion*, came together again in the evening in the limited

space of the conservative Court theatre, with its subdued colouring, where the atmosphere consisted mainly of spirit and soul.

The second stage belonging to the Court was that of the Kärntnertortheater, under the management of an Italian, Domenico Barbaia, who, with Count Palffy, ran also the Theater-an-der-Wien. Those were the palmy days of Italian opera in Vienna. Cherubini, Spontini, and more especially Rossini, the Swan of Pesaro, with his " Othello," " Barber of Seville," and " Tancred," had sent Vienna into a delirium of ecstasy which, while it lasted, put the great German masters in the shade.

Both theatres were given up almost exclusively to the repertory of Italian opera, the stars of which were Rossini's wife, Colbran, Fodor Mainville, and the singers Donzelli, Nozari, and David Lablache. Among these shone two German luminaries, those nightingales Unger and Henriette Sonntag.

A memorable event for German music during the time of the Congress festivities had been the production at last of Beethoven's " Fidelio " at the Theater-an-der-Wien, and its inclusion in the repertory of the Kärntnertortheater. The great success this opera met with at that time confirmed Beethoven in the intention of writing another opera. " In the winter months of 1825," Anton Schindler relates, " the news spread through musical circles in Vienna, to the joy of all friends of music, that the revival after eight years, in November, 1822, of ' Fidelio ' in a series of performances had been such a triumphant success that it had given the administration of the Imperial Opera courage to ask Beethoven to write another opera. Beethoven welcomed the proposal, and expressed a wish to be given a choice of texts. These were forthcoming in great numbers, but all proved unsuitable, because he stipulated that the material should be classic— Greek or Latin. When it was pointed out that these subjects had been used, the choice seemed to the Master so difficult that he confessed his inability to decide from what category to make a selection. At this juncture Grillparzer came forward—not without trepidation—and offered to send the composer his opera book ' Melusina ' which he had just completed. This exceedingly romantic material, with several effective situations, and among the characters a comic servant, delighted Beethoven, and he abandoned altogether his former desire for a classical theme. Poet and composer held various conferences together. Beethoven suggested alterations, omissions, and a closer unity in the scenario, all of which points were gladly acceded to by the author. This brought the two great artists for the first time in contact with each other, and gave them an opportunity of opening their hearts together in melancholy laments over the political and social conditions in their common Fatherland." Almost simultaneously with the commission from the administration of the opera in Vienna came a similar one from the Intendant of the Berlin Theatre Royal, Count Brühl, who left the settlement of fees to the Master. Beethoven, without consulting anyone, sent Count Brühl the Grillparzer libretto, and, though it found favour, the fact that a ballet called " Undine," the same subject as " Melusina," had been given on the Royal Opera stage, led to Beethoven finally giving up the idea of writing another German opera. He even allowed himself to be carried away by the furore caused in the Imperial city by the presence of the Italian princes of song, Lablache, Rubini, Donzelli and the ladies, Fedor Mainville, Dadanelli, Eckerlin, etc. Having witnessed the enthusiasm they excited at the performance of Rossini's " Barbiere," he was almost persuaded by Karoline Unger to write an opera for this phalanx of Italian singers. Indeed, he half-promised the artists to begin one in the following year. But this project came to nothing, as everyone knows. Grillparzer's " Melusina " was later set to music by Conradin Kreutzer.

The ballet at the Kärntnertortheater, at this time, experienced too a brilliant revival. Two stars of the Terpsichorean art scored here their most notable triumphs—Maria Taglioni, who appeared for the first time in June, 1828, in an " anachreontic *divertissement*," and Fanny Elssler, who in the ballet " The Fairy and the Knight " won her first striking success.

Elssler was the great Viennese dancer of the *Biedermeierzeit*. She was as great a favourite as were the Raimunds, Therese Krones, and Schröder in the art of the theatre. Daughter of a court chamberlain and copyist of Haydn's, she learnt her first steps in the children's ballet corps at the Kärntnertortheater, then received instruction from an Italian master in Italy, and toured through Europe and America. She and Taglioni brought the art of dancing in Germany and Austria to the highest perfection. The incarnation of grace and beauty, her undulating movements were rhythmical and the very poetry of motion. Every step was æsthetically perfect. She understood how to convey character, circumstances, conflicting thoughts and ideas with the most consummate mimicry. Her dancing resembled words interpreted by the wonderful play of human limbs. She created the dramatic dance, and her " Cachucha " and " Esmeralda " were famous. " Fanny Elssler dances the Cachucha," wrote Saphir, " with feet, with eyes, with the mouth, and a thousand smiles and a million sweet gestures : That is the Cachucha, and one may say the Cachucha would never have been a dance if Elssler had not danced it." She was called " Fanny I., Queen of the Dance." She was fêted in two hemispheres, painted by famous artists, and her praises sung by the poets.

The finest theatre in Vienna architecturally was the Theater-an-der-Wien, which Schikaneder, with help of funds from a wealthy merchant, Zitterbart by name, built at the beginning of the century. It was opened on June 6th, 1801. During the Congress of Vienna the splendour of its blue-and-silver foyer, the beautiful stage of unusual depth, and its superb technical arrangements excited the wonder and admiration of foreign guests. Then, as now, figures out of Mozart's " Zauberflöte " greeted the audience from the drop-curtain. The owner of the theatre at that time was Count Palffy— " Theatre Palffy," a real cavalier, " a magnificent squanderer, and a dunce at arithmetic and adding up." Loving splendour, he emulated the stages of the Court in mounting plays so expensively that gradually he went financially bankrupt. On this stage, drama and opera, operetta, burlesque and ballet were performed alternately. Memorable especially were the performances of Beethoven's " Fidelio," Grillparzer's " Ahnfrau," and Schubert's fairy play " The Magic Harp," which was first produced here in 1820.

The theatrical splendour of the art-loving Count Palffy came to an end on the last day of May, 1825. Hard pressed by creditors, he closed the theatre. The last performance under his management was Grillparzer's " König Ottokars Glück und Ende." His successor, the Director of the Isartortheater in Munich, had better luck. Karl Carl, with his company, first appeared as guests in Cuno's play " Die Rauber auf dem Kulmerberg." He was a capital man of business, and made a considerable fortune as manager of the Theater-an-der-Wien, so that he was able to purchase the Leopoldstädter Theatres, on the site of which he built in 1847 the Carl Theatre, called after him.

In the little theatre in the Leopoldstadt the *Volksstück* came into vogue. Here the merry Viennese character types, Kasperl and Thaddädl, entered on a triumphant career. The clown, the inexhaustible source of Austrian merriment, came to life once more. Now Viennese humour became associated with romanticism. The spirit world sent its gods and fairies into the everyday world, transfiguring it with divine fantasy. The Viennese Volks-Theater was converted into a temple of gaiety and joyousness, but mingled with the eternal tragedy of humanity. The management of the Leopoldstädter Theaters issued in 1822 instructions to writers for the stage to the effect that what was wanted must appeal to the lower and middle classes. " Satirise follies of the day, manners and customs when these are suitable for friendly satire, in a thoroughly original and attractive way." They are warned against being tedious and dull when they have a moral object in view. " Topical patter, conjuring tricks, powerful witty parodies, light musical comedy, and sketches and schemes for lively pantomimes will be welcomed."

The repertory of the Leopoldstädter-Theater of that time shows that this programme was for the most part faithfully adhered to. As the tragic muse found its classic home in the Burgtheater, so the comic found it in the Leopoldstädter Theater. Grillparzer had his counterpart in Ferdinand Raimund, the classical writer for the Volks-Theater. Besides him, there were three others. Adolf Bauerle, the author of the song " s' gibt nur a Kaiserstadt, s' gibt nur a Wien," gave the Volks-Theater the characteristic figure " Staberl " the umbrella-maker, soon popular on every stage in Germany. Staberl was a caricature of Viennese Philistinism, not exaggerated, but " a flesh and blood creation of Viennese epicene cocksureness with its amusing pretensions of knowing and understanding everything in heaven and earth." Meisl, whose verses " Die Weihe des Hauses " were immortalised by Beethoven's setting them to music in 1822, was the author of numberless farces, burlesques, parodies and mythological travesties. There was a time when his works written for the stage were received with frantic applause in all the suburban theatres. But Meisl reaped small profits from his popularity, for " in those days work like his was poorly remunerated, and for a book that filled the theatre to overflowing for months he only received a sum of from 60 to 89 guldens."

Alois Gleich, Raimund's step-father, made Vienna shudder with his romanticism and laugh happily with his farces. He is said to have written over 400 pieces, among them " Die Musikanten auf dem Hohen Markt," in which Raimund made his reputation as a comedian. But the great Viennese writer for the people of that time was Ferdinand Raimund himself. The son of a cabinet-maker, he was born in Vienna in 1790. Soon left an orphan, he had to earn his living, and was apprenticed to a Viennese confectioner, and part of his duties was to sell sweets in the gallery of the old Burgtheater, where his ardent young soul was awakened and so impressed by what he saw that he cherished all his life the dream of becoming an actor in the Burgtheater and writing for its stage. One day he broke loose from his master and got an engagement in a strolling company of players. For six years he experienced all the ups and downs, squalor and misery of a wandering comedian's life, till, in 1814, he appeared as an unknown actor, first in tragic *rôles*, at the Josefstädter Theater, and then, when Gleich wrote for him the part of the fiddler in the farce " Musikanten am Hohen Markt," he scored a thundering success as a comedian. Soon he was transferred to the Leopoldstadter-Theater, where he formed the famous artistic *ensemble* composed of Ignaz Schuster, Josef Korntheuer and Therese Krones, who gave performances such as have never since been equalled in that particular *genre* on any Viennese stage. The secret of their success was the absolute harmony with which they acted together, putting forth all their best efforts in unison and making the most of every point in the play. The sympathy between the actors and the public was complete. The public enjoyed Raimund's representation, willingly praising to the skies its strong points, and drowning in laughter all blame of its weaknesses.

There was in Raimund's acting something more than the naïve, comic gaiety of the colleagues who acted with him; there was an undercurrent of melancholy which, welling up from a wounded soul, touched the hearts of the spectators. Never lapsing into mannerisms, he absorbed himself in his *rôle*, and infected the whole *ensemble* with his earnest conception of wit and his divine fire.

The most brilliant period of the Leopoldstädter began with Raimund's work, especially as it was there that his creative contributions to the drama first found expression and appreciation. His earliest efforts were " theatre addresses " to the public in prose and

Ferdinand Raimund
Engraving by Michalek after Lampi

verse. Then he wrote " magic " farces, " Der Barometermacher auf dem Zauberinsel," " Der Diamant des Geisterkönigs," which were tremendous successes. They were dramatised fairy tales with echoes of old magic and allegories from the Baroque period. Raimund transformed everyday life into poetry and jest, pouring new wine into old vessels. He would aim at the symbolising of a mere joke into an idea. In " Diamant des Geisterkönigs " he followed the example of Mozart's " Zauberflöte," contrasting the ideal pair Edouard and Amine with the comic pair Florian and Mirande, each pair, like Tamino and Tamina, Papageno and Papagena, in the " Zauberflöte," working out their destiny through trials in their respective ways.

In " Das Mädchen aus der Feenwelt oder Der Bauer als Millionär," Raimund's third piece, his powers came to their full maturity, especially in the wonderful scene when youth, with the Biedmeierean song " Brüderlein fein," takes leave of Wurzel and old age enters into the haughty peasant millionaire and turns him into a poor helpless old dustman. The subtlest stage-craft is used, and all mere theatricality and comic business eschewed in this scene, one of the most affecting surely in the whole literature of the world. In the pieces that followed, " Die gefesselte Phantasie," "Die unheilbringende Krone," etc., he strove in vain to capture tragic laurels, and so returned to the *genre* which was the most fertile ground for the growth of his genius. Once more he plunged into the poetic life of the people, and found in its inexhaustible humour and the treasures of its inner purity of thought copy for artistic presentation. Like Jean Paul, he has often been called the poet of the poor. He entered the dwelling of the man of narrow means, and scattered with a lavish hand the shining pearls of his poesie over the lives of the poor and insignificant. In his profound knowledge of the people and their innermost world, he chose fairy-tale material which he understood how to weave into the conditions of the time with graceful humour, so that the magic world of faerie and allegory, the kingdom of unbridled fantasy, were brought into harmony with the common life of every day.

Much in Raimund is Shakespearean, much Goethean, and sometimes his work is reminiscent of the festivals of Calderon. His goddess was the fantasy which gave him the " desire to dream of golden things." And this fantasy was no abstract idea ; she was a confiding soul, a lively, living creature, a Viennese " Susses Mädel " brimming over with loveliness and grace and frivolity, as her character is depicted in Raimund's song :

> " *Ich bin ein Wesen leichter Art,*
> *Ein Kind mit tausend Launen,*
> *Das Niedres mit dem Höchsten paart,*
> *Mein Witz erregt Erstaunen.*
> *Im dichterischen Übermut*
> *Durchschweb'ich Himmelsfernen*
> *Ich steck die Sonne auf den Hut*
> *Und würfle mit den Sternen."*

The world of his fancy is a fairy kingdom, a magic world full of gardens, meadows, hills, wind angels with blown-out cheeks, full of blue lakes, snowy peaks and shining glaciers.   Here are the islands of Tuto and of Truth, the Arcadian island of Flora, and the House of Contentment shimmering in the gay landscape.   Under its roof dwell Prince Aphio, Moisasur, the good fairies Cheristane and Lacrimosa, the two pale brothers Envy and Hate, and the Genius of the Past, a gloomy, haughty spirit, draped in a long black tunic, his face white and grave, with a serpent wound round his dark curls.   But in the midst of this magic world lies Vienna, the gay Vienna of the Biedermeier time, and, moreover, the theatre of the Leopoldstädt—

> " *Die Jägerzeil' lieb ich vor allem,*
> *Dort wünsch ich den Leuten zu gefallen,*
> *Dort habe ich ein einziges Haus,*
> *Da zieh ich mein Lebtag nicht aus."*

There it was that Raimund played himself the parts of Wurzel, the Harfenstein Nachtigall, and later, as Valentin, sang the " Dustman's Song " and Valentin's *Hobellied,* and with him sang and laughed Therese Krones, the prototype of all great Viennese soubrettes.   She sang the song of youth, " Brüderlein fein." Krones was more than brilliant, she was radiant ; she did not shine, but pierced into the ears and the senses of her listeners. . . . She was a joyous incendiary.   She laid the fire, and the flames crackled, and the sparks flew up.   She incarnated the pleasure-loving youth of Vienna.   Fêted and worshipped, a tragic shadow was cast over her bright life when the murderer Jaro-

schinsky, who was one of her numerous admirers, was arrested at a
banquet at which she was present. Raimund was certainly one of the most famous actors of the old
Vienna. It is true that he possessed no very striking stage-presence;
neither was his voice melodious, and he was lacking in that inborn
power of comic expression which Nature sometimes extracts from
the most unpromising material. But these deficiencies only incited
him to make the very most of what gifts he had, and to *use*
them with wise economy and artistic skill, such as the play of his
extraordinary expressive and clever eyes and the gestures and
movements of his elastic and supple body. His impersonations
were full of character and absolutely true to Nature. In the middle
of the most mirth-provoking joke, he knew how to touch a pathetic
note. His most famous part was the millionaire peasant changed
into an old man, and no one could help being touched when with
shaking voice he sang his song of the old dustman. He belonged
to the small category of students of the *genre* who have above all
things the accurate presentation of character at heart. All the
figures he delineated were illumined by a Hogarthian realism. His
pictures were no Cruikshank caricatures, but character portraits,
like those of Teniers, painted with Nature's colours, the brush
dipped into the palette of Truth. Every feature, every *nuance* was
observed and taken from an original type, and the charm and grace
of the picture was enhanced by the *vis comica* and the rosy reflection
of his humour.

As well as on the Leopoldstädter stage, the Viennese Volks-
play flourished in the Josafstadt Theatre. In the year 1815 there
was a group here of first-rate representatives of the national dramatic
art. Besides Josef Huber, the Director, there were Alois Gleich
as Sub-director, Ferdinand Raimund, who had become famous
in the "Musikanten am Hohen Markt," Karl Mayer, and the
demoiselles Gleich and Habermann. With Schiller's "Raüber"
and "Kabale und Liebe," such Viennese pieces as "Der Schöne
Wiener Nazel," "Hans in Wien," etc., were popular. In the year
1822 Karl Friedrich Hensler made his entry as Director, and the
theatre, thanks to the munificence of the landlord of the "Zum
Straussen," was rebuilt and handsomely decorated. The "house
warming" took place on October 3rd, and, amidst the brand new
golden pillars, the boxes hung with indigo blue, and the beautiful
stage setting of the "Spinnerin am Kreuz," Beethoven's overture,

" Die Weihe des Hauses," conducted by the Master himself, was heard in the new temple of Apollo. Very charming must have sounded Beethoven's graceful dance measure :

> " *Wo sich die Pulse*
> *Jugendlich jagen—*
> *Schwebet im Tanz*
> *Das Leben dahin !*
> *Leicht ist die Freude—*
> *Hüpfend die Jugend,*
> *Frohsinn heisst Tanzen—*
> *Kriechen heisst Schuld.*
> *Lasst uns im Tanze*
> *Das fliehende Leben*
> *Neckend erhaschend—*
> *Dem Drucke entschweben.*
> *Ist es im Herzen*
> *Arglos und jung—*
> *Ist selbst das Streben,*
> *Zur Ruhe ein Sprung !* "

After the death of Hensler, the thoroughly routined theatre-man Carl took over the management, and under him two world-renowned Viennese masters made their *début*—Wenzel Scholz and Nestroy. At the close of the Biedermeier period the Josefstadt gave a run of opera. Conrad in Kreutzer was the conductor, and his " Nachtlager von Granada " enjoyed a series of successes.

Then once more the bright star of the Vienna Volkspoesie shed its radiance on the stage : Raimund's masterpiece, " Der Verschwender," was produced, with himself in the leading part of Valentin, in which alternated humour and melancholy. The effect was greatly heightened by the new artistic richly-coloured background, and all Vienna crowded to the Josefstadt to hear Valentin's great song, and to applaud and admire the famous poet of the people, the actor and author Raimund.

Next to the two classical authors, the dramatist Grillparzer and the *Volks dichter* Raimund, ranked the comedy-writer of the Biedermeier time, Bauernfeld the intimate friend of Schubert, Schwind and Grillparzer. He depicted the Viennese society of the day, drawing impartially its coarsest and its most refined sides, its immortal merits and demerits. He studied it in the office, in the street, the drawing-room, the theatre, and in political and literary circles. He was a journalist and brilliant essayist as well as a writer for the stage. The spirit and culture of Vienna's early springtime are in everything he wrote, from his comedies, essays, satirical verse down to the articles he contributed to newspapers, reviews and almanacks. Much can be learned about the social and political condition of those days from his writings. In his reminiscences, which are of special value, he pictures in lively style the circle round Schubert and Schwind, and gives a loving account of that old Viennese life, so full of romantic beauty and harmless gaiety, such as Schwind painted in his fairy-tale pictures and fantasies, and Schubert glorified with the magic of his melodies.

The beginnings, also, of old Vienna's caricaturist of genius and distinguished satirist, Johann Nestroy, belong to the Biedermeier time, though his masterpieces, of course, came later. He was the son of a Vienna lawyer, and read for the law, but soon gave it up and devoted himself entirely to the actor's art. In his young days he appeared oftenest as a singer. He sang first bass once at a concert given by the Society of Music Friends in Schubert's quartette for men's voices, " Das Dörfchen." He was spared the " wander " years of sordid wretchedness which had fallen to Raimund's lot. Amsterdam, Brünn and Graz were the stations of his artistic training. In Graz, where he met Schubert, he completed the transition from bass singer to comedian, and won his first laurels at the Josefstadt Theater in his own adaptation of " 12 Mädchen in Uniform," and as Adam in " Dorfbarbier." He was enthusiastically received, and Director Carl engaged him for the Theater-an-der-Wien, where he remained fourteen years as actor and farce-writer. He was transferred then to the Leopold-städter, now called, after its rebuilding, the " Carl-Theater." As an actor he achieved wonderful effects, owing to his tall, lanky figure, which he could make still taller and lankier at will. He electrified his audiences by his sudden quick changes from heaviness to agility. His command of language was stupendous, and he amazed his hearers with torrents of words and fiery brilliant improvisations. Even more eloquent than his dialogue was his dumb show, whereby he often fooled the Censor. By a wrinkling of the forehead, the lifting of the eyebrows, a thrusting out of the lips and chin he contrived to give his *rôle* emphasis which meant something quite different from the spoken words. As an actor

Nestroy was, as Öttinger brilliantly expressed it, "from the crown of his head to the sole of his feet a caricature, every inch of him. Every grimace, every gesture, every fibre, every nerve, a scathing satire, a biting, provocative irony, a savage maliciousness, a blood-curdling persiflage, an unheard-of scorning of everything that had hitherto been heard of in Art. He was no Hogarth, no Gillray, no Goya, no Gavarni. . . . Nestroy was more than all these put together ; in him was combined the spirit, the acidity, the caustic scorn, the mocking contempt of all these masters, and he was the born eleven and a half of Caricature, an encyclopædia of Satire, the quintessence of Irony, the refined bouquet of Parody."

Nestroy's works reflect what was ironical and parody-loving in the Viennese nature. He was the embodiment of the old clown of Vienna households, whose comic spirit, humour and wit babbled like foaming champagne and glistened with pearls. His work, like that of all actors, was based on the traditions of the theatre. From the theatre Nestroy adopted old forms and types for his creations, but he invested them with new ingredients. Magic plays, parodies, farces and moralities were the kind of things he recast and made the scaffold for his incomparable dialogue, sparkling with wit. It was not only in Thalia's kingdom, but in the magical garden of Euterpe, that the Biedermeier spirit was richly productive.

The young Grillparzer, caught in the snares of love, chiselled his verses " Allgegenwart," " Als sie zuhörend am Klavier sass," " Der Bann," " Abschied von Gastein " like sculpture ; they were in every mouth. Feuchtersleben, Collin, Castelli, Schober, Seidl, Mayrhofer, Vogl composed their Biedermeier songs, the words of which inspired Franz Schubert to pour out the inex-haustible music of his soul. And the Muse at that time endowed lavishly the young student, Nicholas Lenau, with her laurels.

Lenau came from Hungary. He was the most celebrated lyric writer of the Biedermeier age—the Viennese springtime. The poetic ideals of his fiery and melancholy temperament were in constant strife with reality. He looked with hope towards the new movements and awakening of the time, and yet lamented in elegiacs the lost peacefulness of older days. He gave expression with passionate ardour and sometimes too effeminate feeling to ever-varying emotions, in lyrical poems and lyrical epics full of melodious charm and glorious colour. His verse had the characteristics of perfect poetry ; it was a harmonious blend of the psychic and

Nestroy
Lithograph by Prinzhofer
(Vienna National Library)

picturesque. It had the winged inspiration that weds earthly things with the divine.

The Viennese novels of the Biedermeier period were written by a poetical, talented woman, Karoline Pichler. Both Viennese men and women novel-readers swore by her fiction, although there was an Adalbert Stifter beginning to make his mark. He came to the Vienna University in 1826 when he was twenty-one. Stifter's narratives were Austrian idylls. He spun into them beautiful dreams of the silent grandeur of forest and mountain scenery; he drew with the silver point the most delicate pictures of Vienna and the graceful landscape surrounding her, and gradually out of the heart of the Austrian people and the pure ether of Austrian Alpine air he began to create those figures in his novels known as "Stiftermenschen," so purely characteristic of Austria's national character and so beloved by Austrian readers.

In the realm of music, Vienna during the Biedermeier period experienced a new and hitherto unrivalled renaissance. Beethoven was still at work, and strode through the streets in a condition of absolute detachment from the world, possessed by the dæmon of Dionysian music. It was then that he wrote the powerful "Hammer" sonata for the Archduke Rudolf, and his soul sang the wonderful song group "An die ferne Geliebte." He composed his last deeply significant quartet, and then created, as if seeking release from the burden of his earthly suffering, the mighty Mass. The Credo with the great fugue raged forth from the intoxicated soul of the stormy Colossus, gigantic stone was laid upon stone till a new God-given temple towered into the heavens. It was no Mass in the ordinary sense of the word, but intended to be more a pendant to Goethe's "Faust," something leviathan, unheard of, unique. *Von Herzen, mag sie zu Herzen gehen* was its motto. And at the same time he brought forth the glorious Ninth, the world symphony which rang out sorrow and sighing, and the tragedy of suffering, and rang in jubilantly joy for all mankind. His work, commanding like his personality, the great artist of the Napoleonic era departed this life in the midst of thunder, hail and lightning in the old Schwarzspanierhaus. Europe's music city, which he had filled with the greatness of his genius, went into mourning. Schubert, Raimund, Lenau, Schwind, Grillparzer walked behind Beethoven's coffin. The last-named had composed the funeral oration, which was recited by Anschütz in a thrilling, powerful voice. "He was an artist . . . and who is there to come near him ? . . . As Behemoth streamed through the ocean, so he soared over the boundaries of his art. . . . His genius irradiates to this day every dwelling and every street in the town, and the homes, hills and vales of the Wienerwald."

Next to Beethoven's, the star of the Viennese genius, Franz Schubert, rose on the bright firmament of the Biedermeier period. Here the Viennese atmosphere lent wings to the artist's music-soul and inner inexhaustible wealth of creative power, and he spread these wings in miracles of melody and song. In the steps of these two great men of genius, Beethoven and Schubert, belonging to the first rank, there followed a little group of striving aspirants—Weigl, Gyrowetz, Umlauf, Assmayer, Seyfried, Eybler, and the Abbé Stadler. From abroad, Rossini, the celebrated Italian composer, who lived at this time in Vienna, continued his gallopades of tuneful fireworks, and, as has been mentioned before, reigned with Cherubini and Spontini as first favourite at the Viennese opera, filling for a considerable period the repertory. But then a great German composer appeared upon the scene, "like a beautiful day in the life of the people, a warm drop of their own blood, a bit of their heart"—Karl Maria Weber. Vienna was soon raving about the airs in the "Freischütz," and listened enthralled, like a child drinking in the stories and legends told by its grandmother, to the music that welled direct from the soul of the German people. "I am received everywhere," he wrote, "as if I were some prodigy of a wild animal. I am the god of the hour. A public like this is a joy. Such enthusiastic admiration combined with so much good nature is to be met with nowhere except in Vienna."

He conducted the "Freischütz" at the Kärntnertortheater on the occasion of the benefit of the great Schröder-Devrient. "Wreaths were thrown and poems spouted," wrote Bauernfeld in his diary, and Costenoble the actor adds thereto : "The Viennese forgot their Rossini mania and went mad about Weber, hailing their German compatriot with as much applause as if he had been a foreigner." Schubert met Weber, who was interested in the young tone-poet, and who promised to produce his opera "Alfonso and Estrella" in Dresden. In the following year the German master again came to Vienna, bringing with him his new opera "Euryanthe," which had been ordered by the management of the

Kärntnertortheater. Here he wrote the splendid overture, the most brilliant thing in all his works. The enthusiastic reception given to his "Freischütz" was not repeated in the case of "Euryanthe." "The 'Freischütz,'" criticised Schubert, "was so tender and sincere. Its loveliness charmed, but in 'Euryanthe' there is little 'Gemütlichkeit.'"

Another early master of German romanticism, Ludwig Spohr, in whom the romantic sentiment came to the fore with conscious power, made his entry into Vienna at this time. He first appeared as a brilliant violinist and as conductor in the Theater-an-der-Wien. As a composer his operas "Faust" and "Jessonda" found great favour.

The Viennese stage also was famous for its Biedermeier romantic opera in the musical comedy *genre*. We meet its purest type first in Weigl's at that time extremely popular "Schweizerfamilie," and later it was developed in Schubert's song-pieces and the operas of Conradin Kreutzer. The latter came to Vienna in 1804 as pupil of Albrechtsberger. He made concert tours in Germany, where he acted as conductor at Stuttgart. In 1822 he came back to Vienna and conducted at the Kärntnertortheater and the Josefstadt. He wrote a great many operas and choral pieces, but his chief success as a composer was "Das Nachtlager von Granada." His songs "Der Tag des Herrn," "Die Kapelle," and others from Raimund's "Verschwender" attained great popularity. His was a homely, genuinely Biedermeierish talent, whose works full of romance bordered on sentimentality. Another Biedermeierrer of music in the days of Schubert and Schwind was Franz Lachner, who came to Vienna from Germany, and, breathing the city's atmosphere and that of its surrounding landscape, matured into an artist. The genius of his friend Schubert, the educating intercourse with Simon Sechter and Abbé Stadler, his activity as conductor at the Kärntnertort-theater, all contributed to the productiveness of his artistic talent which afterwards came to richer and fuller development in Munich.

The great renaissance in the Viennese dance and the Viennese Volksmusic, which had their origin in long-past times, also occurred in the Biedermeier epoch. In the far-off days of the Babenberger, the nobility and citizens of Vienna used to greet the spring together on the Kahlenberg with music and dancing at the great Feast of Violets. Niedhardt von Reuenthal's peasant songs intoxicated the multitude, and citizen and noble joined in the dances of the Minnesinger kind. The Zeiselmauer also attracted the dance-loving nobles and burghers, where on a meadow plain in the sunset they danced the " Springtanz-Rattenfängers " in circles till the stars came out. On the subject of Vienna's dancing craze at the beginning of the nineteenth century and the crowds in the dance resorts, Eipeldauer, in one of his lively satirical letters, wrote to his cousin in 1800 in Kagran : " Wherever one goes a ball programme invites one to a music-hall. But to find a table to sit at is a baffling business and cools one's ardour. They are always chock full. . . . People must have more money now than they used to have. . . ."

Much cultivated at that time in the suburbs were the Country Dance and the Polster Tanz. The last combined with Volks melodies grace and merriment. The old Viennese Polster Tanz (Bolster dance) is described in the naïve text of the song :

> " I werf mei Polsterl hin und her,
> i lass mei Polsterl fliag'n
> und wer mei Polsterl haben will
> der mauss a Busserl kriag'n."

One of the most genuine and charming offspring of the Viennese spirit of music was the Viennese waltz. Its origin, its soul lies in the Austrian Volkslied, in the character and dances of the people living in the mountains and country round the city. Alpine wandering musicians of Steiermark (Styria) brought the music of the mountains and woodlands into the town. The violin players from Linz, a quartette consisting of two violins, guitar and double bass, or of violin, guitar, 'cello and clarinet, played, as they came sailing down the Danube on board the steamers the instrumental songs of the mountains, in slow $\frac{3}{4}$ time. When they arrived in Vienna they visited inn after inn in the suburbs and played for the dancers. The influx of this fresh primitive talent, mingled with Viennese grace, gave birth to the Viennese waltz. With its light swaying rhythm, its infectious swing, it was a mirror which reflected the pastoral Viennese landscape, and was the ultra-expression of the soul of the Viennese people. It was evolved from the minuet, the time of which it quickened from the even $\frac{3}{4}$-$\frac{4}{4}$ of the " Allemande." The " Deutschen Tänze," called for short " Teutschen," were the prototype of the Wiener Walzer, and had the same architectural construction, each consisting of 16 bars with *da capo*, but a more even and slower tempo than the Viennese waltzes, which moved quickly to the so-called "deuxtemps." Josef Lanner and Johann Strauss (father) were chiefly responsible for the renaissance of the Viennese waltz. Their forerunner of genius in this department was Franz Schubert with his "Deutschen Tänze," *Valse nobles and sentimental, Hommage aux belles Viennoises*, and Weber with his immortal "Invitation." Schubert played his waltzes in the circle of his friends at the Schubert evenings—"Schubertiaden." His waltzes are true echoes of Nature, but not music intended to be danced to; much more were they meant as *caviare* for the ears of musical gourmets. Josef Lanner and Johann Strauss the elder were chosen by Fate to free the Viennese waltz from anything that might have crept in to corrupt it in the way of vulgarity or commonplaceness, and to raise it to the high standard of a pure native art. They created waltz music in the highest sense. Following Franz Schubert's example, they were the musical apostles of Viennese *joie de vivre*.

Josef Lanner was born on April 12th in the Vorstadt St. Ulrich, No. 20, not far from the birthplace of Raimund. His father, Martin Lanner, was a glove manufacturer. At twelve years old he played in the band of Michael Pamer, a Viennese musician of the suburbs. The latter was a popular composer of dance music, and his "Tempete" and "Eccossaises" had hosts of admirers. His was a real Viennese music nature, full of talent and frivolity. The demons of alcohol and cards degraded him from the elevated position to which his great gifts had deservedly raised him.

The intolerable state of things in the band owing to their chief's unsatisfactory mode of life soon caused Lanner to sever his connection with Pamer. In the "Laim-grube," whither the Lanner family moved, he gave with several comrades, musical like himself, concerts of chamber music in the house of his parents. His dream of himself getting together a little band like Pamer's and to appear with it in public was soon realised. In the spring of 1819 the fair-haired young son of the glovemaker made his *début* in the garden of a *café*, a favourite resort of youth near the Schlagbrücke, in the Leopoldstadt. It was hardly to be called a band, but rather a terzet consisting of Lanner as the leader and two brothers called Dahanek from Bohemia, the elder of whom played the guitar and the younger second violin. It had a very successful beginning. The young musicians were tremendously applauded, and Lanner's Terzet quickly won the approval of the town. He was soon in great request, and played at the " Grünen Jäger," at " Wellischen Bierhaus " in the Prater, at " Rebhuhn " in the Goldschmiedgasse. And before long the terzet became a quartet, Lanner engaging, through the medium of the younger Dahanek, Johann Strauss, senior, as fourth player. Strauss was three years younger than Lanner. He had first seen the light on March 14th, 1804, in the little beer-shop " Zum Guten Hirten," where the Linzer musicians from the Danube ships often put up and played their fiddles in the evening to a company composed not only of people of the working class, but of many of old Vienna's artists and authors, such as Bäuerle, Perinet, Castelli, who were frequenters of the comfortable little hostel. Johann Strauss senior's infancy was full of dance music, and no wonder that the boy dreamed of becoming a musician. His father, through reverses in business, committed suicide, and his mother married again the innkeeper Golder ; but she would not tolerate the idea of the boy adopting music as his profession, and apprenticed him to the bookbinder Lichtschiedl. The boy ran away from his master and wandered about the streets, where he was found by a frequenter of the " Guten Hirten," the musician Polischanky, who adopted him and gave him violin lessons. Next young Strauss joined, as Lanner had done, Pamer's band, and shortly afterwards, when not more than fifteen, played the viola in the quartet under Lanner, whom he idolised. He soon won the recognition and friendship of the now famous master. He and Lanner shared a modest room at No. 18, Windmühle. Theirs was a gay Bohemian life, in which debts, romance, love affairs, youthful frivolity, communism in clothes and laundry played a part in a careless joyous existence. The quartet in due course became a quintet, being joined by another 'cellist. At the " Rebhuhn," Franz Schubert, who came there with his friends on balmy spring evenings to drink a glass of wine, listened with the greatest interest and delight to the dance music of the Lanner Quartet. How soft and exquisite in their rhythm the waltzes must have sounded on those spring evenings, like a spring-song of infinite youth, full of the grace and joyousness of the *wienerisch* temperament. Schubert and his friends, drowned in wine and music, made Lanner happy with their hearty applause.

Already in 1824 Lanner, fired by his success and countless engagements, enlarged his quintet into a string orchestra, which first played in the Prater's leading coffee-house with instant success.

The necessity of further increasing the orchestra and dividing it when it became such a great success led to friction and finally estrangement between Lanner and Strauss, whose nature was irritable and ambitious. One day Lanner dismissed him from his orchestra, and on September 1st, 1825, it came to a stormy parting between them. The Lanner Orchestra was playing at the "Bock," and this was made the scene of a violent altercation, musicians and public took sides, and a miniature music battle, during which chairs were overturned and a looking-glass broken, took place. It ended in separation, Strauss became chief of his own orchestra and Lanner, who had taken to heart what had happened between them, commemorated artistically the painful event in true Biedermeierish fashion. He composed his "Trennungswalzer," in which he set to music in four parts the scene at the "Bock."

A few years later, outwardly at least, there was a reconciliation on the occasion of Lanner's marriage with the daughter of the Viennese glove manufacturer, Franziska. The wedding breakfast was in progress at the "Bock," and the newly-married pair were being enthusiastically honoured by Lanner's friends, when Johann Strauss appeared to offer his congratulations. The two artists fell on each other's bosoms and wept for joy.

Strauss conducted his orchestra, consisting of fourteen members, first at the "Swan," then at the "Tauben" on the Glacis road, where his first waltz, the "Täuberlwalzer," was produced. This was followed by many new compositions, "Döblinger Reunion-Walzer," "Wiener Karneval," the "Kettenbrücken Walzer," the last rapturously received by the Viennese. The Strauss Orchestra and dances won an ever-increasing audience of admirers, and was overwhelmed with concert engagements; publishers clamoured for the latest Strauss compositions. An artistic rivalry between Lanner and Strauss arose which had a blessed influence on the upward growth of the old Viennese Volks music. Lanner, the fair-haired troubadour of the waltz, was, like Schubert, Raimund and Schwind, a romanticist. In his dream-like music all the woes and raptures of love laughed and wept; it was wreathed with joyous grace and melancholy yearning. Very Biedermeierisch are the titles of his five dance numbers in several parts with short introductions and a grand finale—"Terpsichore," "Flora," "Blumen der Lust," "Hoffnungsstrahlen," "Schönbrunner," "Abendstern," He was a favourite in Vienna, beloved and fêted. He was made music director of the Redoubt-halls. But in spite of the honours that were heaped on him, he remained the child of Nature, the typical Viennese of the suburb. Only once did he give concerts abroad and step over the frontiers of Vienna and Austria. That was in the year 1858, when he was asked to direct the music in Milan for the coronation of the Emperor Ferdinand. He made then a triumphal tour, giving concerts at Linz, Innsbruck, Trieste and Venice before he got to Milan. Otherwise he rarely gave a concert out of Vienna. In the years 1854 and 1855 he was in Budapest, where he composed the celebrated " Pester Walzer," and dedicated them to the Hungarian nation. In 1857 he was welcomed with enthusiasm in Graz, the Styrian capital.

Quite differently constituted was Johann Strauss, senior, with his black " Negro head." The important *rôle* that he played in the musical life of Vienna is related by Richard Wagner on his first visit to Vienna : " I shall never forget the passion bordering on mad fury with which the wonderful Johann Strauss conducted. This Daemon of the ancient Viennese Volks-spirit trembled at the beginning of a new waltz like a python preparing to spring, and it was more the ecstasy produced by the music than the drinks among the enchanted audience that stimulated the magical first violin to almost dangerous flights. . . ."

Strauss was more a man of the world than Lanner, he had the fiery nature that sighs for more worlds to conquer, and the bounds of the Fatherland were too narrow for his burning ambition. He toured through half Europe. He carried into foreign lands and great capitals the fame of the Viennese waltz, and the sweet cult of the divine gaiety of old Vienna.

In art and painting, as well as in music and poesie, the Biedermeier period was abundantly fruitful. At that time Vienna brought forth her most famous painters. After the close of the Congress of Vienna, the transition from classicism in art to home-grown romanticism was complete. Nearly everywhere in the circle of young artists awoke an overmastering enthusiasm for the Middle Ages. The romanticists, Franz Pforr, Philipp Veit, Friedrich Overbeck, came to the front and studied in Vienna, where romance in the realm of painting flourished in the works of Schwind, Steinle and Führich. In Schwind, of whom we shall have much to say later in connection with his friend Schubert, the romantic spirit found pure expression full of a dreamy, tender atmosphere, nearly associated with the old Volkslied and fragrant with the charm of the Austrian landscape. The Viennese Eduard Jakob von Steinle painted religious fresco pictures, and romantic *genre* studies, like the " Violin-player." His water-colours owed much to the inspiration of his early connection with Clemens Brentano, who had converted him to it. These were the " Rheinmänchen," " Schneeweiss und Rosenrot," the " Parzival Zyklus," and many others. He had studied in the Vienna Academy of Art, and had been a pupil of Kupelwiesers. Then he went to Rome, where Overbeck's works exercised a strong influence on the young painter. He came back to Vienna counting on an industrious and successful artist's career, which, however, he seems to have abandoned hope of fulfilling. He married in 1854 and moved to Frankfurt-am-Main on the advice of his friend Huber, afterwards Ambassador. The third great romanticist painter whose genius began to unfold in Vienna at that time was the " Shepherd Boy from Kratzau," Josef von Führich, who was in his youth one of the Schubert and Schwind circle. He studied first at the Prague Academy, where Dürer's genuinely German work exercised a fascinating influence on the young artist. Then he read eagerly the works and poetry of the German romanticists, Tieck, Novalis, and Schlegel. It was his illustration of Tieck's " Genoveva " by which he first attracted notice, and the interest of Prince Metternich, who sent him to Rome to paint there in the circle of Overbeck, Julius Schnorr, Philipp Veit, Thorwaldsen, and others. On the recommendation of Overbeck, he painted in Rome scenes from Tasso for the Villa Massimi, the Roman Wartburg at that time of the young German school. Back in Vienna he was appointed through Metternich second custodian in the Academy Gallery. The Chancellor's understanding and sympathy for Führich's creations is shown in the following extract from the diary of Princess Melanie published in Metternich's literary remains in 1882 : " Clemens brought me sketches by a young painter . . . who is of peasant extraction. Clemens (Prince Metternich) has had him educated. His name is Führich, and he has done some charming things. The young man has made a sketch for a great painting, the subject of which is the coming of the Messiah and the founding of the Church. It is magnificent, most touching. . . . The impression it made on Clemens is equally extraordinary, for in describing this young painter's depth of thought and idealism, and in pointing out some of the figures in the picture, his eyes filled with tears."

In Vienna there were two great spiritual movements at this time, the so-called Josephinism, which was evolved in the eighteenth century and influenced a wide circle of the cultured, and the strictly Catholic, which found an apostle of genius in P. Clemens Maria Hoffbauer—a poor peasant's son and baker's apprentice who acted as errand boy in a monastery in order to attend the monastic school and then lived and worked in Vienna as a member of the most abstemious order of the priesthood. Hoffbauer, a strong personality, exercised by his purity and depth of faith an unusual influence on religious people. Führich, through his friend, Madlener, a favourite pupil of Hoffbauer's, became enthusiastic for the ideas of this saint. Intercourse with Friedrich August von Klinkowström, Guido Görres and others, led to a still further intensifying of the religious emotions of the young painter . . . Führich became known as the real " Christian artist " of that day, " not because," as his biographer Moriz Dreger, writes, " he always painted Christian subjects, but because he embodied in his works the two qualities which are at the root of all Christianity—Humility and Love." " The Meeting of Jacob and Rachel " and " Mary's Passing over the Mountain " are two of his most impressive religious pictures. His monumental work was the decoration with paintings of the Altlerchenfelder Kirche.

In the same manner as Führich painted Schubert's friend, Kupelweiser. He had, like Führich, pilgrimaged as a youth to Rome, where he came under the influence of Overbeck and the " Nazarene " comrades. When he came back to Vienna he occupied himself chiefly with the painting of church pictures. He also did some interesting portraits, and a cycle for Klopstock's " Messiah," to the order of the Empress Karoline Augusta, in remembrance of her husband, the Emperor Franz. In good old Wienerisch style are the signs he painted for shops—" Die schöne Schäferin " and the " Heilung des Tobias " (at the Waldheim apothecary's). Besides pious pictures, he drew many lively sketches for the gay " Schubertiade."

Other young painters of the Viennese school eschewed the representation of the wonderful and romantic. They plunged from the restraint of the academic training straight into the giddy whirlpool of life. They went in search of material in which the

Zeitgeist still preserved a few lingering ideas of the French Revolution. They mixed with the people, copied in the Belvedere Gallery, where they studied the glorious colour of the old Dutch masters. Here they found the wonderful varied life of the common people as those great artists had depicted it, a subject that appealed to their natural bent. And this newly-discovered material opened their artistic eyes to the enchanting romance of the everyday world around them, to the poetry that lies in the life of ordinary simple folk, the world from which they themselves had sprung, the Biedermeierisch world, full of strength and weakness, full of humour, poesie and sentiment. The technique which they had acquired in the Academy was applied to the producing of the colour-wealth found in the new *milieu*. They began painting all kinds of little scenes from the citizens' everyday life, scenes from military life, beginning with the recruiting sergeant and ending with the aged pensioners. They painted maternal bliss, betrothal and wedding festivities, holiday crowds at country fairs, drawing prizes in a lottery, and such-like small things. Theirs was the art which was the soul of the Biedermeier period, the same as we meet in Raimund's writings, in Nestroy's satires, the stories of Adalbert Stifter, the music of Lanner and Strauss, and in old almanacks and letters.

The most famous of these painters of the Biedermeier time was Ferdinand Georg Waldmüller. Born in the year 1795, the son of a brewer in the Tiefen Graben, he was to have been, according to his mother's wishes, a priest, but he had contrary ideas to hers for his future. He showed strong inclinations to art when still a boy, took lessons in drawing, and then, against the wishes of his parents, entered the Academy of Arts as a student. He procured the means to pay for his studies by colouring bonbons and cakes. But his youthful impetuous temperament rebelled against the discipline of the school and he had to leave it. Several successful miniature portraits which he completed in Pressburg, where he went at the bidding of the Landtag, attracted the notice of the Bans of Croatia, Count Gyulai, who sent for him to give his children drawing lessons in Agram. There he married a singer, with whom he toured in a number of provincial towns, and, on his wife getting an engagement in Vienna, he returned to his native town, where he passed his time in making copies in the various picture galleries and painting commissioned portraits. While he was working thus, he became convinced of the necessity of studying from Nature. A Captain Stierle-Holzmeister ordered a portrait of his mother, and desired that it should be absolutely true to Nature. "It was now," he himself records, "that the first ray of light dawned on me—alas! that it should have come so late—by which I saw the truth. Through a mere chance I started on the right road. The scales fell from my eyes, and I realised that the goal of all art is observation, conception and understanding of Nature. What had for long been merely a supposition sounding in my soul awakened now to full consciousness, and, though it was owing to this knowledge that I could not conceal from myself how far I had wandered from the right path, all the stronger was my resolution never again to stray from it, and with all my strength to make up for the time I had lost."

Waldmüller studied further in Paris and Italy, and afterwards was made Professor at the Academy of the Fine Arts and Custodian of the Academy gallery. As he had rebelled as a pupil, so as a teacher he came in conflict with the antiquated system of the Academy, and the authorities were instituting a formal complaint against him in the law courts when he appealed to Metternich, who, as Curator of the Academy, sent a letter of remonstrance to the Committee containing the following memorable words: "The Academy is not a reformatory in which teachers as well as pupils are forbidden to follow the bent of their own genius."

Waldmüller's was a curious, unbending nature. He lived in the open air and painted in the sun. He was the joyous painter full of inextinguishable vitality of the Biedermeier time. The stately men, the beautiful women and girls of old Vienna he pictured with temperamental and masterly art. Scenes from Austrian village life and Wienerwald landscapes were produced side by side with his society pictures and portraits. He added to the sentiment of the Viennese Biedermeier time a delightful humour, and from all his pictures shines the joyous genius of the warm Viennese sunlight. What nearly half a century later was regarded as the height of modernity he had anticipated in his pictures. He was really the first modern painter of sunshine, the first Viennese "Secessionist." Such works as his "Klostersuppe," the "Kirchtag in Petersdorf," "Die Pfändung," "Die Johannis-andacht," and many of his family groups and portraits belong to the most famous creations of the Austrian art of painting.

Another thoroughly Viennese painter of that day was Josef Danhauser. He studied at the Academy and worked afterwards in the studio of Peter Krafft, who belonged to the circle of Schubert and Schwind. Scenes from the heroic epics of Ladislaus von Pyrkers and Rudolph von Habsburg won him the regard of the latter princely prelate, and he sent him to Venice to study there treasures of art. The impression made by the works of Titian, Paolo Veronese and Tintoretto on the young artist was profound. He came back to Vienna and took over his father's curio business, where for a time his art was idle, though in its minor branches he learnt much through seeing new specimens and arranging them with taste. By the time his two younger brothers were of an age to succeed to the management of the business, Danhauser was free again to follow his profession as an artist. The pictures he showed at public exhibitions soon attracted notice and admiration. They were reproduced in engravings and lithographs. His travels in Germany, Belgium and Holland, where he studied in the galleries, brought him further new impressions. Danhauser, as a *genre* and portrait painter, was very successful. " He has a sense of colour harmony which few other artists possess," wrote Eitelberger, the art critic, after visiting an exhibition of Danhauser's pictures, " and therein lies his strength. He goes far in *genre* pictures. . . . He has had to overcome a rough realism, like many other artists, and has understood how to do it without sacrificing his individuality."

Danhauser is the Raimund among the *genre* painters in old Viennese art. He has often been called the Viennese Hogarth and the Austrian Wilkie. But he was neither a mere satirist, like Hogarth, nor a mere humorist, like Wilkie. He was more versatile, for now and then he revels in idylls reminiscent of Ludwig Richter and Spitzweg—one has only to think of the " Weinkoster "—and often depicts scenes resembling those in Raimund's writings. These are almost social dramas, such as his " Traum," " Klostersuppe " and " Testamentseröffnung." They bring before us in realistic manner the life of the old Biedermeier city and its characters, such as in the " Concert," " Die Schachpartie," " Die Dame am Klavier." A hundred times reproduced in prints and woodcuts was the famous " Liszt am Klavier," showing Liszt playing to a circle of celebrities, Rossini, Berlioz, Dumas, George Sand, Musset, and the Countess D'Agout, with the bust of Beethoven standing on the piano, the last touch lending a certain distinction to the picturesque group. In " Mutterliebe " he has in a brilliant silvery atmosphere glorified maternal love. In the midst of his activity as an artist he died before he was forty. The famous miniature painter of the Biedermeier days was Moriz Michael Daffinger. After he had learnt the rudiments of drawing from his father, a painter in the Imperial Porcelain Manufactory, Daffinger became a pupil at the academy of the celebrated Füger. When he had completed his apprenticeship, he worked for a time in the porcelain factory, and there devoted himself to the art of portraiture, in which he soon won a brilliant reputation. The two well-known painters of the Congress period, Isabey and Lawrence, were his prototypes. His work, generally executed on ivory, is to be met with in thousands of examples. They combine a fine sense of colour with the greatest sureness and delicacy of drawing, a talented conception and lively temperament with an execution not short of genius. He counterfeited all the leading personages of the high aristocracy, the handsomest men, the most beautiful women and young girls of old Vienna. His portraits of the Duke of Reichstadt, the Court actress, Sophie Schröder, Prince Metternich and his family, the Archduchess Sophie and her children are famous. He was the most sought after of all miniature painters in those days, and was called the Austrian Isabey.

The early death of his young and most beloved daughter affected him deeply. From this time onwards he gave up portrait painting, and devoted himself, for his private pleasure, to flowers. He collected all the loveliest specimens of wild blossoms from the Austrian mountains and painted them. He had done nearly 200 of these " Flower Portraits " when, in the year 1849, he died of cholera.

The two painters, Peter Fendi and Franz Eybl, both painted local humble life. Fendi got his early artistic impressions from the collection of the oculist Barth, and from the valuable picture gallery belonging to Count Lamberg, where he copied industriously. Fendi's pictures of Viennese *bourgeois* life, " Vor der Lottobude," " Der arme Geiger," " Die Pfändung," " Das Milchmädchen," " Das Dachstübchen," are small cabinet treasures of distinction in the art of *genre* painting. Famous in the often seen engraving of Johann Passini is his picture " Familienvereinigung im Kaiserhaus," which contains thirty-seven portraits—Kaiser Franz and the whole tribe of his relatives.

Fendi was called the Hebel of *genre* painting, and one of his pictures, "Die Mutter am Christabend," illustrates a story of Hebel's. This artist was, we are told by a contemporary, " small of stature, ugly as Æsop, with a huge gnome-like head on a short neck. Strange that Nature should have endowed such a grotesque creature with so much taste and artistic talent." Eybl was also a humorous portrayer of the life of the small Viennese shop-keeper and other humble people. His best-known pictures are " Heimkehr eines Landmanns," " Die alte Spinnerin," " Der Bettler," etc. As a portrait painter, too, of distinguished people he enjoyed great popularity.

A truly artistic nature was Johann Matthias Ranftl's, the son of an innkeeper in the Favoriten district. He began with romantic canvases, having with a bound sprung from pot-boy to artist, and painted subjects like " Kunz von den Rosen und Kaiser Max," then altar-pieces and portraits, only finding his true *métier* after long searchings and struggles. The speciality which he at last hit upon was the relationship of men to animals, notably to dogs. He became the most celebrated animal painter in Vienna. He was called Vienna's Dog-Raphael, and caricatured the author, M. G. Saphir, as a poodle barking outside the door of an inn, " Zur Konkordia," a satirical commentary on the vain efforts of the witty but unpopular *littérateur* to get into the artists' club, " Konkordia." Many of this artist's dog pictures have been lithographed and widely circulated. It should be mentioned that it was the young Ranftl who, jointly with Danhauser, took Beethoven's mask in clay. The delightful landscape painter of that day was Friedrich Gauermann, born at Miesenbach, near Gutenstein, in Lower Austria. Like most of the painters of the Biedermeier time, he was a copyist, and copied Ruysdael, de Potter, de Jardin, etc. But the surrounding Nature, which he observed, studied and drew diligently, was his true mistress. Gauermann had roamed through the Alpine districts of Styria, Salzburg, and the Salzkanimergut, and sketched the loveliest Alpine scenes from the life of shepherds, fishermen and huntsmen, and made pictures of the animal world and plants. His technique and truth to Nature were remarkable. " Never are his studies lacking," writes Eitelberger, " in the special characteristics of the time and seasons. . . . But the power of his work consists in his grasp of the animal world, his insight into the life and ways of animals. In his pictures he shows how they look in the hour of danger driven by blind instinct; he strives always in a fresh and natural way to bring the landscape into harmony with the animal in the foreground."

The " Gemüthlichkeit," but at the same time the essentially intellectual intercourse of the time, influenced its artistic life. The Congress of Vienna had been the impetus to noble festivities on the grand scale. The Viennese had seen much beauty and exalted elegance, and had modelled themselves thereon. A new standard and style of living were evolved for the citizen class out of this richly endowed atmosphere, a romantic continuation of an heroic empire. A certain specific Viennese style bound in close relationship the music of Schubert and Lanner, the art of Schwind, the writings of Raimund. The Biedermeier Viennese created a home and mode of life for himself, full of grace and comfort. The furniture was of walnut or cherry-wood and brightly polished. The cupboards had at their corners little sculptured pillars of wood. Through the panes of the glass doors glittered the finest porcelain from the Vienna factory, and over them was carved delicately a tiny lute in gold; the backs of the chairs had slender pilasters. The round table, often with inlaid ornamentation, rested on pillared castor legs. Near the door hung a peal of bells decked with pearls. Fancy work of tatting and crochet and the finest native embroidery covered everything—armchairs, cushions, footstools. Of course, in accordance with the musical spirit of the time, the piano of cherry-wood was not missing, or the black alabaster timepiece, whose solemn tick reminded you of the perishableness of all earthly things. There was the dainty work-table, with work-basket of finest china, and there, too, was the big easy chair to rest in and spin dreams. From the walls laughed the portraits of handsome young men with a *soupçon* of romance, and pretty girls' heads and beautiful women by Daffinger, Kriehuber, Rieder, and Teltscher. Black silhouettes looked out dreamily from cherry-wood frames, half-length portraits in oils breathed parental dignity, and above the canopy reigned also in oils the presentment of the worthy patriarch of the kingdom, Kaiser Franz.

Very Biedermeierisch and genial was the social life, full of the flow of soul and easy hospitality. The old Viennese salon flourished then at its best. Its prototype was Goethe's Weimar Court of the Muses. Music, poetry, theatre and philosophy, without any outward ostentation, formed the backbone of social intercourse. The literary salon of the authoress Karoline Pichler was famous. It was the meeting-place of all the cultured in every position of life at home and abroad. Mozart, although he was not actually her teacher, had given the little Karoline Pichler many lessons, and often played at the house of her grandfather, the old Hofrat Greiner. When she grew up and began to write romances, they met with the approval of the best critics. Her lively society and extremely original mind attracted all the best people, men and women, living in the town to her house, among them Grillparzer, Schreyvogel, Collin, Füger, Hammer, Hormayr, Schlegel, Zacharias Werner, Anschütz, Spohr, Castelli, Adam Müller, Schröder-Devrient, and sometimes Schubert and his circle. Every stranger of note passing through Vienna visited the Pichler salon—Karl Maria Weber, Madame de Staël, Tieck, Jakob Grimm, Clemens and Bettina Brentano and Oehlenschläger. And with Goethe himself this talented Viennese woman was also in communication. After reading her "Agathokles," he sent her through Frau Flies a long message, in which he praised her drawing of character. "How very much I was struck by the inborn talent of the authoress is proved by the fact that in the enjoyment of this amiable work of art I forgot how very little the century which she makes live in its pages appeals to me as a rule."

Houses where the artistic and musical world were hospitably entertained were those of the Hofrat Ignaz Mosel and Rafael Kiesewetter, in whose salon old classical music was performed. At these private concerts his daughter, Irene Kiesewetter, came out as a highly interesting pianist, "with the figure of a Juno and of bewitching beauty." She married later the poet and statesman, Count Prokesch-Osten.

A rendezvous of all Vienna's friends of art, especially of musicians, was the house of Grillparzer's relations, Leopold, Josef and Ignaz von Sonnleithner. They were all musical enthusiasts, especially the last-named, a noted lawyer known everywhere in Vienna for his brilliant intellect and "winged" words of wit and wisdom, which long after his death were remembered and quoted in his native city. He was also famed for his unusual musical talent, for he united with his magnificent baritone voice a noble delivery. During the Vienna Congress, in the year 1815, he sang at request in Handel's Oratorio " Timothæus " before an " illustrious *parterre* " audience in the Reitschule. In the house of Ignaz Sonnleithner in Gundelhof, in the market-place, music was passionately cultivated. For many years regular music evenings took place there every fortnight, at which the flower of artistic talent, both native and foreign, was represented. Caroline Unger, Blahetka, Bocklet, Hummel, Hellmesberger, and Nestroy won their spurs first in presence of the select Areopagus assembled there. Franz Schubert accompanied his own songs, and it was here that on November 20th, 1820, his " Dörfchen," and in the following December his " Erlkönig," were first heard. Grillparzer, who was Sonnleithner's nephew and the same age as the eldest son of the house, was an ever-welcome guest, and some of his most beautiful poems were intimately associated with Ignaz Sonnleithner's family. The Society of Music Friends began in the musical entertainments given at the Sonnleithners' house. Josef Sonnleithner, Secretary at the Hoftheater, was the founder; he also rendered valuable services in composing the text for Beethoven's " Leonore."

Houses of old Viennese citizens much visited where Schubert and his friends were frequent guests were, besides the Sonnleithners', the abodes of the sisters Fröhlich, the brothers Spaun, Anschütz, the merchant Bruchmann, the lawyer Hönig, the actress Sophie Müller, the Schober family, and so on. Here the intimate acquaintances and friends of the families came together in the evening, and one heard serious conversations as well as lively repartee. Young poets read aloud the latest verse with which their muse had inspired them. There was singing, dancing and social games. Then shyly, a somewhat corpulent little young man would go to the piano—Franz Schubert, the genius of the party— and begin to improvise. His short thick fingers glided over the keys of the Streicher instrument, from which he brought forth wonderful pictures in sound which flooded the room with beauty. Often he would play duets with the daughter of the house or with his friend the medical practitioner, Josef von Gahy. Sometimes he accompanied the famous singer Vogl, or the elegant Baron Schönstein, or the Civil Service magnate Gymnich, as they sang his songs. And the whole family and all the guests of the house gathered round the little spectacled man, the musician absorbed in the sweet sounds he was producing. Now and again he would raise fiery and melancholy eyes to his spell-bound listeners . . . this prince of genius-land who strewed with generous hands the pearls of his soul before the reverently attentive audience. Walls and doors began to ring, the room changed into an arena for the singing muses and graces. The miracle of human genius transformed this little everyday life into a dream-world of divinest beauty. And late at night when the party broke up still saturated with Schubert's music, humming his melodies to themselves, alone or in groups, the guests, in the light of flickering lanterns, made their way home through the quiet narrow streets and benighted courts and alleys of the deserted Glacis.

A merry, lively meeting-point for the social Viennese bachelor life was the "Ludlamshöhle." "A group of socially inclined youths," relates Castelli in his memoirs, "came together in 1817 to engage in conversation, with songs and heated discussions on the subject of Art." The Society was named "Ludlamshöhle" after a popular drama at the Theater-an-der-Wien. The Chief or Caliph was the Court actor Karl Schwarz. All the members had nicknames. Grillparzer, for instance, was "Sophocles"; Castelli, "Charon"; Zedlitz, who had drawn up the rules, "Columbus"; Ludlams, "Solon," and so on. Nearly every representative of art belonged to the club, hence Schubert and his friends. In course of time the Metternich police began to regard these gay and harmless Biedermeier bachelors as conspirators, and the merry and intellectual meetings were dissolved in 1826 as dangerous to the State, after eight years' existence.

In those days an atmosphere of joyous satisfaction prevailed in the town after the termination of the festivities attending the Congress which had made it the centre of the whole realm. "The whole aspect of the town with its surroundings," wrote Varnhagen von Ense, "has something about it suggestive of riches, well-being and personal contentment. The people here seem healthier and happier than elsewhere, the evil spirits which are generally supposed to accompany, torment and stick to human beings, in this air would find it difficult to breathe, and would be obliged to take up their abode somewhere else. . . ." The spirit of citizenship was strengthened, and trade and industry began greatly to prosper. Recognition and riches rewarded the efforts of Viennese merchants and manufacturers in the Neubau and Schottenfeld. It was the Phœnician epoch of Vienna culture, full of an abundance of talent and genius, full of gladness and enjoyment of life. People concerned themselves little about politics, but revelled in a laughing philosophy of life, in " Wein, Weib und Gesang."

Lanner and Strauss, the music magicians, expended generously their gay and graceful melodies to heighten the brilliance of the Viennese carnival. To the swaying rhythm of their waltzes all Vienna danced and sang in an ecstasy of happiness and bliss. Numberless were the *cafés* where the two artists with their bands gave concerts. Strauss's domain was the " Sperl," a very favourite pleasure resort in the Biedermeier time. It was in the halls of the " Sperl " that he scored his first great triumphs, and several of his celebrated dance pieces, such as " Sperlpolka," the " Sperlwalzer " and the " Fortuna Gallop," came out here. Vast crowds flocked to the Strauss *soirées* which Bauernfeld has immortalised in his " *vers de société*." And to " Tivoli," on the green hills of Obermeidling, near Schönbrunn, the Viennese pilgrimaged in their hundreds on Sunday afternoon to hear Strauss play his waltzes in a splendid hall with gilded pillars and glass walls, and to disport themselves on the switchback and at " Kiss in the Ring." Ferdinand Raimund has described these guileless dissipations in his Biedermeier song of the Carpenters and the Kitchen Fairy, whom he takes to " Tivoli " on Sunday afternoons.

The Eldorado of both society and the people was, above all, the Prater. " There were to be found all the beauties of Nature," wrote at that time the cosmopolitan Count de la Garde, " the sight of which had a wonderfully refreshing and soothing effect on the soul. The Prater is planted with majestic trees more than a hundred years old. They cast a splendid shade on the turf, preserving it from being burnt up by the rays of the sun. It is intersected with glorious avenues, and, as in Schönbrunn, one sees here endless stags and fawns wandering about in the glades, giving these lovely solitudes life and movement. Besides the enjoyment of a sylvan and unspoilt Nature, one is also provided here with all the charming accessories of culture and art. There are to be found here any number of booths, *cafés* and social resorts, where the people of Vienna can indulge their taste for music to their hearts' content. The greatest charm of the Prater for these people is its associations. It is easy to understand what memories are connected with the ancestral oaks that stand here, memories both sympathetic and sentimental. For every one of the aged, this walk under the oak trees is the book of life ; for here in the beginning are played the games of childhood, here youth's dreams of first love unfold. Every evening when the day's work is over, those who have reached maturity may seek here hours of untroubled happiness. But there are pleasures of all kinds to suit the taste of every age."

On fine spring mornings the Viennese used to crowd into the Prater bent on sport. Horsemen in pink with tall hats galloped over the meadows, carriages of the nobility, smart turn-outs with coachmen in livery and haughty, stiff footmen, drove into this open-air drawing-room of Viennese life. *Fiacres* brought the *bourgeoisie* through the green broad walk to the Pavilion of Pleasure. From carriages and coaches decorated with flowers descended beautiful women with bare, gleaming shoulders, clad in bright colours illumined by the sun, wearing wide-brimmed hats like flower-gardens and rustling silks trimmed with lace, carrying tiny parasols, and waving jewelled fans. And here was assembled everybody who was anybody in the town : Kaiser Franz and his lovely young wife Maria Ludovika, the friend of Goethe, the ex-Empress Marie Louisa, and Napoleon's son, the Duke of Reichstadt, the pale Cardinal Archduke Rudolph, the pupil and worshipper of Beethoven, Metternich with his clever aristocratic head, the severe Minister of Police, Count Sedlnitzky, the Biedermeier lady-killer, Hofrat Gentz, with fair women swarming round him, wealthy bankers, magnates of industry from Schottenfeld, and the famous actors and singers from the Court Theatre, Sophie Schröder, Adamberger, Therese Krones, and the delightful young dancer Fanni Elssler. . . . All in the glory of the spring came hither, the powerful and rich, the rulers of money and mind, and were the " observed of all observers "; the Viennese people collected on either side of the avenues watching them, staring and gaping at them in curiosity and admiration. There they listened to the *Vorstadt* musicians, the fiddle and the harp players who, on improvised stages, gave of their best in native art. The game of Pulcinella was played. There were swings and hoops and wax-works. There revolved " Calafatti " the grandpapa of all round games ; there was the dazzling " Gothic Tower," with its coffee-house and camera, in which was reflected a pretty picture of the town and suburbs embedded in green woods and the Wienerwald's chain of gentle hills. They amused themselves, these pleasure-loving folks, with games of ball, in climbing trees and sack-racing. They went into little bars for refreshment—favourite of all was the " grünen Paperl," where for a gulden note one got its famous menu of a dozen dishes—or to the " Schönen Schäferin " with the gay ditty inscribed above its door :

> *" Ich schöne Schäferin ruhe allhier*
> *alle Schäfer setzen sich zu mir,*
> *da kann man lustig seyn*
> *man bekommt gut Bier und Wein."*

Then there was the " Wallfisch " and the " zur Vermählung," where on the sign-board a pair of lovers were seen being joined in holy matrimony by a priest. On May 1st there was a great National Festival, with races and prizes for the postillion runners who ran before the equipages of the nobility and lighted them on the way home at night with torches. The fireworks of the Conjurer Stuwer on Maria-Theresa Days drew half Vienna into the Prater and on to the bastions, or as far as the Mariahilferberg. "When the Fire-artist lets off his fantasticks," relates Adalbert Stifter, " the watching crowd is so thick it looks as if the space was plastered with heads, and all gaze up into the night sky, which is full of zigzags of light from exploding rockets. Suddenly there will appear a star, which floats away on the air in colour, first green, then blue, then gold; it comes down slowly and bursts on the way, sending out a shower of coloured fire-flowers. Or suddenly you see a great burning city, crackling and fizzling, in which to occult vision marvellous things are visible."

" In Vienna the Sunday after the full moon in the July of every year and following days is a regular festival," relates Grillparzer in the " Arme Spielmann." "The people celebrate it, and the people make it what it is. Aristocrats can come to the same only in the capacity of being members of the people. On this day all classes, from Augarten Leopoldstadt to the Prater, join hands in celebrating the *Brigittenkirchtag*. The people count the days from one *St. Bridget* to the next. Long looked forward to, the Saturnalian feast comes at last. Then there arises an uproar in the good-natured, orderly town. A seething crowd fills the streets. Class distinctions are forgotten. Everybody pushes and jostles everyone else, pressing forward to the first trees of the Augarten.

When these are in sight they call out 'Land! Land! Land!'
Those who have come in carriages get out and mix with the
pedestrians. Sounds of distant dance music are greeted with
rapture by the newcomers. On they go, further and further, till
at last they are *there*—there where in wood and meadow music and
dancing, wine and song, are in full swing, where shadow-games,
tight-rope walking, illuminations and fireworks combine to produce
a *Pays de Cokayne*, an Eldorado, a veritable fairy-land."

The life of Vienna in the Prater was designated by Count de la
Garde as a true reflection of his government, " which doubtless
might be called despotic, but which had no other goal in view than
the well-being and material improvement of the people. Contrary
to other States, notably France, the Austrian *régime* was free from
all control and able to become the leader and protector of the
people, and if it was necessary sometimes to act despotically, it
happened, as in private families, with the consent of a peaceful and
sensible population."

Quickly as the Viennese Biedermeier time had come and bloomed
as the blue flower of Viennese romanticism, casting a wonderful
glamour on the life of the city, it as quickly faded away ; its fine
delicate petals fell to the ground, its soft light was extinguished.

First of all the brightest star of the Biedermeier firmament,
Franz Schubert, went out. " Schubert is dead and with him is
gone the brightest and most beautiful thing we possessed! "
exclaimed Schwind, when he heard the news in Munich of
Schubert's death. He was soon followed by the joyous, lively
Therese Krones. At scarcely thirty she took leave of the stage.
The pale-faced magician, Thanatos, came to her sick-bed and
played to her for the last time the song which she had sung so
often with incomparable pathos, "*Brüderlein fein, Brüderlein fein,
einmal muss geschieden sein.*" Raimund's fairy world sank below the
horizon, with all its joyous spirits and goblins ; its young master
and creator, a prey to sordid cares, passed sadly away. And
Lanner's fiddle, with its wonderful tones of gaiety and melancholy,
was now for ever silent. Viennese youth followed the coffin of
their Waltz-Troubadour, whose swaying melodies had lured them
irresistibly to the dance, sorrowfully to the grave. Schreyvogel,
the dramaturgist of genius, left his beloved Burgtheater, where he
had been at the helm for fifteen years, and which he had raised to
the first rank of German theatres. His new chief, a haughty, bad-

tempered count, at whom he once hurled the memorable retort, "You don't understand these things, Excellency," turned him brusquely out of the temple of art which he had reared with so much laborious care. Broken-hearted, he staggered down the stairs, and in his haste left his umbrella and overcoat behind. His eyes full of tears, he went home in a downpour of rain. The chill and excitement made him ill, and he had to take to his bed. When he rose from it after a few weeks, he was a shadow of his former self, and so weak he fell an easy victim to cholera.

And, lastly, the young Duke of Reichstadt, the beloved Prince Charming of the Biedermeier times, the idol of women and maidens, lay on his death-bed out there in Schönbrunn. All Vienna wept for the fair youth, for Napoleon's son, and sang Saphir's elegy:

> "*Im Garten zu Schönbronnen,*
> *Da liegt der König von Rom,*
> *Sieht nicht das Lied der Sonnen*
> *Sieht nicht des Himmels Dom.*"

And like an elegy, too, on the dying Viennese romanticism are the words which Countess Lulu Thürheim, the Prince's friend, wrote, full of sadness, in her diary:

". . . .Blotted out from this earth, and soon out of the memory of men and the records of history, like a trampled-on blossom. Just a name, a borrowed name and nothing more. Insoluble riddle to which God alone holds the solution, which not in the course of this century or in eternity will ever be revealed."

Schubert's Life

THE course of Schubert's life, like that of those other great Austrians, Haydn, Mozart, Grillparzer, Stifter and Bruckner, was simple and uneventful. Outwardly his life presents nothing very remarkable, and can almost be related as an everyday story. It was a life of poverty, and, like his nature, introspective. All the more wonderful, then, were the riches of Schubert's mind and thought, his inner life. What days, full of wistful longing and creative joy, lie hidden in it, what artistic achievements, what hours of joyous gaiety and profoundest melancholy, what pleasures earthly and divine! His life was his art, his art was his life. It was, if we look at it from his earliest childhood, a ceaseless expression of tones, a continual dreaming and creating winged by fantasy, spurred on by a supernatural power, the like of which in the history of the musical arts only finds a parallel in Mozart. Everything round him and in him was music.

Three years before the beginning of the new century, on January 31st, 1797, Franz Schubert was born in the Viennese suburb, Himmelpfortgrund, Pfarre Lichtental, at the house " Zum roten Krebsen," number 72 (to-day 54, Nussdorferstrasse). He was the son of the national schoolmaster, Franz Theodor, from Neudorf in Mähren, who was married to Elizabeth Vietz. She was from Silesia and had been a cook in Vienna. Franz was one of the younger of fourteen children, five of whom, including himself, the brothers Ignaz, Ferdinand and Karl, and the sister Theresa, survived. Himmelpfortgrund was the domain of the Viennese laundry girls, and at that time was quite rustic in character, having flower gardens behind the houses, vines and fields. In the distance could be heard the rustling of trees in the Wienerwald, and the silhouette of the Kahl and Leopold Mountains was discernible against the sky. For the most part the houses were simple suburban dwellings with small windows, backyards and gardens.

The house (still standing) in which Schubert was born was a plain, one-storied building, with yard space on either side. In the background a garden smiled, and in the yard splashed a fountain. In those days there may have been lively times here when there appeared in the yard an organ-grinder or a dancing bear, women selling lavender, the " Evangeliman " singing, children playing, maids hanging out washing to dry, girls coming to the fountain to fetch water and to gossip a little. And if a fiddler or a harp-player came in at the door there would be songs and dances. Then Viennese Volks music would fill the yard, every window would be thrown open, the girls would leave their work and come crowding round the musicians, sing to their tunes and pose gracefully for the dance. This yard was Schubert's merry childhood's kingdom.

Before the boy had begun to have his first music lessons he used, his sister Theresa relates, often to go with a carpenter's apprentice who was connected with the family to a pianoforte manufactory, where he struck chords, according to his childish fancy, on the rows of instruments standing there.

" Before he was five," his father wrote, " I prepared him for elementary instruction, and in his sixth year sent him to school, where he was always higher in the class than his schoolfellows. When he was eight I grounded him in violin-playing, and got him so far advanced that he was able to play easy duets fairly well, and then I sent him for singing lessons to Michael Holzer, choir-master in Lichtenthal. This teacher used to assure me with tears in his eyes that he had never had such a pupil before : ' When I begin to teach him something new, I find that he knows it already,' he said. ' Finally, I have given up teaching him anything, and simply listen to him in amazed silence.' " He was given his first piano lessons by his eldest brother, Ignaz, who tells us : " To my astonishment he came to me after a few months and said he required no further instruction, as he would teach himself in future. And, in fact, he was so far advanced in a short time that I was obliged to acknowledge that he far surpassed myself as a master, and I should have difficulty in overtaking him."

Schubert as a boy had a sweet-sounding soprano voice, and, owing to his father's efforts, little Franz, in the year 1808, after he had several times sung soprano in the parish church to the conducting of the choirmaster, Holzer, was appointed a chorister

Franz Theodore Schubert
Unknown painter
(Schubert Museum, Vienna)

in the chapel of the Imperial Court. On September 30th, 1808, in the Konvikt, Universitätsplatz, No. 796, Schubert underwent the examination at which his clear treble and perfect accuracy of tone attracted the notice of the Court examiners, Anton Salieri and Josef Eybler. Their report in September, 1808, was to the effect that the three vacancies for choristers in the choir of the Court Chapel could not be better filled than by the sopranos, Franz Schubert and Franz Müller, and the alto, Maximilian Weisse.

Five years were now passed by Schubert in the Konvikt of the city on the Jesuitenplatz. For five years he sang in the Court Chapel choir, and these years were of the greatest importance in his later musical training. The Imperial Court Orchestra was one of the oldest musical institutions in Vienna. Even as early as the days of Maximilian I. it had been recruited from the best Viennese musicians to satisfy the taste of the art-loving Imperial Court and its artistically-gifted regents; especially the Baroque Kaiser Leopold I., Josef I. and Karl VI., encouraged its activity. Its performances enjoyed a world-wide reputation. The Konvikt was for the chorister boys a kind of small music conservatoire, reminiscent of the old ecclesiastical singing schools belonging to the monasteries and cathedral chapters, where a classical education and training was provided for the young singers. Music was ardently cultivated. The boys had their own separate orchestra. The pieces practised daily in Schubert's time consisted of an overture (of either Cherubini, Weigl, Méhul or Mozart), a symphony, and, to end the concert, an overture. Song quartets and string quartets from Mozart and Haydn were also practised. In winter these were exclusively house concerts, but in summer, when the windows of the Konvikt stood open, the youthful musicians attracted a large open-air audience. On fine evenings promenaders returning from the Bastions would pause outside to listen entranced to the music coming through the open windows. Schubert played the violin or viola in the Konvikt orchestra, and sometimes, in the absence of the Court musician, Wenzel Ruczizka, wielded the baton. Playing in the orchestra, conducting, and, above all, singing in the choir of the chapel was an invaluable musical training for Schubert, teaching him the sound and different character of every separate instrument, and accuracy of tone.

The divine world of the Viennese classics was opened up to the receptive boy's heart in the Konvikt and the old Imperial Court

Orchestra. From Haydn's symphonies, sonatas and quartets he felt the inspiring breath of idyllic beauty. " One hears the angels singing in Mozart's symphonies," Schubert confided to his faithful school comrade, Spaun. Here he learnt, too, to know and value some of Beethoven's works. The unusually precocious child seems at first to have been somewhat depressed when the Master's mighty tornados of tone first rushed over him. " Sometimes I think," he once confided in Spaun, " that I might myself perhaps bring forth something, but who, after Beethoven, dare try ? " It was not till later that he found his way into the works of this Titan, to whom ever afterward he looked up to as his highest ideal.

Every Sunday and saint's day the young soprano, Franz Schubert, in the uniform worn by the Court choristers, climbed the steep steps of the Schweizerhof to sing under the guidance of the Court conductors, Salieri and Eybler, in the Masses, vespers and litanies in the little choir of the Court Chapel. The mystical power of the Catholic Church music exercised a marvellous fascination on the boy's sensitive temperament. In the Konvikt and at school the foundations of lasting friendships were laid with Josef von Spaun, Albert Stadler, Josef Kenner, Johann Michael Senn, Anton Holzapfel, Franz Bruchmann, Josef von Streinsberg, and Benedikt Ranhartinger, most of whom played a considerable part in Schubert's later life.

Schubert's chief musical mentor in those years was Wenzel Ruczizka. He was the singing-master and piano-teacher of the Court choirboys. His first-class method of instruction was thus flatteringly commented on in a letter from the musical member of the Court, Count von Kuefstein, to the head tutor, written in November, 1809 : " It is much to the credit of the excellent teacher, Ruczizka, that in this troubled half-year he has continued with praiseworthy zeal giving instruction in various branches of music besides the piano, especially in harmony. He is not by his duties bound to teach anything but the piano, but to his extended activity the Konvikt enjoys an all-round fairly organised musical education."

Schubert's circumstances during his years in the Konvikt were very modest. " For a long time," he wrote to his brother Ferdinand, " I have been thinking over my position, and have come to the conclusion that on the whole it is not bad, but might be somewhat improved. You know by experience how one would enjoy now and then devouring a roll and an apple or two when, after an indifferent midday meal, one has to wait eight and a half hours for a miserable supper. This desire is becoming more and more imperative, and I feel I must, *nolens volens*, make some different arrangements. The few groschens I get from our father are gone in the first few days. . . . What am I to do for the rest of the time? To set my hopes on you would be no disgrace, according to St. Matthew, chap. 2, v. 4. What do you say to allowing me a few kreutzers monthly? You would hardly miss them, whereas they would make me happy and content. As I said, I support my case with the words of the Apostle St. Matthew: 'Whosoever hath two cloaks, let him give one to the poor.' Meanwhile, I hope that you will not turn a deaf ear to the voice which unceasingly petitions you not to forget

Your loving, poor, ever-hoping,
BROTHER FRANZ."

The favourite resort in the Konvikt of the little chorister was the music-room. " In the room where the piano was," Kenner, who wrote the text of so many of Schubert's songs, tells us. " After dinner in our own free time we practised, Stadler, myself and Anton Holzapfel, and gave recitals of Beethoven and Zum-steegscher works, in which the whole audience took part. The room in winter was not warmed, and for that reason ghastly cold. Now and then Spaun came, and, after he had left the institute, Schubert. Stadler played the paino, Holzapfel sang, and now and then Schubert seated himself at the piano."

And Josef von Spaun, Schubert's most faithful school-friend, relates in his reminiscences of the master, about the time which they spent together in the Konvikt: " Schubert didn't feel very much at home in the school, for he was a serious, always reserved little boy. He was put into the small orchestra because he could already play the violin quite well. I sat as first violin, next the second, and behind me, standing, little Schubert played from the same notes. Very soon I became aware that the little musician played in far better time than I did. This drew my attention to him, and I noticed how the silent boy, who generally appeared to be indifferent and uninterested, was carried away by the beauty of the music we performed. Once I found him alone in the music-room, sitting at the piano, which, with his small hands, he played very nicely. He was trying over a sonata of Mozart's, and said that he liked it, but found Mozart very difficult to play well. Encouraged by my friendly remarks, he played me a minuet of his own composition. He did it very shyly and blushed crimson, but was pleased when I applauded him. He confided to me that he often expressed his secret thoughts in notes, but his father muśtn't know, as he was altogether againśt his devoting himself to music. I used afterwards to bring him music paper."

Schubert confided to Spaun all the emotions and feelings of his precocious child-soul. He played to him in the music-room, where there was no śtove and which was icily cold in winter, his firśt attempts in composition, and with him he used later to go to the Kärntnertortheater sometimes, and from the gallery liśten with enthusiasm to Weigl's " Schweizerfamilie," Gluck's " Iphigenie," Cherubini's " Medea," and Mozart's " Zauberflöte," and admire the singing and the expressive aćting of the chief performers, Frau Milder and the singer Vogl. " There can't be anything more beautiful than the aria in the third aćt of ' Iphigenie,' with the accompanying chorus of women's voices," he exclaimed, giving vent to his enthusiasm after a performance of Gluck's opera. " The Milder's voice pierces my heart. I should like to know Vogl, so that I might kneel at his feet and thank him for his Oreśtes."

Spaun, his beśt freind, to Schubert's grief, after he had finished his śtudies at the Konvikt left Vienna, and did not return till 1811 when he was appointed to a pośt in the Government. The old bonds of friendship, after two years' separation, were then resumed. " I found my young friend," Spaun tells us, " somewhat grown and in good case. He had long ago been promoted to play firśt violin, and had won regard and respećt in the orcheśtra. Schubert told me that he had composed a great deal : a sonata, a fantasia, a little opera, and he was now going to write a mass. The chief difficulty that he had to overcome was that he had no music paper and no money to buy it with ; he was therefore obliged to use ordinary paper, and even that he often didn't know how to get. I undertook to supply him secretly with music paper, which he consumed in incredibly large quantities. He wrote music with extraordinary rapidity, and the time of śtudy he devoted entirely to composition, so that his scholaśtic attainments lagged behind. Father Schubert, an otherwise worthy man, discovered the reason of his son's backwardness in śtudy, and there was a śtormy scene and a renewed command to the boy to neglect music instead of his other studies, but the young artist's impulse towards this was so strong it was not to be suppressed."

Schubert, entirely absorbed by his musical dreams, began to neglect more than ever his school studies, and his father, angered, forbade him to enter the parental house, in the hopes that this severity would have the effect of making his son work in the direction he thought the right one. But the demon of music had taken possession of the boy's soul. Instead of Latin vocabularies and mathematical problems being committed to memory, reams of paper brought him by his friend Spaun were covered with a flood of notes. Under the influence of the compositions of Johann Rudolf Zumsteeg, about whose songs especially the boy raved, he wrote *lieder*, then fantasias and sonatas, string quartets and masses—all tentative attempts, imitative of his prototypes, as yet without distinctive characteristics and impersonal. Nevertheless, Schubert's amazing productiveness and precocity, his extraordinary musical gifts, attracted the notice of the Court Conductor, Salieri, who suggested that Ruczizka should give him lessons in the theory of music. The latter replied : " I can teach him nothing ; he has learnt everything from God." And now Schubert's father began, too, to respect his son's great talent, and agreed to allow the boy to go in for a higher musical education and become a pupil of Salieri's. Just at this time the little chorister sustained a heavy sorrow in the loss of his mother on Corpus Christi, May 28th, 1812. " She was a quiet, unpretentious woman, but greatly beloved by her children, and esteemed by all." Schubert came now, after a long absence, to the home in the Lichtental. The sad event brought father and son together again in reconciliation, and the Court Chapel chorister was seen from this time forward every Sunday and saint's day after the Mass in the Lichtental. On these occasions chamber music was played in the afternoons with great zeal. Quartets of Haydn, Mozart, Beethoven, later Schubert's own, formed the programme. Franz played the viola, father, 'cello, and the brothers Ignaz and Ferdinand, first and second violin. Franz, as the most musical of them all, was permitted to correct in his modest way the father's inaccurate playing with " I think you've missed out something here, sir." Those were pleasant hours for the simple household of the schoolmaster. The neighbours gathered outside the windows of the little dwelling, and people living in the neighbourhood of Himmelpfortgrund, artisans, burghers, workmen, women and children, listened quietly and full of admiration to the music made by the Lichtentaler schoolmaster's family.

In the year 1815 Schubert, whose voice meanwhile had cracked, left the Konvikt and returned altogether for the time being to his father's house. " *Schubert (Franz) crowed for the last time, 26th July,* 1812," is to be seen scrawled in a boyish hand on the margin of a sheet of music for third alto voice in the music collection of the Vienna National Library. His father had changed his dwelling, and had come into possession of a small house in the Himmelpfortgrund (Säulengasse IX). In accordance with the wishes of his father, who considered a musical career too uncertain and precarious, Franz adopted the calling of a schoolmaster ; also this step seemed the best way of escaping military service, which then lasted for a compulsory period of fourteen years. He therefore attended a training course for teachers at St. Anna's in 1813 and 1814, and then was appointed to the post of assistant master for the junior classes in his father's school. For three years he strove with conscientious industry to initiate the small children of Lichtental in the rudiments of knowledge—a tedious task for a steadily developing genius, who, alongside the barren, unstimulating schoolmastering, lived another secret life devoted to the art of music. It was a tossing hither and thither between two worlds, like Pegasus in harness. One day he was a poor usher, the prey of all the rude ribaldry of an untamed youth ; the next he was a heaven-besieger, lifted above the drab everyday on the wings of his dreams into the divine realm of fantasy. Again and again the slumbering creative power awoke within him, again and again an irresistible impulse drew him to music, and every bit of music paper he could get hold of was covered with the masses, songs, cantatas and quartets which he composed, and more and more frequently the dreamy youth fled from the deadening schoolmaster's yoke to communion with his muse.

We get a picture of the young musician's psychic life in extracts from the diary, to which Schubert confided his thoughts and dreams. " A brilliant, beautiful day, the memory of which will remain with me for my whole life," he recorded on June 15th, 1816, after an evening of chamber music, in which he had taken part. " From distant space echo still within me the magic tones of Mozart's

The Konvikt
From a water-colour by an unknown artist
(Vienna State Museum)

music. How wonderfully powerful and yet gentle and soft was it, played in Schlesinger's masterly style, penetrating deeply into the heart. No time and circumstances can efface from the soul these beautiful imprints, which must everlastingly affect our inner existence. Oh, Mozart! Immortal Mozart! how many and endless are the impressions of a brighter and better life that you have imprinted on our souls? This quintet is, so to speak, one of his *greatest* smaller works. I felt on this occasion that I, too, must contribute something. I played variations of Beethoven, sang Goethe's ' Rastlose Liebe ' and Schiller's ' Amalia.' Although I can congratulate myself on ' Amalia ' being a success, I can't deny that Goethe's poetic genius had the lion's share of applause."

" Man is like a ball," he wrote on September 8th, 1816, " with which chance and passion play games. I have often heard it said by authors, ' Life is like a stage on which every man plays his part. Praise and blame follow in the next world.' A *rôle* is given us, and our *rôles* also come to an end ; who is to say whether we have played them well or badly? It is a bad stage-manager who gives to individuals parts that they are not able to play. There is no question here of not trying ; the world contains no instance of an actor being dismissed because of bad recitation. Directly he gets a part that suits him, he will play it well; whether or no he gains applause depends on the public's thousand moods. Praise or blame is the concern of the world's stage-manager. Natural gifts and education determine what a man's mind and heart shall be like. The heart rules ; the mind ought to rule. Take men as they are, not as they ought to be. Moments of bliss brighten this dull life.

" Up there the blissful moment will be lasting happiness, and more bliss will be the insight into other blissful worlds.

" Happy he who finds a loyal friend. Still happier he who finds a true friend in his wife.

" In these times the idea of marriage is alarming to a single man ; he exchanges it either for sadness or sensuality. Monarchs of the day, you see this and are silent. Or perhaps you don't see it. Then, O God, veil our senses and feelings with gloom, but withdraw once again the veil without penalty."

" A man may bear unhappiness without complaining, but feels it all the more acutely. Wherefore did God endow us with the feeling of sympathy?

"An easy mind, a light heart! But too easy a mind often conceals a heavy heart.

"A mighty antipodes of human sincerity is conventional politeness.

"The greatest misfortune of the wise, and the greatest good fortune of fools, is based on *des convénances*.

"The noble person who is unhappy feels the depth of his unhappiness and happiness, as the noble happy person feels his happiness and unhappiness.

"Now I know nothing else; to-morrow perhaps I shall know something more. What is the meaning of that? Is my mind duller to-day than it will be to-morrow, because I am full and sleepy? Why does my mind not act when my body sleeps? It must be taking exercise. Can the spirit sleep?

> "'*Sonderbare Fragen,*
> *Hör'ich alle sagen?*
> *Es lässt sich hier nichts wagen,*
> *Wir müssen's dulden tragen.*
> *Nun gute Nacht,*
> *Bis ihr erwacht.'*"

At that time genius ripened in Schubert's life and bore its first fruit. It is true that in the Konvikt, as a boy, he had perfected some of his compositions, like the songs "Hagars Klage" and "Der Vatermörder," which attracted the notice of his teachers, and had made attempts in church music, writing masses and quartets, cantatas and choruses. But these were crude imitations, lacking for the most part all originality. Now, however, the creative power within the adolescent began to stir, his genius caught fire, fantasy acquired wings which bore him in an ecstasy into new worlds. The day had come for Schubert when the young soul awakes for the first time to the beauty of things, when life is filled with vague yearnings, sometimes with suffering, but oftener with the effulgent glamour of visionary dreams. Everything was now an inward event. Every book, every poem, every picture awoke a responsive echo within him. His heart sought freedom from the oppression of a thousand contending stormy emotions, and salvation in his music. He flew to music during the intervals in his daily work, and escaped from the prosaic surroundings of school and everyday life and ascended to transcendental heights of the creative spirit. Soon he had found the key to the power of painting in tones, the true form for the expression of the purely romantic sentiment of his time. Melodies streamed from the hidden recesses of his inner being. His soul was the sensitive instrument on which the chords of all human emotions from deepest sorrow to gayest laughter were sounded. An almost unexampled productivity in the history of music was now inaugurated by the dreamy, quiet school usher. Cantatas (like those composed for the celebration of Salieri's jubilee, for his father's birthday, and the one dedicated to the founder of the Widow's Institute, Josef Spendou) several works of sacred music, like the F Major mass which was first performed to celebrate the hundred years' jubilee of the Lichtentaler Parish Church, the beautiful mass in G Major, with the inspiring Credo and Kyrie, the offertory in B Major, a Magnificat, a Stabat Mater, and various compositions for choir, with orchestral accompaniment. Fugues for several voices, symphonies, sonatas, string quartets, operas, choral plays, most of which are lost—all were poured forth in the years 1814 to 1816. Above all, it was now that Schubert found himself in the musical lyric, a *genre* of which he became the consummate master. A huge number of verses by Matthisson, Kosegarten, Schiller, Goethe, Klopstock, Hölty, Ossian, and other less important poets were set to music. Ballads, *lieder*, and lyrics date from this period, many of which belong to the most priceless treasures of German song literature, and have made Schubert's name immortal: the well-known " Röslein, Röslein auf die Heide," " An Mignon," " Trost in Tränen," " Wonne der Wehmut," " Gretchen am Spinnrad," " Erlkönig," " Die Gesänge aus Ossian," " Die Gesänge des Harfners " from Wilhelm Meister, " Der Wanderer," and others. The composition of the " Erlkönig " perhaps exhibits Schubert's sheer creative power at its high-water mark, and is proof of how suddenly his imagination took artistic shape. " One afternoon," relates Spaun in his reminiscences, " I went with Mayrhofer to see Schubert, who at that time was living at his father's in Himmelpfortgrund. We found Schubert with a glowing face reading the ' Erlkönig ' from the book aloud. With the book in his hand, he walked up and down several times. Suddenly he seated himself at the table and in the shortest possible time, as quickly as it could be written, the magnificent ballad was committed to paper. We ran with it, as Schubert at that time had no piano, to the Konvikt and there the same evening the 'Erlkönig' was sung and hailed with enthusiasm."

In April, 1816, Schubert made a formal application to the municipal authorities for the post of musical director in the newly-founded Music Department of the German Normal School Institute in Laibach, with a salary of 450 florins weekly and a yearly remuneration of 80 florins. He supported his claim by stating the following qualifications :

" 1. Applicant has been brought up at the Konvikt, and was a Court chorister and pupil in composition of Salieri—first Court Conductor (first Hofkapellmeister) on whose kind recommendation he applies for this post.

" 2. He has gained such thorough knowledge and experience in every class of composition for organ, violin and the voice that, as the enclosed references testify, he is considered in every way the most capable among all competitors for the post.

" 3. He promises the best possible application of his abilities to the carrying out of his duties should he be graciously considered a fitting applicant to fill the post.

FRANZ SCHUBERT

(at the present time assistant schoolmaster on the staff of his father's school in Vienna, Himmelpfortgrund, No. 12)."

In spite of being warmly supported by a testimonial from Salieri and a letter of recommendation from the Vienna Town Council addressed to the Landesregierung of Lower Austria, Schubert failed to procure this post. But though this first step towards obtaining a salaried musical position came to nothing, there were friends who came forward at this time to release him from the fetters of the, to him, more and more intolerable drudgery of schoolmastering. Franz von Schober, a University student of almost the same age as Schubert, by birth a Swede, a talented amateur musician, painter, actor and man of letters, the friend of his youth, Josef von Spaun, and the gifted writer Johann Mayrhofer, all full of enthusiasm for Schubert's compositions, espoused the cause of the young genius. One day Schober and Spaun together looked up the school assistant in Lichtental and found him engaged in correcting exercises. Without further delay the friends set about freeing in an unselfish and practical manner the musician of genius from this distasteful drudgery on which he was wasting time and energies. Schober arranged a room rent-free for him in his mother's house, and in other ways did all he could to help Schubert. Spaun exerted himself to interest distinguished personages in his friend's work, in the importance of which he had never ceased to have unswerving faith. He made propaganda for the struggling young genius in the exclusive circles of Viennese society, and he succeeded in interesting in him, among others, the highly esteemed æsthete and tutor of the Duke of Reichstadt, Matthäus von Collin, in whose house he met influential men and women in Viennese social life, such as the Oriental scholar, Josef von Hammer-Purgstall, Hofrat Ignaz von Mosel, the authoress Karoline Pichler, the poet Ladislaus Pyrker, the Court musician Moritz Graf von Dietrichstein, who played several of his works in public. Spaun also started musical evenings in his own house at which Schubert's compositions were brought to the notice of art-loving audiences. Spaun even sought to win the approval of the great prince of poets, Goethe, for the muse of Schubert when his first collection of songs was published, in a letter dated April 17th, 1817, a touching document dictated by true friendship :

" YOUR EXCELLENCY,—

The undersigned ventures by means of these lines to deprive you of your precious time for a few minutes in the hope that the enclosed collection of songs may prove not a quite unwelcome gift to your Excellency, and that therefore you will excuse the great liberty he is taking.

The songs collected in this copybook are by a composer named Franz Schubert. He is nineteen years of age, and Nature has from his earliest childhood endowed him with the most decided gifts for music, and these have been trained by the Nestor of composers, Salieri, out of disinterested love for art. The universal applause which the young artist's songs, those which I send herewith and others of his numerous compositions, have gained among connoisseurs and non-connoisseurs of both sexes has encouraged his friends in the wish that the modest youth should begin in earnest his musical career through the publication of a portion of his compositions, whereby there is no doubt that in a short time he will rise to the high position his talent merits. It is proposed to begin with a selection of German songs, which are to be followed by more important instrumental compositions. These would fill eight volumes. The two first (of which the first is here enclosed as a sample) contain poems from Schiller; the fourth and fifth, Klopstock; the sixth, Matthison, Hölty and others. The seventh and eighth contain songs of Ossian, which last are the best of all. The artist cherishes the wish to dedicate these in all humility to your Excellency, to whose glorious poems he attributes not only the inspiration of the greater part of them, but his own success as a German singer.

Being too modest himself to deem his work worthy of the great honour of bearing on its front the highly esteemed name known throughout the world wherever the German language is spoken, he has not the courage to ask himself this great favour, and so I, one of his friends, saturated with his melodies, dare in his name to beg it of your Excellency. A special edition worthy of this honour will be prepared. I forbear from any further eulogy of these songs, as they will speak for themselves. I would only add that those which are to follow in no wise fall short of them with regard to melody—in fact, perhaps, surpass these in appropriateness and expression, as the pianist who plays the songs to your Excellency will demonstrate.

Should the young artist be fortunate enough to win the approval of him who more than any other in the wide world he honours, I would venture the request that the permission sought may, in a few words, be graciously communicated.

I remain in all reverence,
Your obedient servant,
JOSEF EDLER VON SPAUN
(dweller in the Landskrongasse No. 622, 2nd floor)."

This well-meant effort met with no success. The letter remained unanswered. The aged poet, who was perpetually immersed in appeals of this kind took no notice. Also Spaun's endeavours to interest the Leipzig publishers Breitkopf & Härtel in the " worthy edition " mentioned in the above letter failed. Indeed, the firm thought that it had " scotched " a swindling misuse of the name of a concert conductor in Dresden called Franz Schubert, who, on the proof of the " Erlkönig " being sent to him, replied : " I have never composed a cantata on the ' Erlkönig,' but will try to find out who the sender of this patchwork is and to discover who has appropriated my name for such base uses." The Leipzig firm consequently ignored the letter of Schubert's friend, and he received no answer.

Under June 17th, 1816, Schubert wrote in his diary : " To-day I composed for the first time for money. That is to say, a cantata for the celebration of the birthday of Professor Watterroth von Dröxler has brought me an honorarium of 100 florins." The first performance of this cantata, " Prometheus " took place on July 14th, 1816, in the garden of the Professor in the Landstrasse Erdbergstrasse 96. The function was organised by the Society of Solicitors, among whom were Schubert's friends, Franz von Schlechta, Leopold Sonnleithner and Albert Stadler. Schubert conducted the work. Schlechta wrote in commemoration of this event a poem that was published in the Vienna *Theaterzeitung :*

To HERR FRANZ SCHUBERT.

the occasion of his Cantata " Prometheus " being performed.)

" *In der Töne tiefem Beben,*
Wie die Saiten jubelnd klangen,
Ist ein unbekanntes Leben
In der Brust mir aufgegangen.

" *In dem Sturmeston der Lieder*
Klagt der Menschheit jammernd Ach—
Kämpfend steigt Prometheus nieder
Und das schwere Dunkel brach !

" *Mich hat's wunderbar erhoben*
Und der Wehmut neue Lust,
Wie ein schimmernd Licht von oben,
Kam in die bewegte Brust !

" *Und in Tranen und Entzücken*
Fühlte ich mein Herz zerstücken,
Jauchzend hatte ich mein Leben
Wie Prometheus hingegeben ! "

Besides Schober and Spaun, Schubert found in the poet and Censor official Johann Mayrhofer, himself artistically gifted, a friend who exercised an important influence on the young tone-poet.

His was a serious and deep nature, and he had at his command a thoroughly erudite knowledge, to which the young Schubert owed many inspirations for composition and choice of material.

Mayrhofer wrote in 1829, a year after Schubert's death, concerning their friendship : " My connection with Schubert began with a young friend giving him the song ' Am See ' to compose. He came, led by this friend, into the room which five years later we were to share. It was in the Wipplingerstrasse. Both house and room had felt the weight of time ; the ceiling was low, and the light shadowed by opposite buildings. A much-played-on piano, a small book-shelf, furnished the room in which hours were passed that will never fade from my memory. For in the same way that spring moves the earth to bring forth abundantly her foliage and flowers, so man is roused to productivity by the awakening to a consciousness of his powers. Then comes into force Goethe's lines :

" ' *Weit, hoch, herrlich der Blick*
Rings ins Leben hinein,
Von Gebirg' zu Gebirg'
Schwebet der ewige Geist
Ewigen Lebens ahndevoll.'

" This inner bond and our mutual love for poetry and music made our relations closer. He composed what I wrote, and the origin of many of his melodies, their continuance and extension, arose from the material I thus gave him. At the time when he was still a teacher he occupied a poky little room in his father's house, with a wretched old piano. How often I visited him there ! The pressure of circumstances, social engagements, illness and altered views of life afterwards separated us, but what once had been could never be wiped out."

The friends who rallied round Schubert were not discouraged in their efforts to help him by Goethe's silence and the rebuff given by the publishers Breitkopf & Härtel. They now left no stone unturned to find a singer of repute who would sing the *lieder* of their *protégé* in public.

Through the instrumentality of Schober, who was related to the opera singer Josef Siboni, they succeeded in interesting the great and generally most inaccessible singer Michael Vogl in the young composer, of whose artistic creations they spoke to him in terms of glowing enthusiasm. Vogl was engaged at that time at the

Kärntnertortheater with his colleagues, the distinguished artists Baumann, Saal, Wild, Anna Milder, Wilhelmine Schröder and Karoline Unger. He appeared in Italian and French operas and *Singspielen*, and scored brilliant and triumphant successes in Weigl's operas "Das Waisenhaus" and "Die Schweizerfamilie," and as Orestes in Gluck's "Iphigenie auf Tauris." In 1822 he retired, and appeared henceforth only as a *lieder* singer. Vogl was a man of wide culture and somewhat eccentric character; his outward appearance was that of a powerful and imposing personality. His features had extraordinary expressiveness, and his carriage was noble and dignified. The monastic education which he had received in his youth at the Kremsmünster had not a little influenced the formation of his character, which always at bottom inclined to seriousness. His disposition presented a striking contrast to his external circumstances. The keystone of his inner soul was a moral scepticism, a meditative dissection of himself and the world. The companions he chose to guide and advise him through life were the Old and New Testaments, the Gospels, Epictetus, Marcus Aurelius, and Thomas à Kempis. He translated into German the book "Von der Nachfolge Christi," and had extracts therefrom circulated in leaflets among his friends. A work of Epictetus' he had with his own hand copied in four languages (Greek, Latin, English and German). Religion and philosophy composed the fibres of his existence. It was a wonderful sight to see the admired opera-singer sitting in his dressing-room in the classic costume of Orestes, reading attentively the works of the Greek poets and philosophers. All his life he kept diaries. When Vogl first made Schubert's acquaintance through Schober he was fifty-five and Schubert twenty-four. They soon felt drawn to each other, and the prejudice which the critical and mature master-singer may have harboured in the beginning against the overflowing exuberance of the young composer's heart was easily overcome and nonplussed by kindly acts. "Vogl came," Spaun relates, "punctually to Schober's, looking very dignified, and when little insignificant Schubert made a somewhat furtive inclination, something between a bow and a nod, and stammered out a few disjointed remarks about the honour the introduction did him, Vogl rather turned up his nose, and the beginning of the acquaintance filled us with misgivings. At last Vogl remarked : 'Well, what have you there ? Come and accompany me,' and thereupon he seized the nearest notes containing Mayrhofer's verses 'Augenlied,' a pretty, very tuneful, but not specially remarkable song.

" Vogl hummed more than he sang and then said indifferently, 'Not bad.' But he grew more and more friendly as he went on, only singing in an undertone 'Memnon' and 'Ganymed,' but still he departed without promising to come again. He patted Schubert, however, on the shoulder at parting, and said : ' There's something in you . . . but you are too little of a comedian, too little of a charlatan. You waste your beautiful thoughts without making the most of them.' "

Vogl expressed himself much more favourably to others. When he came across the " Lied eines Schiffers an die Dioskuren " (words by Mayrhofer) he said it was a magnificent song, and wondered how such mature work could proceed from the little youth.

" The impression made on Vogl by the songs of Schubert was soon overwhelming, and he came frequently to our circle without being asked, invited Schubert to his house, studied songs with him, and when he became aware of how tremendous the charm was which his interpretation exercised on Schubert himself and all who heard it, his enthusiasm for the songs became so intense that he now ranked among Schubert's most ardent admirers. It had been his intention before to give up music, but now he was enamoured of it afresh." Vogl from this time onwards was a faithful Schubertian whose name was immortally associated with Schubert's artistic creations. " The delights which were now in store for us cannot be described," relates Spaun apropos of Vogl's rendering of the songs.

The Viennese Nightingale, Franz Schubert, was thus discovered for the public by this great singer. At a concert in the Kärntnertor-theater on March 7th, 1821, he sang the " Erlkönig," and the success of the young composer who till then had only been known to an intimate circle of friends and amateurs was assured. Vogl, who, according to the opinion of Hofrat von Mosel, was one of the greatest dramatic singers of that day, accompanied his truly en-chanting singing with learned remarks on the right rendering and presentation of the German song. Especially did he insist on a clear pronunciation of the text, with the winged words : " If you have nothing to say to me, then you have nothing to sing to me." Schubert undertook at Vogl's recitals the pianoforte accompaniments. Without being what is called a *virtuoso*, he made the very most of the music, atoning a thousandfold for any lack of technique by his sentiment and expression. Schubert's " Memnon," " Philoktet," " Erlkönig," " Wanderer," " Ganymed," " An Schwager Kronos," " Der Einsame," the " Müllerlieder," " Die Winterreise " were all, as it were, created for Vogl's voice. The publicity given to Schubert's muse brought him now, in addition to the friends he already had, many new comrades, artists, poets, composers, friends of music, amateurs in art, and, more valued than all, the brothers Anselm and Josef Hüttenbrenner, who were soon to be counted among the truest Schubertians. At the same time the master lost two friends of his boyhood, Stadler and Ebner, who left Vienna. And Schober, too, to Schubert's grief, deserted the gay circle of friends to spend a year in his native Sweden. Farewell entertainments were given, and Schubert composed music in memory of Stadler to his poem " Der Strom," and for the much-loved Schober he wrote both words and music of the following " Abschied " :

> " *Lebe wohl, du lieber Freund !*
> *Ziehe hin in fernes Land,*
> *Nimm der Freundschaft trautes Band—*
> *Und bewahr's in treuer Hand !*
> *Lebe wohl ! Du lieber Freund !*

> " *Lebe wohl, du lieber Freund !*
> *Hör' in diesem Trauersang*
> *Meines Herzens innern Drang,*
> *Tönt er doch so dumpf und bang.*
> *Lebe wohl, du lieber Freund !*

> " *Lebe wohl, du lieber Freund !*
> *Scheiden heisst das bittre Wort,*
> *Weh, es ruft dich von uns fort,*
> *Hin an den Bestimmungsort.*
> *Lebe wohl, du lieber Freund !*

> " *Lebe wohl, du lieber Freund !*
> *Wenn dies Lied dein Herz ergreift,*
> *Freundesschatten näher schweift,*
> *Meiner Seele Saiten streift.*
> *Lebe wohl, du lieber Freund ! "*

In those years Schubert's output was amazingly prolific: a group of songs, to the text of Mayrhofer and Schober, among them the glorious " An die Musik," a Preislied for the gentle art of tones ; from Schiller, the mighty group from " Tartarus " ; Goethe's vibrating hymns, " Ganymed" and " An Schwager Kronos " ; the Sixth Symphony in C Major, several sonatas for piano. Among these are that famous Op. 147 in B Flat Major and the lovely Sonata in A Minor, with the romantic, melody-radiating andante, the B Major Trio for stringed instruments, sonatinas for piano and violin and twelve German Dances. Also the popular Trauer and Sehnsuchtswalzer, which, till it was printed, was often taken for a work of Beethoven's, came into being at this time. " It was for long," as Anselm Hüttenbrenner tells us, " thought to be a piece by Beethoven, who, when asked about it, repudiated all knowledge of the composition. By chance I learned that Schubert had composed this waltz, and I asked him to put it on paper for me, because there were so many divergent copies of it in existence. He granted me the favour and wrote on the margin of the music paper : ' Written for my dear Coffee, Wine and Punch Brother, 14 March, in the year of our Lord, 1818, in his own particular house, 30 florins monthly.' Another authentic copy of the Trauer-waltz was presented to friend Assmayer with the title, ' Deutscher von Franz Schubert, March, 1818,' and the humorous verse :

> " Hier haßt Du diesen Deutschen,
> Mein allerliebster Asma'r !
> Sonst möchst Du mich noch peitschen,
> Vermaledeyter Asma'r ! '

Illistrissimo, doctissimo, sapentissimo, prudentissimo, maximoque Compositori in devotissima, humillimaque reverentiae expressione dedicatum oblatumque di Servorum Servo Francisco Seraphico vulgo Schubert nominato."

The year 1818 was important for Schubert, for now one of his works was published for the first time. It was the lied " Erlafsee," by Mayrhofer, which appeared as a supplement to Sartori's " Malerischem Tagebuch für Freunde interessanter Gegenden, Natur- und Kunstmerkwürdigkeiten der österreichischen Monarchie." Another work, an overture in Italian style, was the first Schubert composition to be performed at a concert in public. This took place in the violinist Eduard Jaell's Academy for Declamatory

Music on March 1st, 1818. The Viennese Press gave it the following notice : " The second part began with the loveliest overture by a young composer, Franz Schubert, a pupil of the famous Salieri. He understands how to touch and move to emotion all hearts. Although the theme is simple enough, it contains an astonishing wealth of pleasant thoughts."

The post of assistant schoolmaster, which for three years, to please his father and to escape from military service, he had filled, was given up in the autumn of 1817. His father had obtained for him from the educational authorities a grace year in the hope that Franz, at the expiration of this period, would come back refreshed to the scholastic profession. The master, being now without any sort of income, as his compositions brought him in next to nothing, had to look round for another situation. This led to his following the example of his great forerunners in the realm of music, Mozart and Beethoven, by giving music lessons in order to earn the necessary means for a modest living. A favourable opportunity offered itself, which, besides the honorarium of two guldens for a lesson, opened out a prospect of enjoying a pleasant summer change to the country. It was through the recommendation of the father of Karoline Unger, the famous *diva* and *fiancée* of Nikolaus Lenau, that he was engaged as music teacher in the family of the Count Johann Karl Esterhazy von Galantha, and passed the summer with this family on their estate in Hungary. His duties consisted in giving the two Countesses, Marie and Karoline, music instruction, as well as to take part in the musical performances given in the castle.

" Our castle," he wrote to his Viennese friends, " is not one on the grand scale, but very charmingly built. It is surrounded by a beautiful garden. My quarters are in the Inspector's department. It is tolerably quiet till 40 geese begin to cackle all at once, when one can hardly hear oneself speak. The people about me are thoroughly good. Seldom, I should think, has a Count had a more harmonious staff of servants and employees. They all get on well together. The Herr Inspector is a Slavonian, an honest fellow who prides himself much on the talent for music he once had. He is playing now on the lute two Deutsche solos in three-four time. His son, who is studying philosophy, was here for the holidays. I want to be friends with him. His wife is like all wives who like to be called *Gnädige*. The rent-collector is altogether suitable to his office, a man with quite a number of extraordinary opinions in his pocket. The doctor, who is really clever, is at 24 invalidish like an old lady. The surgeon is the nicest, a hale and hearty old gentleman of 75, always merry and happy. God grant us all such a happy old age. The Hofrichter is an unaffected, good sort of fellow. I often enjoy the society of a comrade of the Count's, a gay old bachelor and good musician. Then there are the *chef*, the valet, the parlour-maid, the nurse, the porter, etc.; two stable grooms are decent fellows. The chef is rather convivial, the valet thirty years old, the parlour-maid very pretty, often my companion, the nurse a good old soul; the porter is my rival. The two grooms are much better company for the horses than for human beings. The Count is a little rough, the Countess proud, though of gentler feeling; the young Countesses are good children. Now I have nothing more to say, except that, as you can well understand, I want, with my usual sincerity, to get on well with all these people."

Music was ardently cultivated in the Count's household, and many of Schubert's compositions were performed there. His songs were sung by Baron Karl von Schönstein, who was sometimes a guest, and with his beautiful tenor was soon a devoted ally of Schubert's muse, and with Vogl one of the best interpreters of his songs. Countess Karoline, who was an excellent pianist, accompanied him on the piano, or Schubert himself. The composer owed to his visit to the Zselesz estate inspiration for several songs like " Einsamkeit," " Blondel zu Marien," " Der Blumenbrief," " Das Marienbild," " Das Abendrot," " Die schöne Litanei auf das Fest Allerseelen," as well as two sonnets of Petrarch's in a translation of Schlegel's. Also eight variations for four hands on the theme of an old French romance, " Réposez-vous, bon chevalier," afterwards dedicated to Beethoven, date from this time. Many touching letters from the master to his friends and brothers and sisters testify to Schubert's not having forgotten them during his stay in Hungary. He gives them detailed accounts of his visits and his doings in Zselesz. Thus, under date of August 3rd, 1818, he writes, full of longing for his faithful Schubertians :

" DEAREST AND BELOVED FRIENDS,—

How could I ever forget you ? You who are all in all to me—dear Spaun, Schober, Mayrhofer, Senn—how fares it with you all ?

Vogl and Schubert
Pencil sketch by Moriz von Schwind

I am getting on splendidly. I live and compose like a god, as if I was born to it. Mayrhofer's 'Einskameit' is finished, and I think it is my best, because I've been without cares. I hope that you are all in good health and as content as I am. Now I really *live*. Thank God, it was time, for otherwise there would have become of me a musician *manqué*. Schober, please give Herr Vogl my respectful regards. I will next take the liberty of writing to him. If you can possibly manage it, propose to him that he should have the kindness to sing one of my songs at the Kunzische Concert in November, whichever he likes. Remember me to everyone. With deepest respect to your mother and sister. Write soon. Every line from you is precious to me.

Your ever-faithful friend,

FRANZ SCHUBERT."

He wrote to his brother Ferdinand, under date August 24th, the following :

" DEAR BROTHER FERDINAND,—

It is half-past eleven at night and I've finished your ' Trauer-messe.' It made me sad, you can believe me, for I sang it from an overflowing heart. If there's anything wrong, put the text under-neath and mark it above. If you would have many repeats, you can make them without asking me here in Zselesz. Things are not going well with you ? I wish I could change places with you ; that would make you happy again. Every burden of care would soon be cast off here. Dear brother, I sympathise with you heartily. My foot has gone to sleep and I am very cross thereat. It wouldn't sleep if Talk was writing. . . . Good morning, dear brother, I have now been to sleep with my foot, and continue my letter at 8 o'clock on the 25th. In exchange for your request, I have one to make. Love to my dear parents, brothers and sisters, friends and acquaintances ; in particular don't forget Karl. Did he not remember me in his letter ?

Remind my town friends to write to me. Tell my mother that my linen is very well looked after, that her motherly care makes me grateful. But if I could have a little more linen it would please me uncommonly. If she could send me an extra supply of handker-chiefs, neck-ties and stockings I should be glad. I require, too, very urgently two pairs of cashmere trousers ; Hart can make them to my measure. I'll send the money for these at once. During the month of July I took together with journey money 200 guldens. It is beginning to be cold here, but still we shall not come to Vienna till the middle of November. I hope next month to spend a few weeks at Freystadt, which belongs to Count Erdödy, the uncle of my Count. It is said to be a wonderfully pretty place. I also expect to be in Budapest, as we shall stop at Boszmedjer Weinlese, which isn't far from there. I should like to meet there Administrator Tsigele, but in any case I look forward to Weinlese, having heard so much that's amusing about it. The harvest here is very beautiful. They don't put the corn here in barns, as in Austria, but pile it up in the open field in huge stacks, which are called ' Triften.' They are often 40 or 50 feet long and 15 high. They understand how to build it up so skilfully that the rain runs off it and can do it no harm. . . . Although I am so happy here and my health so good, and all the people about me are good and kind, I shall rejoice when the word of command comes, ' To Vienna ! To Vienna ! '

Yes, dear Vienna, within your narrow limits is contained all that's dearest and loveliest, and only seeing you again will still the longing within me. Once more I remind you, dear brother, of my above-mentioned wishes, and

Remain in truest affection,
Everybody's sincere and faithful,
FRANZ."

A hearty greeting to Frau   A thousand greetings to your
Muhme Schubert and daughter.   good wife and your dear Resi."

On September 8th, 1818, he replied to a letter from his friends in the usual hearty tone :

" DEAR SCHOBER, DEAR SPAUN, DEAR MAYRHOFER, DEAR SENN,
    DEAR STREINSBERG, DEAR WAYSS, DEAR WEIDLICH,—

How can I express the delight your letters jointly and separately have given me. I was at a cattle show when your thick envelope was handed to me. I gave a loud cry of joy as I broke the seal and saw the name of Schober. With perpetual laughter and child-like delight I read it in a neighbouring barn. It was almost as if I had my dear friends themselves at my elbow. But now I will answer you all in correct order :

"Dear Schobert,—I see that this little change in your name is permanent. Well, then, dear Schobert, your letter from beginning to end was very dear and precious to me, especially the last sheet. Yes, yes, the last sheet gave me ecstasies. You are a really divine boy (in Swedish, of course), and, believe me, friend, your feeling for art is the purest, truest conceivable. . . . That the opera managers in Vienna are so stupid and produce beautiful operas without mine puts me in a rage. In Zselesz I must be everything myself, composer, editor, auditor, and I don't know what else. With the exception of the Countess (if I am not mistaken) no one here has the slightest true conception of art. Therefore, I am forced to be alone with my beloved, and must hide her in my room, in my piano and in my breast. Though this makes me a little sad, on the other hand it stimulates me to go on and up. You need have no fears that anything but the grimmest necessity will hold me back. A good many songs, very successful ones, I hope, have been evolved in this time. That critical Vogl is lingering in Upper Austria doesn't surprise me, for it is his native air and he is on holiday. I wish I was with him; I should then make the best of my time and strike roots. But that you should think my brother is kicking his heels there without a guide or any agreeable society does surprise me. In the first place, because an artist generally likes to be left to himself; in the second, because there are so many beautiful spots in Upper Austria that he can't help finding out the most beautiful for himself; and, thirdly, because in H. Forstmayer in Linz he has a very sociable acquaintance. He is, therefore, assuredly in the right place.

"If you can give Maxen greetings from me without hypochondria it will rejoice me, and, as you will soon be seeing his mother and sister, give them my respectful compliments. It is possible that this letter will not find you any longer in Vienna, for yours reached me in the beginning of September, when you were starting on your travels. I will have it forwarded to you. Among other things, I am pleased that you think Milder cannot be replaced. I am also of that opinion. She sings beautifully, but trills badly. . . .

"Dear Spaun,—It delighted me to know that you can still build palaces in which little courtiers jump about. You'll probably do a quartet of mine. Greet H. Gahy from me,

"DEAR MAYRHOFER,—My longing for November won't be second to yours. Stop being sick, or, at any rate, taking medicine, and the rest will follow.

"DEAR HANS SENN,—Read the above.

Friend Streinsberg might be already dead, so doesn't write. Friend Weidlich, darn his name on a coat-tail!

Good Waiss I remember with gratitude. An honest fellow.

*　　*

*

And now, dear friends, goodbye to you all. Write again soon. It is my chief and dearest amusement to read your letters ten times over. Give my love to my dear parents, and tell them I long for a letter from them.

> With eternal love,
> Your faithful friend,
> FRANZ SCHUBERT."

And his brothers, Ferdinand and Ignaz, also answer his letters. The latter writes to him on October 12th :

"DEAR BROTHER,—

At last you will see the sight of my handwriting and get a few lines from me. Yes, but I believe you wouldn't have them if it weren't, to my intense relief, again vacation, so that I have leisure to write a proper letter without worrying interruptions.

You happy creature! How I envy your lot! You are enjoying a delicious, golden time of freedom and can give wing to your musical genius; you may throw off your thoughts as you like, and are beloved, admired, idolised; whereas we, miserable school-ushers, the butt of undisciplined youth, have to endure all kinds of rudeness and humiliations, and are in subjection to a public of blockheads. You will hardly believe it when I tell you that it has come to this, that one mayn't laugh, when one is giving religious instruction, at some ridiculous story of superstition. You may imagine that in such circumstances I am often boiling with inward indignation and longing to be free in something more than name. You have escaped all these annoyances. You are out of it all, and

quit of the Bonzes, and so don't require consolation from Herr
Bürger's rhyme :

> ' *Beneide nicht das Bonzenheer*
> *Um seine dicken Köpfe,*
> *Die meisten sind ja hohl und leer*
> *Wie ihre Kirchturmknöpfe.*'

But to turn to another subject. We celebrated the birthday of
our Herr papa in lively fashion. The whole school staff, with
wives, brother Ferdinand and wife, besides our Mühmchen and
Lenchen and the whole Gumpendorfer lot of relations, were invited
to a supper at which we ate and drank and were very merry. On
this occasion my slender stock of wit as a poet was brought into
requisition when we drank our father's health :

> ' *Es lebe Vater Franz noch lang in unserer Mitte ;*
> *Doch vergönn, er wohl uns heut, auch eine Bitte :*
> *Er stell' aufs Jahr sich wieder ein*
> *Mit Hendel, Strudel, Konfekt und Wein.*'

Before the gorge, we played quartets, and heartily lamented that
our master, Franz, was not in our midst ; we soon stopped.

A few days later was the feast of our patron saint, Franziskus
Seraphitus. It was solemnly commemorated. The pupils *en masse*
had to be brought to Confession, and at five o'clock in the afternoon the elder ones assembled in the school. An altar was erected,
and two school flags were arranged to right and left of it. There
was a short sermon, the upshot of which was that one must learn
to distinguish the difference between good and evil, and that one
had every reason to be indebted to the laborious schoolmaster.
A litany for the Saint was sung—a litany the curious nature of which
rather astonished me. To end with there was singing, and relics
of the saint were brought out to be kissed, but most of the adults
slunk out at the door before this part of the ceremony, it apparently
not being to their taste. Now a few words about the Hollpein-
schen. Both husband and wife send you hearty greetings, and
have inquired if you still remember them and think of them sometimes. When you come back to Vienna you will probably not be
paying them visits so frequently as you used to do, as your new
circumstances may prevent you. This will be much regretted by

them, for they love you dearly, as we all do, and often speak with sympathy of you in your present fortunate position.

I haven't referred to your birthday, but you will understand that I love you now and always. You know me.

Farewell now, and come soon in person. I have still much to say, but will keep it till we can have a verbal conversation.

Your brother,
IGNAZ.

If you should write to papa and myself at the same time, be sure not to touch on religious subjects. Mühmchen and Lenchen send their love."

Ferdinand wrote, too, at about the same time as follows :

" DEAR BROTHER FRANZ,—

I am delighted that things are going well with you. But make haste and come back soon, as I am always being asked how long you are going to be away. Our good father said the other day that your little sisters Marie and Pepi think you've been away too long, and ask every day, ' When is Franz coming ? ' It's the same with all your music friends. So the sooner you can settle the day of your arrival the better. Your friends in the town have all been away in the country. Our papa read your last letter to Mayrhofer, and the secret that Schober is devoting himself to agriculture and farming has come out.

Among other things, I must tell you about some musical events. Your overture to Claudine, which was given at a Jaell Concert in Baden, Doppler tells me, has been much criticised. It is too heavy for the harmony, so that oboes and bassoons could not play in it. Others say (Radecki too) that it was only too difficult for the Baden Orchestra. Now it is to be given on October 11th in Vienna, so it is announced, but it won't go any better. In my opinion, this is unpleasant news for you, but you have to thank Doppler. But much the same is now said here, and a certain Scheidel has declared (So I hear from Jaell) that the effect is irregular, and certain well-known themes occur in it. But to turn to another subject. Your overture from Hoheisel's Cantata at the first performance in the ' Orphanage ' was very well received, and my ' Prüfung's ' song was very well sung. Afterwards the prize were given away. Twelve silver medals, three of which were honours orders with scarf and ribbon, had to be given back after the pupils who had won the distinction had worn them for a certain time; but the other nine remained in possession of the awardees. One of the latter was besides presented with a watch. In conclusion, ' God save Franz the Kaiser ' was sung.

Our Director's Name Day I wanted to celebrate with a grand concert. But as both singers and finances failed me, it ended in a very small affair. The whole orchestra, which besides the violins had only cornets and oboes, consisted of thirteen persons. Grob Theres refused to sing; she wanted, on this occasion, only to listen. I should have liked to have done the overture to your ' Prometheus,' the chorus that follows and other big things; but, as it was, the items of the programme were as follows :

    I.   Overture from Mozart's ' L'Idomeneo.'
   II.   Two Songs, Ferdinand Schubert.
  III.   Polonaise in B for violin, Franz Schubert.
  IV.   First movement of a Rosetische Symphony.
   V.   Overture from Mozart's ' Figaro '; and that's all.

And one thing more: My pianoforte has been sold. Now I would like to have yours, so quote a price and payment will follow. Now with a thousand embraces, farewell, and when you come back to Vienna don't leave me to the last. You will always be welcome at my house, and doubly welcome if you would pass the winter with us.

With true love,
Your truly affectionate brother,
FERDINAND.

I, father, mother, sisters and brothers and friends all send you heartiest greetings.

Note.—Father warns you not to send money without receipt, as the transit is uncertain."

Schubert replied in a letter addressed to his brothers Ignaz, Ferdinand and sister Theresa :

" DEAR BROTHER FERDINAND,—

I had already forgiven you your first letter. There was no reason, therefore, why you should have been so long in writing, unless it was your tender conscience. You liked the mass, you

cried over it, and perhaps at exactly the same place as I cried, dear
brother, that is the most beautiful reward I could ask for my present,
don't talk of any other. If I didn't get to know these people
around me here better and better every day, everything would
please me as much as it did at first. But I see now that I am really
entirely alone among them, with the exception of a couple of nice
girls. My longing for Vienna increases every day. In the first
half of November we shall start. Kiss the dear little creatures,
Pepi and Marie, for me, and greet my good parents. Musical
events leave me cold. I only admire the blind, mistaken zeal of
my somewhat tactless friend Doppler, who with his friendship does
me more harm than good. For the rest I shall never consider and
mince matters with the feelings of my heart. What is in me I give
forth, and there's an end of it.

Take my pianoforte by all means; I shall be pleased to give it to
you. Only don't vex me by saying that you think I don't like
your letters. That is devilish—to think such a thing of your brother,
much more to write it. And then you are always speaking about
payment, reward and thanks.

To a brother—*Pfui!* Kiss your dear wife for me, and your
little Resi. Good-bye, Ferdinand.

I was right glad to get letters from you, Ignaz and Resi. You,
Ignaz, are still the old man of iron. Your irreconcilable hatred of the
Bonze clique does you honour. But you can have no conception
of what the priests here are like—bigotted as old cattle, stupid as an
arch-donkey, uncultured as a buffalo. Such sermons as they
preach—they play on the *canaille* and bring carrion into the pulpit."

Back in Vienna the tone-poet would again have crept into
the schoolmaster's yoke if he had listened to his father, but this
time Franz was not to be intimidated. So there was renewed
friction between father and son, and Franz, to whom the parental
house was closed, and who was too poor to rent a room for himself,
had to take refuge with his friends. It was with Spaun and
Schober that he now first found a temporary domicile. Then he
migrated to Mayrhofer, with whom he shared for two years the
room in which the poet Körner had formerly lodged. The two
friends were then joined by a third, Josef Hüttenbrenner from
Graz, who rented rooms in the same house and was in future the
faithful factotum who took in hand all Schubert's business affairs.

Now that the master was an outcast from his father's house, and, thanks to his friends, had a roof over his head, he composed afresh, as Bauernfeld relates, "Amidst all sorts of cares and torments, unknown, nameless, his genius only recognised by a few friends." Work by day, amusement in the evening, such was the course of the young artist's life. Hüttenbrenner, who visited him constantly, found him in a "nearly dark, damp, unheated little room, huddled up in an old threadbare dressing-gown, freezing and composing." In the evening Schubert would go to the inn, "Zur ungarischen Krone," after having accomplished the composition of innumerable songs to poems of Schiller and Schlegel (among them "Sehnsucht," "Der Jüngling am Bache," "Hoffnung"), four hymns from Novalis, Goethe ("Prometheus"), Mayrhofer ("Beim Winde," "Sternennächte," "Trost" "Nachstück") all written at about this time, and there the Schubertians gathered together and enjoyed themselves merrily, forgetful of care.

In the summer of 1819, Schubert, with Vogl the singer, made an expedition into Upper Austria. Both friends of Nature, they gloried in the country so full of fruit and flowers. They put up in little quaint towns where Schubert played his sonatas and fantasies to the astonished and delighted citizens, and Vogl sang to them his friend's songs. Once the wandering artists came to a great monastic building which, like the Temple of the Holy Grail, stood on the slope of a mountain, commanding a view of the fertile flowery plain. Like pilgrims, they climbed the steep village street, till between great shady ancient elm trees they saw before them the monastery with its hundred windows and mighty Baroque towers. The monks received and entertained the musicians courteously, and listened with artistic understanding in the glorious cool refectory to their music and song. Then one day the pair of artists reached the old and very beautifully situated town of Steyr. Here they stayed a long time and were shown hospitality by the music-loving families of Paumgartner, Koller, Schellmann and Stadler.

"I think this letter will reach you in Vienna," Schubert wrote to his brother Ferdinand on July 15th, 1819, from Steyr. "I am writing to ask you to send as soon as possible the 'Stabat Mater,' which we are going to give here. I feel very well so far, if only the weather were a little better. We had a very heavy thunder-storm yesterday, which broke over Steyr, killed a girl and injured two men. In the house where we are lodging there are eight girls, nearly all of them pretty. So, you see, we've something to do. Herr von Koller's daughter is very pretty, too, and plays the piano excellently. I and Vogl take our meals at Koller's every day."

On August 10th the birthday of the singer Vogl, a native of Steyr, was celebrated. Schubert composed in his honour a cantata based on the poem of Stadler's with its playful allusions to Vogl's famous *rôles*. Soon afterwards he travelled further to Linz, where, on August 19th, 1819, he wrote to the poet Mayrhofer :

" DEAR MAYRHOFER,—

If you are feeling as well as I do, you must be in good health. I am at present in Linz, have been at the Spauns' and have met Kenner, Kreil and Forstmayer. I was introduced to Spaun's mother and Ottenwald, to whom I sang the *Berceuse* which I composed to his words. In Steyr I enjoyed myself very much, and shall again. The scenery is heavenly, and here round Linz it is very beautiful. We, Vogl and I, in the next few days go on to Salzburg. The bearer of this letter is a student from Kremmünster called Kahl, who is going *viâ* Vienna to his parents in Idria. I commend him to you, and beg that you will let him have my bed during the few days he is in town. Please show him friendly attention, for he is a very good, dear fellow.

My compliments to the Frau von Sanssouci. Have you made way ? I hope so. Vogl's birthday we celebrated with a cantata composed by me to words by Stadler. It was quite a success. Now goodbye till the middle of September.

Herr v. Vogl sends greetings to you.　　　　　Your friend,
Greet for me Spaun.　　　　　　　　　　FRANZ SCHUBERT."

In Steyr and Linz much music was made of a serious kind, but also there was dancing, laughter and merriment in the social gatherings organised in honour of the two musicians from Vienna. Everywhere beautiful young married women and maidens swarmed round the famous singer and the composer of genius, among them Pepi Koller, Fritzi Kornfeld, Kathi Stadler. Those were charming, joyous travel days. A lover's springtime was in full blossom. An abundance of exalted impressions received from the brilliant landscape, from love and enthusiasm kindled by newly-acquired friends, rushed on Schubert's soul, and his genius created at that time, reflecting the wonderful experiences of those halcyon summer days as in a brightly flashing mirror, the celebrated " Forellen " quintet for piano and stringed instruments. The magic of the gardens, orchards and hills of Steyr, the romance of the magnificent old monastery, the blue lakes of Upper Austria set in their frame of rocks—all are in the foaming melody of the quintet, especially in the andante with the enchanting variations on the " Forellenlied."

Quickly the beautiful summer dream came to an end. Schubert boarded at Linz the post-ship and floated over the silver waves of the Nibelungen River. The green hills of Wachau, the old towns of Dürnstein, Krems, the Baroque splendour of the convents of Melk and Götweig, greeted him from the banks. Melancholy may have crept over him again as he looked on the lovely landscape. His thoughts had soared beyond this life. Melodies still rang in his ears, echoes from the summer days, of the dances and songs that he had played and sung of an evening in the circle of the friends in Steyr, and elaborated in the solitude of fragrant dawns. He became more and more meditative as the towers of Klosterneuburg began to gleam in the distance. Vienna was drawing near, the great city in which he was again to be faced with the banalities and prosaic demands of everyday life, where neglect, poverty and care awaited him, where there was only one bright spot, the love and constancy of his friends.

Back in Vienna, Schubert lived apparently quiet and uneventful days, but an inner fire consumed him, and with passionate zeal he devoted himself to his creative genius.

If when evening came the young master was lured to seek gay company and to worship Bacchus and Eros, the day was always dedicated to earnest artistic work and the divine muse.

" While Schubert and Mayrhofer were living together in Wipplingerstrasse," writes Hüttenbrenner, " the former, every day at 6 o'clock in the morning, seated himself at his writing-desk and composed without a break till 1 o'clock in the afternoon, smoking a few small pipes. If I came to see him in the morning he would play to me what he had ready and wanted to hear my opinion. If I praised any song specially he would say : ' Yes, that was a good poem, and when one has something good the music comes easily, melodies just stream into one, so that it is a real joy. With a bad poem everything sticks ; one may make a martyrdom of it, and nothing but dry stuff comes forth. I have often rejected dozens of poems that have been pressed on me.' "

And Spaun relates : " When I spent the night with Schubert he wore his eyeglasses on his nose while he slept, and began work in the morning in complete *négligé*, so that he might be ready to capture on paper the ideas that came to him in the night." A glance at the enormous amount of Schubert's compositions composed at that time testify to the creative power and unceasing industry, the earnest effort which he expended on his work. As in his earliest youth, he attempted operas and choral works, such as " Die Beiden Freunde von Salamanka," " Des Teufel's Lustschloss," " Der vierjährige Posten," " Adrast," " Der Minnesänger." So he was still strongly attracted to the theatre, and exerted himself zealously to attract the attention of the public to one of his creations for the stage. But the great almighty public hitherto would have nothing to do with the musician of genius. In the year 1820, however, his muse did at last enter the portals of the theatre. Through Vogl's intercession, the directors of the Vienna Opera commissioned him to write a farce with songs— " Die Zwillingsbrüder." It was performed for the first time at the Kärntnertortheater on June 14th with doubtful success, and, after being repeated five times, was withdrawn from the repertory. But Anselm Hüttenbrenner gives the following glowing account of it : " An operetta by Schubert, in which the Court opera singer, Vogl, sang the chief part, was given several time at the Kärntnertortheater and greatly applauded. At the first performance I sat beside Schubert in the last row of the gallery. He was quite pleased that the operetta was being received with loud applause. All the solos and scenes in which Vogl took part were clapped vigorously. At the end Schubert was called, but he refused to come before the curtain, because he had on an old shabby overcoat. I took off my black tail-coat and tried to persuade him to put it on, and to present himself to the audience, which would have been a good thing for him, but he was too irresolute and bashful. As the calls became more and more insistent, the producer at last had to appear before the curtain and announce that Schubert was not in the house. Schubert laughed when he heard this. Afterwards we foregathered at Lenkay's inn in the Liliengasse, where we commemorated the success of the operetta in a few bottles of Nessmüller."

The newspaper critics noticed the performance. "The *Hofoper* gave a little play with songs, 'Die Zwillingsbrüder,' adapted from the French ('Les deux Valentins')," wrote the Vienna correspondent of the *Dresdener Abendzeitung*. "A young composer made his *début* in public with the music composed for the book. I would warn this talented young man that too much praise is unwholesome. For the public received the operetta as if it were a great masterpiece, which, of course, it was not. Certainly there is evidence in his composition of thoroughness and well-thought-out sequence of new themes, but, just as light frivolous music is not suitable to illustrate heroic subjects, so his music is far too grave and exalted to illustrate this very frivolous subject. Generally speaking, I am of opinion that this young composer (he calls himself Schubert) will employ his talent more happily in the heroic than in the comic line. With regard to the performance itself, our master, Vogl, on this occasion did not appear at his best. He played the part of the twin-brothers in such a way that one could see he was always the same actor. He, too, is not at home in comedy."

The critic of the *Wiener Sammler* called the music a "pretty trifle," the work of a young composer of promise. "It shows signs of a mastery of the art of composition, for the style of the opera is undoubtedly pure and sure, and proves that the composer is no novice in harmony. But many of the melodies are somewhat antiquated, and many unmelodious."

Yet another attempt: Schubert's music to the three-act piece, "Die Zauberharfe," which was given on August 19th, 1820, in the Theater-an-der-Wien, met with no success.

Bauernfeld wrote in his diary about the first night : "Aug. 19th, 1820, Theater-an-der-Wien. The 'Zauberharfe'—a decorative and mechanical piece. Music by Schubert. Capital ! "

The newspaper critics were of a less favourable opinion. The correspondent of the *Leipziger Allgemeinen Musikalischen Zeitung* wrote of the performance : "The melodrama 'Zauberharfe,' with music by Herr Schubert, was rather coldly received. A few astonishingly effective decorations did not atone for the dull, too monotonous subject, the treatment of which was without interest. The composition here and there showed talent, but as a whole it lacks evidence of the experience which can weld material together ; it is much too long, ineffective and fatiguing, the harmonies are too sudden, the instrumentation overloaded, the chorus tame and wanting in strength. The introductory adagio and the romance for tenor are the most successful phrases, and give an impression of deep feeling and noble simplicity, also of delicate modulations. A more idyllic material would suit the young composer infinitely better, and it must be regarded as a mistake that he should have attempted a subject which requires an intimate acquaintance with the secrets of stagecraft to be effectively dealt with." Only the Schubertian Baron Schlechta, in a long article in the *Konversationsblatt*, wrote in a tone of enthusiastic admiration : " Schubert has been given ample opportunities here of exhibiting in song his poetic powers and has done so very happily and thoroughly. Now we hear his notes coming to us in a dreamy dance measure ; now the most powerful rush of melody sweeps the strings of the magic harp. The most convincing proof of the merits of his composition is that in spite of the performance being, for the most part, mediocre, it shone out in such brilliant contrast. Even the unfortunate Palmerin was unable quite to ruin his *rôle*. I should like to be allowed, in conclusion, to express a wish that Schubert may often repeat his efforts to awaken us from the stupor into which we have sunk in these degenerate days by giving us melody on the stage from the endless riches of his genius."

All that remains to-day of the " Zauberharfe " music is the glorious " Rosamunde " overture, which ranks among the composer's most masterly creations.

The year 1821 brought many radical changes in the circle of Schubert's friends. The master separated from Mayrhofer, with whom he had for so long lived ; their joint housekeeping was given up. The cause, as has been before mentioned in Mayrhofer's words, " circumstances, social engagements and changed views of life." Schubert then again went to Schober, who readily put a room at his disposal. The faithful Anselm Hüttenbrenner, too, pressed his hand in farewell and went away to Graz, there to inherit the estate of his father, who was a landed proprietor of importance. Spaun was obliged to go to Linz, whither he was transferred, and where for two years he was to hold a Government appointment. Thus, to the master's sorrow, the circle of Schubertians was sadly reduced, but, all the same, friendship, the one consolation in Schubert's outer life, continued in other ties. He found new comrades, who were soon enthusiastic Schubertians. Especially

was this the case with the two young painters, Leopold Kupelwieser and Moritz von Schwind; and then later came the poet
Eduard Bauernfeld and the musician Franz Lachner.

Less fortunate than in friends was Schubert in his endeavours
to gain recognition for his artistic creativeness. In spite of the
not very favourable criticisms of his first attempts for the stage,
he tried once more to place new works for the theatre, in the hopes
that these would give him a little relief in his narrow circumstances. But still without success. The opera he next undertook,
" Sakuntala," remained a fragment. In the following year he
composed " Alfonso und Estrella," for which his friend Schober
had supplied the text, but, notwithstanding the strenuous efforts
of the Schubertians and the many beauties it contained, it failed to
get performed. It was partly written (Acts 1 and 2) at the
Castle of Ochsenburg, near Pölten, where Schubert and Schober,
in September, 1821, were guests of the Bishop of St. Pölten,
Johann Nepomuk, Knight of Dankesreither, a relative of Schober's.
Ochsenburg was a favourite resort of the people of St. Pölten, on
account of its romantic position and charms. In his topography
of the year 1815, Strohmayr praises the castle thus : " It is really
in one of the most picturesque and lovely neighbourhoods it is
possible to see anywhere, and the panorama deserves to be sketched
by an artist. Fruitful fields, wooded hills, flowery meadows,
through which streams babble, the most magnificent park, the
village of St. Georgen am Steinfeld, the Markt Wilhelmsburg,
and groups of farmhouses, make the near view as pleasant as that
of St. Pölten, seen veiled in the blue ether of distance. Here one
can breathe freely and forget all the petty harassing cares of
existence ; here are no intrigues, envy, hatred and malice, but a
pure unadulterated atmosphere in which one can live and enjoy
life."

The castle is still standing there, almost the same as in the bright,
happy days of the Schubert idyll. The old linden trees, under
which Schubert dreamed, still cast their shade and blossoms on the
grass. The old posting road, along which the two young friends
drove in the carriage with galloping horses to visit the art-loving
Bishop, is unaltered and shows almost the same ruts in which their
wheels revolved. St. Pölten's narrow streets, with Baroque gables
and spires at odd corners, have the same old-world dreamy aspect
as in the autumn of Schubert's visit. At Ochsenburg the two

friends worked together on their opera. Schubert produced many immortal melodies; many a bumper of sparkling wine, amidst laughter and jest, was emptied in all joyousness and harmony, and many a "Schubertiade" celebrated in the precincts of the episcopal castle.

"In Ochsenburg," Schober told Spaun, "we were very busy seeing the beautiful neighbourhood and attending balls and concerts in St. Pölten; nevertheless, we were industrious, especially Schubert, who composed nearly two acts. . . . I only wish you had been there to hear the glorious melodies as they came; it is wonderful how rich and ever-fresh thoughts pour from him. The room we had in St. Pölten was uncommonly charming: two double beds, a sofa near the cosy stove, a grand piano, everything as comfortable and homelike as could be. In the evening we compared notes about what we had done in the day; then we sent for beer, smoked our pipes and read, or Sofie and Nettel would come over and we would have singing. We had 'Schubertiades' at the Bishop's, and at Baron Mink's, whom I like immensely, and there were present a princess, two countesses and three baronesses. All were charmed. Now we have come here with my mother. We were given a dinner in Heiligen-Eich, and Heaven gave us the most splendid weather for travelling which we have enjoyed for eight whole days. Now the Bishop has followed. S. and my mother send you love. You can imagine that Kupel (the painter Kupelwieser) not turning up after promising to come was a great disappointment. And so is not to have you, for we would specially have liked your criticism of our work. . . ."

Schubert, in gratitude for being so hospitably entertained in Ochsenburg, dedicated his Harfnerlieder to Bishop Danksreither, for which the princely ecclesiastic thanked the composer in the following undated lines :

"You have done me a really remarkable and undeserved honour, dear sir, in that you dedicate to me the twelve operas of your everywhere valued and admired musical productions. Accept my heartiest thanks for this mark of your regard and for the kind letter which accompanied the copy of your excellent work, and believe that I feel greatly indebted to you. God, from whom all good gifts come, has endowed you with such rare and exalted musical talent that its further employment should

form the foundation of your future happiness and lasting good
fortune. With every good wish and assurance of my high
esteem.

I am,

Your very humble servant,

JOHANN NEPOMUK m.p. Bishop."

Despite the fact that the theatre directors had refused "Alfonso
und Estrella," Schubert, in order to improve his financial position,
tried composing for the stage again. He wrote a song-piece called
"Die Verschworenen" (the Conspirators) to the text of a dialect
poet of repute, Ignaz Franz Castelli. The Censor regarded the
title as dangerous to the State and changed it to "Der häusliche
Krieg." Schubert expended on the tame, undistinguished text an
abundance of splendid music, and sent the work to the Opera-
direction. After repeated urgent requests, it was returned un-
opened. The friends of Schubert had set their hopes on the
influential Castelli. "Castelli has reported in some foreign
papers," wrote Schober, "that you have set his words to an opera.
He should open his mouth and say something about it." But the
author of the text seems not to have done this. Not till years later
was the work first performed—on March 1st, 1861, in a Viennese
concert hall, and next at the Court Opera. But even this new
failure did not prevent the master from finishing another opera,
"Fierrabras." The text was by Josef Kupelwieser, brother of the
painter. It was an heroical romantic opera in three acts. The
quite mediocre text lacked any sort of stage-effectiveness, and again
if did not come to a performance.

"Your brother's opera is pronounced unworkable," Schubert
wrote to his friend Kupelwieser, "and with it my music." Schubert
had certainly no luck with the theatre. Again he had written two
operas without result. But in these days of disappointment a ray
of encouragement brightened the master's hard lot. It came from
Graz, the capital of green Styria, where the brothers Hüttenbrenner
and the Court official, Dr. Johann Jenger, made an active propaganda
for Schubert's work. Jenger, who was secretary to the Styrian
Society of Musicians, had obtained for the Master the distinction
of honorary membership. The diploma was handed to Schubert
through Hüttenbrenner with the following address :

" Your Highly Born,—

The services which you have rendered to the art of music are too well known for the Committee of the Styrian Society of Musicians to be in ignorance thereof. In their name I am therefore deputed to inform you that as a proof of their recognition and esteem, you are elected an honorary member of the Styrian Society of Musicians. A copy of the rules of the Society will follow the Diploma sent herewith.

From Secretary Jenger,
Kalchberg."

Schubert was at that time travelling in Upper Austria. Again he had set out with Vogl " to combat and victory," as Schober, in an amusing caricature in pencil, commemorated the journey. He shows the proudly striding patron of the shy little master, who trots behind him, nearly annihilated by the majesty of the opera singer's imposing figure. There were merry parties in Linz and Steyr among the friends, and new triumphs. He wrote at the time from Steyr to the faithful Schober, who was about to leave Vienna, to Schubert's intense regret, on August 14th, 1825 :

" Dear Schober,—

Although I am writing rather late, I hope this will find you still in Vienna. I am corresponding diligently with Schäffer, and I am pretty well. Whether I shall ever again be quite strong, I rather doubt. I am living here in every way very simply ; I take regular exercise, write a good deal of my opera, and read Walter Scott. I get on splendidly with Vogl. I was with him in Linz, where he sang much and very beautifully. Bruchmann, Sturm and Streinsburg came to see us a few days ago in Steyr, and went away loaded with songs. As I think I shall scarcely see you before you depart on your travels, I wish you now every good fortune in your enterprise, and assure you of my unchanging affection, and of how sadly I shall miss you. Wherever you are, let me hear from you sometimes.

Your friend,
Franz Schubert.

Greetings to Kupelwieser, Schwind, Mohn, etc., to all of whom I've written.

Address :
Stadt Steyr, an Platz, c/o H. V. Vogl."

In Linz the tone-poet visited his old friend Spaun and his family, as well as the Schubertianer Stadler. There was much music in the capital of Upper Austria just then, played to audiences bursting with enthusiasm. " Women and girls, after the performance of some melancholy songs, wept till they swam in tears." Schubert was elected member of the Linz Music Society.

On his return to Vienna Schubert went to his father at the Rossauer Schoolhouse. A very great event in the musical life of the capital was the arrival of Karl Maria von Weber, the celebrated composer of the " Freischütz." He came on September 21st, 1825, bringing with him the completed score of " Euryanthe," the composition of which had been commissioned by the Director of the Kärntnertortheater. In those days in the department of opera, admirers respectively of Italian and German music were ranged in hostile camps. Babaja's new opera company consisted of first-rate artists even in the smallest parts. Rossini himself conducted the works which had taken Viennese hearts by storm. With his imposing artistic appearance, he was the hero of the musical world, and the monarch of the operatic stage. Now came into rivalry with him Weber, a German of insignificant figure, who from his earliest youth upwards had struggled for success and money, and had not been spoilt by the favours of the great and the happiness of riches. On October 25th the first performance of " Euryanthe " took place, at which Schubert was present. " My reception when I stepped into the orchestra," wrote Weber to his wife, " was enthusiastic, and the applause tremendous. There was no end to it till I gave the sign to begin, when dead silence followed. The overture was wildly applauded. And at the conclusion . . . oh ! my beloved wife, how can I describe the scene ? All were besides themselves with ecstasy—singers, chorus, orchestra were intoxicated with delight, and nearly suffocated me with caresses." Of course, Weber had exaggerated the success of " Euryanthe." The critics compared it unfavourably with the beautiful national airs of the " Freischütz," and so it happened that the success soon fizzled out. Schubert, too, who had been ravished by the " Freischütz," went away disappointed from the performance of Weber's " Euryanthe," and when he met Weber the next day and the latter asked him for his opinion, he seems to have pointed out faults in the melodies which in the " Freischütz " had been so perfect, and to have remarked to others : " The ' Freischütz ' was tender and touching ;

it enchanted through sheer loveliness; but in ' Euryanthe ' there is little that is really appealing."

These frank expressions of opinion on Schubert's part may probably have caused a coolness between him and Weber, who had before interested himself in the Viennese composer's dramatic efforts and led Schubert to build hopes on their production in Dresden. " The prospects for my two operas are at present bad," wrote Schubert to his friend Schober. " Kupelwieser has suddenly left his post at this theatre. Weber's ' Euryanthe ' was a failure, and, in my opinion, deserved a poor reception. These circumstances, and a new difference which has arisen between Palffy and Babaja, leave me little hope for my opera."

But all these failures in the sphere of the theatre could not stem the tide of Schubert's creative activity. Perpetually new works streamed from the rich mine of his divine imagination—dances for the piano, Ecossaisen, Ländler, German pianoforte sonatas—and once more, but for the last time, a work was consecrated to the stage, the music to the play " Rosamunde, Fürstin von Cypern," written by the authoress who supplied the book of " Euryanthe," Wilhelmine Chezy. It was again the occasion of a benefit performance for the actress Emilie Neumann at the Theater-an-der-Wien.

On December 19th, 1825, the theatre bills announced :

" *For the First Time.*

ROSAMUNDE, PRINCESS OF CYPRUS.

Great romantic drama in four acts.

Musical accompaniments, choruses and dances by Helmine von Chezy, *née* Freiherrin Klencke.

Music by Herr Schubert.

Emilie Neumann.

Actress, the Imperial and Royal Private Theatre, Vienna."

On December 30th the performance took place. The text proved to be extremely poor and ineffective, and the piece only survived two representations. But this time Schubert's music was not so adversely criticised. For instance, the *Sammler* wrote :

" The composer Herr Schubert met with a good deal of encouragement, an overture and a chorus had to be repeated, and a song sung by Madame Vogl was very happy. Herr Schubert displays in his compositions originality, but, unfortunately, also *bizarrerie*. The young man is at a stage of development in his art which we wish may proceed satisfactorily. On this occasion he got too much applause. May he never have to deplore getting too little. The choruses were somewhat uncertain, and especially the intonation of the female chorus was vacillating and lame."

The *Wiener Zeitschrift* criticised thus :

" The music accompaniment by Schubert did not disgrace the genius of this popular master. The overture and a chorus in the last act were so irresistibly lovely that amidst excessive clapping an encore was demanded. The charming romance of Axa is likely without doubt to be a favourite piece in the singing world."

Yet this time again Schubert's efforts remained fruitless. As Weber had not succeeded with his " Euryanthe," so Schubert failed to displace Italian opera from the stage. Rossini continued to reign supreme in the repertory. The captivating, easy-to-sing airs by the Swan of Pesaro so bewitched the Vienna public that Beethoven and other German masters were forgotten. Schubert, who with such generous hands had scattered the glorious pearls of his genius before an ungrateful world without claiming thanks or recognition, while his own talent remained neglected, granted Rossini's its due. Though he saw plainly that the Italian *maestro's* popularity was a set-back to German opera (Schubert praised the "Barber of Seville" as excellent), " he consoled himself," said Anselm Hüttenbrenner, "with the reflection that lack of inner stability would prevent the favour which the Rossini operas enjoyed being of a lasting nature, and that people would one day return to their earlier loves, like ' Don Juan,' ' Zauberflöte ' and ' Fidelio.' "

If the master met with little success in his works for the stage, the fertility of his lyrical muse continued its produtivity. Now came the songs of " Frühlingsglaube " of Uhland, in which are expressed in divine music the breath of balmy spring zephyrs, the radiance and sweetness of a night in May ; the " Waldesnacht " of Schlegel, which makes one feel in tones the cool, shivering woodland air ; and Goethe's " Gesang der Geister über den Wassern," with accompaniment for viola, cello and double-bass, paints in sound a mysterious unearthly magic. For Anna Fröhlich, the concert singer, who every Thursday produced songs of Schubert's in the Musikvereinssaal, he wrote at the end of 1820 music to the

Twenty-fifth Psalm, " God is my strength." During the months that followed were set to music Goethe's " Grenzen der Menschheit," one of the finest of all musical hymns ; Schiller's " Sehnsucht " (a second setting) ; the Suleika-Lieder " Was bedeutet die Bewegung " and " Ach, um deine feuchten Schwingen " ; from Rückerts's " Östlichen Rosen," the " Sei mir gegrüsst," so overflowing with the sentiment of love ; Goethe's " Musensohn," " Willkommen und Abschied " ; Mayrhofer's " An Heliopolis " ; " Geist der Liebe," by Matthisson ; and, lastly, the famous *lieder* cycle, " Die schöne Müllerin," after the poems of the romantic writer Wilhelm Müller.

Worthy to rank with " Die schöne Müllerin " were the songs " Du bist die Ruh " by Rückert, " Auf dem Wasser zu singen," a lace-work of the finest notes, the moving ballad " Der Zwerg " by Collin, the chorale " Gott in der Natur," and " Geist der Liebe." In the year 1820 the choicest product of his pianoforte compositions was the C Major Fantasia, also called " Wanderer." In Church music he composed the beautiful mass in A flat major and the offertorium " Salve Regina " : in chamber music and instrumental works, part of the quartette for strings in C minor and the " Unfinished " Symphony.

These years were memorable for Schubert's life and creation, because in the course of them he succeeded not only in being heard as a composer of opera by a greater public, but in getting recognition as a composer of *lieder*. Then he had the satisfaction of getting several of his works published, and this extended considerably the circle of his admirers. There were two houses especially open to him in Vienna at this time, where two old Viennese musical families gave performances of his works to large gatherings of music friends, and to whose help he owed the printing of several of his compositions. These were the family of Sonnleithner and the house of Grillparzer's intimate friends, the sisters Fröhlich.

It was Cappi and Diabelli, art and music dealers in Graben No. 1133, who issued in quick succession the first twelve books of Schubert's songs. The remuneration was mainly used for the purpose of clearing off old debts of the master's. On the advice of his friends, he sought, too, to strengthen his financial position by dedicating separate items of his compositions to notabilities. The " Erlkönig " ballad was dedicated to the Count von Dietrichstein, " Gretchen am Spinnrad " to the Reichsgraf Moriz Friess,

" Der Wanderer " to the Poet-patriarch of Venice, Johann Ladislaus Pyrker. For these dedications he received various presents. In a letter to his friend Spaun of November 2nd, 1821, he writes : " Now I have something to tell you : that is, my dedications, the idea of which I owe to you, have brought me fees from the Patriarch of 12, and from Friess, through Vogl's influence, 20 ducates, which is very satisfactory to me."

On March 7th, 1821, the " Erlkönig " for the first time was heard by a large audience, at an Ash Wednesday concert which Vogl organised for the Society of Noble Ladies for Promoting Good and Useful Charities, which held its reunion annually at the Kärntnertortheater. The " Erlkönig " was an enormous success, and other Schubert compositions—" Das Dörfchen," by Burger, " Der Gesang der Geister über den Wassern " (Goethe)— were given. The last, according to the critical Rosenbaum's note in his diary on the performance, totally failed to charm. Wilhelmine Schröder gave recitations at this concert, and Fanny Elsler took part in it as a dancer. The accompanist was Schubert's friend, Anselm Hüttenbrenner, on a new grand piano made by Conrad Graf. " Schubert could have played his own compositions better than myself," Hüttenbrenner relates in his reminiscences, " but was too shy to be induced to do so. He contented himself with standing beside me and turning over."

Schubert's music was heard now at many other important functions, both private and public—at concerts of the Society of Music Friends, in the " Römischen Kaiser " and Kärntnertortheater, at a performance by the pupils of the Vienna Conservatorium, at the Music Academy on the occasion of the Kaiser Franz's birthday, and on many other occasions his work gained the ear and admiration of large distinguished audiences. The critics of the leading music and art periodicals, too, began to busy themselves more and more frequently with Schubert, and his name headed innumerable articles and essays.

Thus *Der Wiener Zeitschrift für Kunst*, on March 25th, 1822, occurred a detailed criticism of the master's lyrics, entitled, " A Glance at Schubert's Songs," by Friedrich von Hentl : ". . . Schubert's *lieder* rank through their undisputable merits with the very highest masterpieces of genius ; they are calculated to raise the present lowered standard of taste to its former level, for the power of real genius never fails in the long run to have effect on the human mind. The divine sparks may be deeply hidden in the ashes smouldering before the altar on which the idols are sacrificed, but a breath of genius will fan them into a glorious flame of enthusiasm which cannot be described, but only felt." Then the critic goes on to speak in detail of every published ballad and song of Schubert's, and to praise their characteristic melody. In conclusion, he sums up his judgment with the following memorable remarks : " I think that I have said enough without going further into the general characteristics of the Schubertian muse. Everyone must at a first glance discover for himself in his works the character and thought of an artist of genius, and when the innermost depths of the cultivated mind are so strongly impressed and struck with what is here so perfectly and beautifully produced in tones, it is better to silence the questions of the cavilling understanding, such as, ' Is this the right manner ? Couldn't a better have been found ? Have other masters anticipated it or not ? ' Every genius has his own criterion, and is inspired by a feeling which contains within it the deepest inner consciousness, the highest wisdom, the only true source of knowledge in appraising works of fine and exalted art."

At that time possibilities arose for Schubert to better considerably his unfavourable material position and to free himself from the harassing cares of his narrow circumstances. But he did not understand how to utilise his artistic successes by seeking the recommendations of the influential personages whose attention had been drawn to him. He was a man of introspective nature, too unpractical and unworldly wise to make the most of such opportunities ; he was without energy, always dreaming and absorbed in his artistic creations. There are, besides his musical works, many literary documents dating from that time from which one can learn something of the dreamy romantic inner life of the composer. " My Dream," for instance, written evidently in memory of the beloved mother lost in childhood :

" I was a brother of many brothers and sisters. Our father and our mother were good. I loved them all dearly. Once our father took us to an entertainment. The brothers enjoyed it. But I was sad. My father came to me and ordered me to eat of the good things. I couldn't, which made him angry, and he banished me from his sight. I went my way full of love for those who despised it, and wandered in far-off lands. I felt for long torn by the greatest pain and the greatest love. Then came the news that my mother was dead. I hurried to see her, and my father, softened by sorrow, did not forbid my coming to the house. Tears rained from my eyes. I saw her lying there and she seemed to me to look just the same as in the past when living, and we followed her in sorrow to the grave, and the coffin was lowered. From this time onwards I stayed at home. Then one day my father led me into his favourite garden. He asked me if I liked it. But I couldn't bear it, though I dared not say so. Again he asked me if the garden pleased me, and, trembling, I answered ' No ! ' I hated it. Then my father struck me and I fled. And again I wandered forth with a heart full of love for those who scorned it, and I went into strange lands. For years I sang songs. If I sang of love it became pain, and if I wanted to sing only of pain it became love.

" So I was torn between love and pain. And once I was told of a pious virgin who had just died, and that round her grave a circle of many young and old people had drawn who felt eternally blissful, and who spoke softly, so as not to wake the virgin. Heavenly thoughts seemed perpetually to irradiate from her grave and shower on the young men sparks of glory. This made me long to find my way there too. But people said that only by a miracle could one enter this circle, the tone of which was so wonderfully soft and lovely, and, all in a moment, I felt overwhelmed with this everlasting blissfulness. I beheld my father, too, reconciled and loving. He clasped me in his arms and wept. But I wept still more."

A poem of Schubert's, written in 1825, gives expression to his profound, romantic longing to rise above this earthly life into the fair worlds of ideality. It is called " Mein Gebet " (My Prayer) :

My Prayer

" Deepest longing, holy fears,
　　Striving up to lovelier spheres,
　　Would fill the darkling space above
　　With the almighty dream of love.

" Give thy son, O mighty Father,
　　As reward thy sorrows rather
　　And at last, him to redeem,
　　Thy love's eternal beam.

" See, in dust destroyed alway,
An unheard-of horror's prey,
Lies my life, its mortal woe
Nearing endless overthrow.

" Slay it and slay me at last,
In the stream of Lethe cast.
And, O great One, let me then
Stronger and purer rise again."

His sensitive, shy character and want of practical experience prevented him from turning to business account his artistic successes. Friends assisted him, it is true, to get his works printed, as has been mentioned before, by Cappi and Diabelli in Graben, and by the art and music publishers, Sauer and Leidesdorf in Kärntnerstrasse No. 941, and later by Pennauer and Matthias Artaria. But he had no idea of negotiating with publishers for an increase in honorariums, or of making efforts to give lucrative lessons in the houses of the wealthy, or appearing at public concerts, or fighting with dogged persistence for a post in a musical institute. Very rarely did he rouse himself to stand out energetically for some point of business concerning his compositions, as in the following letter, which he addressed in April, 1825, to his publishers, Cappi and Diabelli :

" Sir,—Your letter really astonished me. I had concluded that with Herr Cappi's own consent the account was closed. As I have not been particularly struck in former transactions over the publication of the waltzes by the honest intentions of my publisher, I am in a position to explain what may seem to you to need explanation, and that is that I have entered into a permanent agreement with another publisher. It is hardly clear to me why I should be presented with a bill for 150 florins when the cost of copying the opera was fixed by you at 100 florins. But, be that as it may, I think that the extremely small fees received for the earlier things—50 florins, for instance, for the Fantasia—has long ago nullified the debt unjustly attributed to me. But, as it is doubtful that you will cherish any such humane opinion, I respectfully draw your attention to my just claim to 20 copies of the last and 13 of the earlier printed works. If you will kindly reckon in with these the 50 florins which you have tried to lure out of me by other means, you will see that my demand is greater and more justified than yours, but I should not have made it if you had not reminded me in such an unpleasant manner. The debt, as you will oblige me by admitting, has thus long ago been wiped out. There can be no question of another edition of songs for you to remunerate as cheaply as possible. I am now receiving two hundred florins for a volume, and H. V. Steiner has repeatedly made me an offer for the publication rights of my work. In conclusion, I must request you to return all the manuscripts you have of mine, whether already set up or not, with the least possible delay.

Respectfully,

FRANZ SCHUBERT."

In the year 1822 another attempt was made to interest a foreign firm in Schubert's compositions. The faithful *Famulus*, Josef Hüttenbrenner, drew the attention of C. E. Peters to Schubert as a "Second Beethoven." The shrewd Peters replied very evasively. He was already negotiating with many well-known musicians, like Spohr, Romberg, Hummel, etc., and must approach unknown talent with caution; the composer, anyhow, might submit works for "consideration" with a view to publication. The matter was not followed up.

"One reason why Schubert's talent during his lifetime was mostly hidden under a bushel," writes Anton Schindler, "was a certain pig-headed obstinacy, an exaggerated sense of independence, which rendered him often deaf to the good and practical advice of his well-intentioned friends." Thus it happened that Schubert's outward circumstances, in spite of many hard-won successes, and notwithstanding intercourse with distinguished persons, remained limited. Poverty and care were his inseparable companions, and to these was added ill-health. He suffered repeatedly from attacks of anæmia, fits of giddiness and weak nerves—forerunners of his approaching last fatal illness. Disappointments in life and in art gnawed at his heart-strings, luckless love depressed his sensitive and gentle spirit.

On the subject of Schubert's illness, Schwind wrote in a letter to Schober in March, 1824: "He (Schubert) says that the new treatment in a few days did him good and he felt quite different. He still lives on vegetables one day and a *schnitzel* the next, and drinks gallons of tea; he takes a great many baths and is tremendously industrious. His new quartet was produced on Sunday by Schuppanzigh and very well played. It is quite inspired. Now he is working enthusiastically on an octet. If anyone comes to see him during the day he merely says, ' *Grüss dich Gott*, how are you ? ' and goes on writing. Naturally he is soon left alone. He has set two very beautiful poems of Müllers, and three of Mayrhofer's, whose poetry has lately appeared, ' Gondalfahrt,' ' Abendstern ' and ' Sieg,' besides he has composed 20 ' Deutsche,' each lovelier than the last, gallant, delightful, Bacchanalian. God ! it's wonderful ! I go to him nearly every evening."

A letter of the master's on March 31st, 1824, to his friend Leopold Kupelwieser, who was studying at the time in Rome, gives a touching picture of the state of melancholy in which Schubert found himself in those days :

" Dear Kupelwieser,—

I have long been wanting to write to you, but never knew how to manage it. Now an opportunity offers itself through Smirsch, and I can once more pour out my soul to someone. You are so good and kind. I am sure you'll forgive what many would not take in good part. In short, I am feeling just now the unhappiest and most miserable of men : health will never be right again, and I'm in despair at things going from bad to worse. Picture to yourself, I say, a man whose brilliant hopes have come to nothing, to whom fortune, love and friendship give little but pain and inspiration, for the beautiful becoming less active, threatens to forsake me altogether. I ask you if that is not being a miserable, unhappy creature ? ' *Meine Ruhe ist hin, mein Herz ist schwer, ich finde sie nie und nimmermehr.*' * I can sing those lines with truth now every day, for every night when I go to bed I hope I may never wake again, and every morning the depression of yesterday reoccurs. So, joyless and friendless, I pass my days, unless Schwind visits me and brings a ray of those old past sweet times with him."

In this letter he mentions, too, that he has composed few new *lieder*, but a string quartet and an octet, and that these may be stepping-stones to a great symphony. As a special piece of news, he tells his friend that Beethoven is to give a concert at which his Ninth Symphony and extracts from the new Mass (Missa Solemnis) and a new overture are to be performed. " If God wills it," he

* Gretchen's song in Goethe's " Faust."—*Translator*.

concludes, " I too will give a like concert next year." In his
diary Schubert wrote, March (1824), the following melancholy
reflections : " Not one of us knows what the other suffers, not one
understands another's pain or joy. We think we are finding our
way into each other's hearts, but we are really only with, not near,
each other. It is torture to realise this. My musical productions
come into existence through the understanding and through pain.
Those which pain has brought forth seem to please the world most.
. . . Oh, Fantasy ! most precious of all jewels, to humanity the
inexhaustible well from which learned men as well as artists drink,
don't desert us, who are recognised and valued by few, and save
us from that so-called ' enlightenment,' a hateful skeleton without
flesh and blood."

The summer of 1824 saw our master again in Hungary in the
Esterhazy household at Zselesz. Again he gave the two young
Countesses music lessons and arranged music for the evening concerts. The letters which he wrote from the Hungarian castle to
his friends and relations give an idea of Schubert's state of mind at
that time, and also tell much of the artistic work that occupied him
at Zselesz. In July his brother Ferdinand wrote to him :

" BELOVED BROTHER,—

" ' Now at last here is a letter from Ferdinand. What a lazy
fellow, how cold and unfeeling to leave his brother unnoticed for
so many weeks ! ' So, I hear you saying. But forgive me and don't
be angry. I am always thinking of you and really have been in your
company, since I have begun to play your quartets again, and hear
when I go to the ' Ungärischen Krone ' once a week so many of your
compositions played by Uhr. I was not a little surprised the first
time I heard this Uhr play quite unexpectedly while I was in the
middle of dinner some of your waltzes. I felt at that moment a
curious sensation. I wasn't in the least merry ; much more was my
heart wrung with melancholy longing, a sort of pain . . . I can't
describe.

Now, dear Franz, write (specially to me) and tell me how you
are, if you are quite in good health, and what you are doing. To-
day I have sent off to you the Bach Fugues and ' Der Kurze Mantel,'
the opera book which Herr von Leidesdorf wishes submitted to you.
Make haste and let us have from you soon something splendid on
the operatic stage.

About a month ago Herr von Mohn was here with me and I handed him the following books of songs :

1. Geheimnis, by Schiller, 1823.
2. An der Frühling, 1817.
3. Die Lebens-Melodien, 1816.
4. Beim Winde, von Mayrhofer, 1819.
5. Frohsinn, 1817.
6. Wanderer's Nachtlied.
7. Trost, 1817.
8. Frühlingslied, 1816.
9. Der entführte Orest, 1820.
10. Sprache der Liebe, by Schlegel, 1816.

A few days afterwards I handed over to H. v. Kupelwieser, at his request and at your suggestion, the score of your new opera.

Besides these two gentlemen, a Herr von Hugelmann came with the request that I would restore to him the scores of the Mozart quartets which you gave me to take care of. But as, after searching for them three times, I could not find them, he had to go away without his wish being gratified. I have seen him twice since, once in the corridor of the Normalschule and once again in my dwelling, where he has caused me not a little unpleasantness, for he began to abuse you and used such coarse language and kicked up such a row that I very much regretted the honour of having made his acquaintance. So will you be so good as to tell me where you think the above-mentioned music scores are to be found, that I may pacify this raving wild beast.

Now I must tell you how it goes with myself, which I am glad to do, because, thank God, I am very well indeed. Of course my office gives me a great deal to do ; but I don't object to that, and I like the post. Out of school hours there are exercises to go through and lessons to be prepared, but all the more enjoyable for that reason are my free hours, which I spend generally in the society of my dear Rieder, my one real friend. The latter greets you and is meditating performing your last Mass, in such a way, be it understood, as will crown you with laurels, but not till you are back in Vienna.

Now farewell! Write soon. Have a good time and keep well till I see you again.

Your faithful brother,
FERDINAND."

Schubert's answer was as follows :

"DEAREST BROTHER,—

Certainly I was a little hurt at not hearing for so long from home or from you. Leidesdorf, too, is silent, and I have written to him more than once. Be so kind as to look him up in the Art Shop and get him to send what I've written to him about ; also you might inquire about the third book of the ' Müllerlieder.' I see nothing in the newspapers. What you tell me about your Quartet Society surprises me, all the more because you've prevailed on Ignaz ! ! ! It would be better, however, if you played other quartets than mine, for these please you only because you like all my things. Still it delights me most to be remembered in this way, especially as you don't seem to have been so affected by the quartets as by the waltzes in the ' Ungärischen Krone.' Was it sorrow at my absence that drew tears from you so that you couldn't trust yourself to write ? Or did all the tears that you have ever seen me shed occur to your memory ? Be that as it may, I feel at this moment clearly that you, if anybody, are my most inward friend, bound to me by every fibre of my soul. In case these lines should induce you to believe that I am not well or in the best of moods, I hasten to assure you to the contrary. It is true that these are no longer those happy times when everything shone in a youthful glory, but are rather those of fatal acquaintance with a miserable reality, which I try with my ' Fantasy ' (I thank God for it) to beautify as much as possible. One is apt to believe that in the place where one has been once happy happiness is to be found again, when it really lies in oneself. So I have experienced here an unpleasant disappointment, the repetition of an experience in Steyr—but now I am more in a condition to find inward peace and happiness than I was then. A proof of this you will see in a sonata with variations on an original theme for four hands which I have just composed. The variations in particular are very much appreciated. With regard to the songs handed over to Mohn I console myself with the fact that only a few of them seem to me to have been good, i.e., ' Geheimnis,' ' Wanderer's Nachtlied,' and ' Der entsuhnte (not entführte) Orest.' The mistake made me laugh. Try at least to get these back. Hasn't Kupelwieser said what he intends to do with the opera, or where he is going to send it ? The quintets (or quartets), through the stupidity of that consummate ass Hugelthier, have come here with me, and by God! he'll not get them back till he has apologised either in writing or by word of mouth for his gross rudeness. If you get an opportunity of administering a dressing down to this unclean sow let me know ; I'll gladly take a part in it. But enough of this wretch. I am very glad to hear that you are feeling so well, and hope that in the coming winter my health, too, will become stronger. Give parents, brothers and sisters my dearest love and a hundred embraces for yourself. Write as soon as possible. Goodbye now, goodbye.

N.B.—What are Karl and Ignaz doing ? Tell them to write to me.

With everlasting love,
Your Brother FRANZ."

In August a letter was despatched from Zselesz to Schwind :

" DEAR SCHWIND,—

At last a letter from Schubert, you'll say, after three months ! It is true that is a pretty long time, but as my life here is as simple as can be I haven't much to write about, either to you or others. And if I weren't so anxious to hear something of you and the other dear friends, especially Schober and Kupelwieser, I should, perhaps, if you'll excuse my saying so, not be writing to you now. How goes it with Schober's enterprise ? Is Kupelwieser in Vienna or still in Rome ? Does the Reading Society still continue or is it, as is only likely, entirely broken up ? What are you doing ? I am, thank God, still well. If I only had you, Schober and Kupelwieser with me ! The cursed yearning for Vienna possesses me sometimes in spite of the presence here of the all-attractive star. At the end of September I hope to see you again. I have composed a big sonata with variations for four hands. Everyone here likes it, though I don't altogether trust the taste of the Hungarians, and therefore shall leave it to you and the Viennese to decide. How is Leidesdorf ? Is he progressing or are things at a standstill ? Please answer all these questions in detail and as soon as possible. You can't think how I long for a letter from you. You are in a position to tell me so much that I want to hear about our friends and a thousand other things that it is impossible for me to get news of. It wouldn't have hurt you to have told me a little, always supposing that you knew my address. Above everything, I put it on your conscience to elucidate the Leidesdorf scandal, as he neither answers my letter nor sends what I ask for. What does that mean? The Devil only knows! The 'Müllerlieder' is a slow affair. Here is quarter of a year gone by since the book was dispatched. And now goodbye and write soon.

Your true friend,

FRZ. SCHUBERT."

And to his other friend of the Vienna confidential circle, Schober, who was at that time in Breslau, he poured out his despondent heart:

" DEAR SCHOBER,—

I hear that you are not happy and that you have to deaden the tumult of your despair with sleep? So Schwind writes. Although this grieves me greatly, I am not surprised, for such is the lot of every intelligent man in this most miserable of worlds. And what should we do with happiness when unhappiness is the one charm left to us in life? If only we were together, you, Schwind, Kuppel and myself, then every misfortune would seem supportable ; but we are separated, each far from the other in some out-of-the-way corner, and that is what is really my misfortune. I feel inclined to exclaim with Goethe : ' Oh! could we but call back an hour of those dear old times!' Those times when we sat together so confidingly, and with motherly pride submitted each to the other the children of our artistic creation, waiting, not without anxiety, the opinion that would be given in all sincerity and love ; that time when we inspired each other and were all striving mutually after the most beautiful and highest of ideals. Now here I sit alone in the wilds of Hungary-land, because I've let myself, to my regret, be beguiled hither a second time, and there isn't a single creature with whom I can converse sensibly. Since you went away I've hardly composed a song, but have tried my hand at several instrumental things. What will happen about my opera, Heaven only knows. Notwithstanding all this, my health is now good and has been so for three months. Only my gaiety is eclipsed through your and Kuppel's absence. I have many bad days when I am in the lowest spirits. In one of these hours of despondency, when I have been more than usual painfully conscious of the barrenness of this present-day existence, the following poem escaped me, and I only transmit it to you because I know you'll judge my weaknesses with love and toleration :

COMPLAINT TO THE PEOPLE

Undone art thou, O youth of this our day !
And waste and spent the countless peoples' starkness,
Not one stands out from all that mass of darkness
Which, without meaning, floods along the way.

It is too great a pain that gnaws at me,
Of all my one-time strength the last poor fraction ;
It is the age that dooms me to inaction,
Preventing all the greatness that might be.

Decrepit, old, the people crawl around,
The deeds of youth seem to them but a vision,
On their own golden rhymes they cast derision,
Nor heed the mighty sense behind the sound.

But thou, O sacred art, canst still dictate
That pictured deed of the old strength shall borrow,
And partially assuage the heavy sorrow
That never can again be friends with fate.

Up to the present things are going badly with Leidesdorf; he can't pay, and no one will buy things, either of mine or anybody else's at a wretched bric-à-brac shop. I have now described my present position pretty fully to you, and I await with longing to hear about yours as soon as possible. What I would like most would be to have you back in Vienna. I've no doubt that you are quite well. And now goodbye, and write to me quickly.

THY SCHUBERT,
Adieu ! ! ! "

As can be gathered from these letters, Schubert's genius brought forth in Zselesz many compositions of value. There were several pianoforte pieces for four hands, such as Variations on an Original Theme in A Sharp Major, the beautiful B Major Sonata, the grand Duet in C Major, and the famous " Divertissement à la Hongroise," filled with echoes of Hungarian folk music. A good many string quartets were partly begun and partly finished, among them the romantic A Minor, a favourite to-day with all chamber musicians, with its impressions of the idyllic country life and magic of the Hungarian national atmosphere. To these belong a group of dances, which are tender and joyous children of the impromptu inspiration of Schubert's rich fancy. For the Count's House Quartet he composed the beautiful chorale " Gebet vor der Schlacht." The composition of this work proved how the master's creative spirit was ever spreading its wings, and how quickly he was able to produce the most precious pearls from the treasure-trove of his genius. The Countess, at breakfast, had laid before him the poem by de la Motte Fouquée beginning with the lines " Du Urquell aller Güte," and asked him to set it to music. Schubert withdrew, and, after wandering for a few hours dreaming in the park, he found the wonderful accompaniment to the words. The same day the quartet was written down, and the two Countesses, the Count and Baron Schönstein sang it in the evening in the Countess's salon.

Before his return to Vienna, Schubert received another very Biedermeierisch letter from his brother Ferdinand, telling him about the performance of a mass in Hainburg :

" In Hainburg I was hospitably entertained by the amiable parish priest, Reinberger. He gave me meals and a bed, and gave himself a great deal of trouble to amuse me. The first day he took us (Mayseder was there too) to the Castle and into the Castle grounds ; the second day we went to Pressburg, and in a meadow caught *litmice*, not less than two hundred, and in the afternoon shot hares on Hainburgerberg. This offered an opportunity of making the acquaintance of Regenschori and his son, who are schoolmasters there. They are a rare couple. The former asked me to a service on the following Sunday, and, when I asked him what the mass was to be, he answered, ' A very beautiful one by a well-known and famous composer—only just at the moment I can't remember his name.' And now what do you think the mass was ? If only you had been with me I know you would have been very pleased, as I was, for it was the Mass in B by you ! You can imagine my feelings. And what unusual and nice people those were. . . . The mass, moreover, was given with extreme reverence and very well performed. Regenschori conducted, and led the time so accurately that it couldn't have been better. His son, who is a finished violin-player, played in the band of musicians, and the priest sang second; I, as usual, played the organ. The choir was good on the whole, but the tenor was somewhat nervous and his voice weak. It rained the whole day without ceasing. The afternoon had to be spent indoors and we had string and voice quartets, and in the evening amused ourselves with games and charades."

In the middle of October Schubert went back to Vienna with Baron von Schönstein. "The greater part of our journey," wrote Schönstein to Count Esterhazy in a letter of October 20th, 1824, "was soothing as a lullaby. Morpheus wrapt us in beneficent slumber, till we were disturbed by fears of being upset in the dark. One of the lead horses cast a shoe, and we had to stop at a blacksmith's to get another. . . . As up till then we had travelled with closed eyes, afterwards we were not in so much need of sleep, and played in the evening a rubber of *Mariage*. The second day we arrived punctually at Pressburg, where I only stopped till the horses were changed. The coachman must have anticipated my generosity, for he drove the rest of the way so excellently that we were in the metropolis by 4 in the afternoon. . . . Apropos of the cold, I've nearly forgotten to tell you that on the second day our caravan was perished with cold. It was terrible. Schmetter was nearly frozen, and, if he had really been a *schmetterling* (butterfly), would have flown for the rest of the journey, as nothing would have induced him to stick on the box. Schubert, to make matters worse, had smashed the window at the back of the carriage before we got to Dioszeg, so that the most horrible cold wind played about our ears."

Again in Vienna, the composer was in less melancholy humour. "Schubert is here," Schwind announced to his friend Schober in a letter dated November 8th, 1824, "well and in a heavenly mood, rejuvenated through bliss and woe and a gay life." At that time Schubert was living on the Wieden, near the Karlkirche, in a former public-house (to-day Technikerstrasse 9), where his neighbour was his friend, Moritz von Schwind. A lively intercourse was carried on between the two artists of genius. "Schubert is in good health," Schwind told Schober in a letter on February 14th, 1825, "and after a pause again very busy. He has been living recently in the house near us, on the second floor, and has a pretty room. We see each other every day, and, in as far as I am able, I share his life. In the spring we are going to

Dornbach, where we shall stay in the house of a good friend of mine. Every week-end we have a Schubertiade, that is to say, the singer Vogl sings. The company besides him consists of Wittelscheck, Esch and Mayrhofer, and Gahy turns up often. The nine variations for four hands are something quite unusual. . . . You'll be astonished at the characterisation of the little march and the intense loveliness of the trio. Now he is working on songs. If you would care to make an operetta or opera out of David and Abigail or anything else, he wants a text, but with not many words."

Schubert's life just now was careless and gay. Artistic toil alternated with convivial society when the friend of his boyhood, Josef von Spaun, came from Linz for a few weeks on leave in Vienna. At Schwind's the Schubertians spent a merry Christmas, and on Twelfth Night in the year 1825 a masquerade was organised for which Bauernfeld supplied the verse, Schwind humorous drawings, and the three kings in full fancy costume played dice. And there were lively Schubertiades with music, dancing and humour at Karl von Enderes' and Witteczek's. Schubert and Vogl were often invited to the house of the young and admired Court actress, Sophie Müller, where music was made and Schubert's latest songs sung by the artist or by Vogl. It was at that time, too, that the singer Anna Milder, famous in Berlin, began to correspond with Schubert. She was an enthusiastic admirer of his songs, and had sung several with great success at a concert in Berlin. She asked him if he could not compose an opera for Berlin. When he sent her " Alfonso und Estrella," she gave him, on sending back the score, the well-meant advice " to compose something new with a non-Oriental setting in which the soprano would be the leading character." Naturally, Schubert did not accede to the proposal.

He still craved for recognition by the great gods in art, and so once more he tried Goethe. He dedicated to him the songs "An Schwager Kronos," "An Mignon" and "Ganymed," which had recently been published by the firm of Diabelli & Co., and sent them to Weimar with the touching letter :

" YOUR EXCELLENCY,—Should I succeed through the dedication of these compositions in proving to the world my unbounded reverence for your Excellency, and perhaps gaining from you a little esteem for my insignificant work, I should value the granting of this wish above all things, and regard it as the happiest event of my life. With my deepest respect,

Your humble servant,

FRANZ SCHUBERT."

Goethe accepted the songs without further acknowledgment, and merely noted in his diary : " Music to my songs sent by Schubert from Vienna."

A pleasant change in Schubert's life was an invitation from the singer Vogl to accompany him on an Alpine tour. Again, as two years before, they went to their beloved Upper Austria—to Steyr and then to Gmunden, Linz, St. Florian, and Steyieregg, where Schubert stayed a week as guest on the estate of Count Weissenwolf. This journey was then continued as far as Salzburg and Gastein. Everywhere the artists were received with hearty applause. Schubertiades were the order of the day ; there was singing, dancing and love-making, and the dear little master was made much of in the exclusive circle of music friends. Several letters tell us of those days of Schubert's artistic touring and happy travels. " I am now in Steyr again," he wrote on June 25th, 1825, to his parents in Vienna, " but I was six weeks in Gmunden, where the scenery is really heavenly, and whose dear inhabitants, especially good Traweger, touched me deeply with their kindness. At Traweger's I was made quite at home. Afterwards, when Herr Hofrat von Schiller, who is monarch of the whole Salzkammergut, came back, Vogl and I dined every day in his house and played music there, as well as at Traweger's. Especially appreciated were my new songs from Walter Scott's ' Lady of the Lake.' Also my piety excited great wonder, in that I had composed a Hymn to the Virgin, which appeared to touch all hearts and promote a religious feeling. I believe the reason of this is that I never force myself to compose these hymns and prayers, and only do so when carried away by a true and real sentiment of reverence. From Gmunden we went by Puschberg, where we met some friends and stayed a few days, to Linz, where we spent several days, which were sometimes passed in Steyieregg. At Linz I was quartered in the house of Spaun's family, where Spaun's transference to Lemberg is very much deplored. I was given some letters that he had written from Lemberg to read, and they were full of homesickness and very sad. I wrote to him at Lemberg, and joked over his

Sophie Müller
Lithograph by Kriehuber, 1830
(Vienna National Library)

babyish behaviour, but probably were I in his place I should be still more miserable and pitiable than he is. In Steyieregg we met the Countess Weissenwolf, who is a great admirer of my small work, possesses all my things, and sings a great many very prettily. Walter Scott's songs made such a favourable impression on her that she half-hinted the dedication of them to herself would not be disagreeable. I contemplate making a change with the publication of these songs by having Scott's name printed prominently on the cover to excite curiosity, and the English text given, so that I may be better known in England. . . . If only one could make an honest arrangement with the art dealers, but the wise and just ordering of the State takes care that every artist shall be eternally the slave of every despicable tradesman.

Everywhere in Upper Austria I find that my compositions are known, especially in the convents of Florian and Kremsmünster, where I, with the help of a fine pianist, produced with success my four-hand variations and marches. The variations from my solo sonata, which I performed myself, were specially liked, and I was happy when several people assured me that the notes under my hands became singing voices. No compliment could please me better, because the cursed hammering which even some of the most famous piano-players indulge in is to me intolerable, being neither pleasing to the ear nor soothing to the mind. I am again in Steyr, and if you will give me the happiness of hearing from you soon the letter will reach me here. We only stay here for 10 or 14 days, and then start on the journey to Gastein, one of the most famous *Bads*, about three days' distance from Steyr. This journey gives me extraordinary pleasure, for we've got to know the loveliest places, and on the way back shall visit Salzburg, with its glorious surroundings. As we shall not return from this tour till the beginning of September, and then have promised to go again to Gmunden, Linz, Steyreck and Florian, it's hardly likely that I shall be in Vienna before the end of October. Meanwhile, I beg that you will pay the rent of my quarters near the Karlskirche— 28 florins—which on my return I will gratefully repay, because I have promised that I may come back sooner than I expected. The weather was very uncertain here the whole of June and July ; then for 14 days extremely hot, so that I got thin from sheer sweating, and now it has been raining again for four days on end. Give my love to Ferdinand, his wife and children. He can't tear himself away, I suppose, from Dornbach, and, of course, he will have been ill seventy times and seven, and nine times thinking himself in a dying condition, as if dying was the worst thing in store for us mortals. If he could but see these divinely beautiful mountains and lakes, which threaten to overpower us with their grandeur, he wouldn't be so in love with this petty little life, and would feel how the incomprehensible mightiness of the earth can give us confidence to live anew."

To Josef Spaun, whom to his great regret he had not met in Linz, he writes :

" DEAR SPAUN,—

You can't think how it vexes me that I have to write to you a letter from Linz to Lemberg ! ! ! The Devil take the infamous system which tears friends apart so cruelly before they have as much as sipped from the cup of friendship. Here I am in Linz, perspiring till I'm half-dead in this ghastly heat, have ready half a book of *lieder*, and you are not here to enjoy them ! Aren't you ashamed of yourself ? Linz without you is like a rider without a horse or soup without salt. If it wasn't for Jägermeyer I should hang myself on the promenade with the explanation : ' Out of sorrow for the flown Linzer soul.' You see that I am very unjust towards the rest of the Linz folk, for in your mother's house, in the circle of your sisters of Ottenwald and Max, I have been very contented, and from the flesh of other Linzers shafts of your spirit have radiated. . . . Don't let being so far from us turn your hair grey ; bid your fate defiance and let your gifted mind blossom like a flower garden, so that you distribute warm rays in the cold northern atmosphere and advertise your godly descent.

Curious, almost comical, things have been reported of Schober. To begin with, I read in the Vienna theatrical newspaper of a pseudonym, Torupsohn ? ? ? What does that mean ? He won't have married ? That would be too amusing. Secondly, the Casperl-Rolle in the travestied Aline is said to be his *Fors-Rolle*. Rather a come-down from the sublime heights of his plans and expectations. And, thirdly and lastly, that he is coming back to Vienna ? Now I ask, what is he going to do there ? Nevertheless I rejoice thereat, and trust that he will quicken and infuse new life into our somewhat compressed social circle.

I have been in Upper Austria since May 20th and was annoyed

to find that you had left Linz a few days before. I should so much have liked to see you before you migrated to the Polish devils. In Steyr I was only 14 days; from there we, Vogl and I, went to Gmunden, where we spent a whole six weeks very pleasantly. We were domiciled at Traweger's, who has a splendid piano and, you know, is a great admirer of my little self. I lived there very simply and comfortably.

At Hofrat von Schiller's we made much music, and, among others, some of my new songs to Walter Scott's ' Lady of the Lake ' were greatly appreciated, especially the Hymn to Maria. I am glad that you have met young Mozart; greet him from me; and now farewell my dear, good Spaun. Think often of your

Sincere friend,

SCHUBERT."

A letter also from Anton Ottenwald to Josef von Spaun in Lemberg gives an account of how friendly was the reception of Schubert and Vogl in Linz. It is dated July 27th, 1825 :

" I have lots to tell you about our Schubert, though, of course, his own letters give you the best information. I don't think I ever enjoyed so much dispensing hospitality as in those days when he was staying with me and was our guest at lunch and in the evening at the castle. . . . We heard Vogl three times, and Schubert himself after breakfast sang to us and performed his variations for two and four hands on the piano and an overture—all compositions of such supreme interest that I don't know terms of sufficient praise to speak of them in. Neither can I do justice in words to his last songs after W[alter] Scott, and yet I can't be silent on the subject. 1. Ave Maria, Ellen's prayer for her father in the wilderness, where they live concealed ; 2. Warrior's Rest, an ingratiating lullaby such as Armida might sing to Rinaldine's magic harp ; 3. Huntsman's Rest, another slumber song, simpler and even more moving, so it seems to me. The accompaniment, the song of the horn as it were, the echo of the hunting song in a dream of great beauty. ' Mein Ross im Stalle so müde sich steht, meine Dogge traurig das Futter verschmäht . . . an mir zehrt des Turmes Einsamkeit." Accompaniment ? It is more. Who shall describe the broken chords, tremulous with wrath ? I am almost ashamed of attempting it ; and now I come to the last, Norman's Song, song of the warrior who, with the sacrificial torch symbol of the arrière-ban, rides through the field, restless, in haste, thinking as he goes of the bride whom he has left at the altar, the morrow's battle and victory, and the return and meeting. Schubert himself thinks the melody and accompaniment the most successful of all the Scotch *lieder*. Vogl finds it difficult to deliver (every note a syllable, frequently a word), but sings it magnificently. Most attractive of all, through the grace of the melody and the rocking sound of the horns, is the Huntsman's Rest. Dear fellow, how we wished every time that you could hear it. If only the fairies could bring it to you in your dreams, as it sounded in our ears till far in the night. Schubert was so friendly, so communicative, not only with Max, which is natural, but with us. On Sunday when Vogl, at half-past ten, had departed, he sat on with us, Max, myself, Marie and mama, who between 10 and 11 o'clock retired. We sat up till long past midnight, and I have never seen him or heard him to such advantage. He was serious, deep, and as if inspired when he talked of art, poetry, his youth and friends, and of other men of mark ; of the relation of ideals to life, and so on. I could not help being amazed at the brilliance of his mind, from which such outpourings on art come almost unconsciously, and all so simply. I cannot speak of the extent of his convictions as a whole, but he gave us glimpses into a not unoriginal way of looking at the world, and the part that his best friends may have therein in no wise robs it of its originality. And thus it gave me intense pleasure that he seemed to like to be with me and to show himself to us from a side which one only discloses to congenial temperaments, and I felt as if I must write and tell you about it. . . ."

In two letters to his brother Ferdinand, Schubert describes the continuance of the journey to Salzburg and Gastein. From Gmunden, under date of September 12th, 1825, he writes :

" DEAR BROTHER,—

In accordance with your wishes, I should like to give you a detailed account of our journey to Salzburg and Gastein, but you know what a poor hand I am at narrative and description ; but as I should be obliged in any case to tell you all about it on my return to Vienna, I would rather attempt in writing than by word of mouth to give you some faint idea of all the beauties I have seen, hoping that I shall succeed better with the pen than I should with the tongue.

We started about the middle of August from Steyr, passing Kremsmünster, which, it is true, I have often seen before, but which, on account of its lovely situation, I can't leave out. One has a view there of a charming valley, with small, softly undulating ranges of hills here and there and one mountain of considerable height, on the peaks of which stands, with its mathematical tower, the Monastery, a glorious view of which we had already admired from the high road. Here we have long been known, as Vogl studied in the Monastery, and we had a very friendly reception there, but didn't stay, and continued our journey without anything remarkable happening to Vöcklabruck, where we arrived in the evening. In that deplorable little hole there was nothing to see. The next morning we came through Stasswalchen and Franken-markt to Neumarkt, where we had our midday meal. These places are all in the Salzburg district, and the houses are built alike, after a curious architectural pattern, of wood. Everything belonging to them is made of wood ; the wooden kitchen utensils are ranged on wooden shelves outside the houses, and the paths round the houses are floored with wood. And they hang, too, outside their houses old targets which have been shot through and through and are preserved as trophies of victory from long past-times. Frequently one sees on them the dates 1600 and 1500. Here, too, we began getting Bavarian coins. From Neumarkt, which is the last posting-place before coming to Salzburg, the mountain peaks of the Salz-burger Thal were visible, covered with snow. The scenery was beautiful in about an hour's drive from Neumarkt. The Waller-See, which, to the right of the road, stretches its blue-greenish sur-face like a mirror, adds greatly to the charm of the landscape. The country is very hilly, and from this point goes downhill all the way as far as Salzburg. Mountains become higher and higher, and the fabulous Untersberg especially stands out majestically. The villages show traces of former wealth and prosperity. The commonest peasant houses boast marble windows and porches and many have steps of red marble. Clouds hide the sun and wraiths creep over the dark mountain-sides like spirits of the mist. The wide-stretch-ing valley, with its hundreds of castles, churches and farmsteads, becomes more and more visible to the delighted vision. Towers and palaces come into view, and at last we pass the Kapuzinerberge, the gigantic rocky walls of which rise perpendicularly from the roadside. The grandeur of the Untersberg almost threatens to fall on us. And now under glorious avenues we come to the town itself. Fortifications of time-worn freestone encompass this famous seat of the former Kurfürsts. The gates of the city, with their inscriptions, speak of the vanished power of the Papacy. Houses 4 and 5 storeys high crowd the fairly wide streets, and we passed the wonderful mansion of Theophrastus Paracelsus, with its ornate façade, before crossing the bridge over the Salzach, which rushed along, its waters troubled and overcast. The town itself made rather a melancholy impression on me, as dull and rainy weather made the ancient buildings look even gloomier than they are, and the overhanging fortifications on the highest point of the Mönchsberg seemed to send down greetings from uncanny spirits. Then, as often happens, rain set in in earnest as we entered the town, so that, besides the many palaces and fine churches we drove past, there was not much to be seen.

We were introduced through Herr Pauernfeind, a merchant of the town whom Vogl knows, to the Count von Platz, President of the *Landrechte*, whose family had heard of us by name, and received us very hospitably. Vogl sang *lieder* of mine, and the following evening we were invited to supper and asked to perform to a very select audience, who were specially delighted and touched with the ' Ave Maria' which I mentioned in another letter. The way in which Vogl sings and I play the accompaniments as if we were one person is something quite new to these people and unheard of. After we had climbed the Mönchsberg the next morning, from where one looks down on the whole town, I could not help marvelling at the number of splendid buildings, palaces and churches. Still, there are not many inhabitants here, many of the buildings are empty, and many are only occupied by two or three families. In the squares grass grows between the paving-stones, so seldom are they walked on. The Cathedral is a heavenly edifice, built after the style of St. Peter's in Rome, on a smaller scale. The nave of the church is in the form of a cross, and it has outside four huge courtyards, each one of which forms a separate square. Over the entrance stand the Apostles, carved in stone and of gigantic size. The inside of the church has marble pillars, adorned with the portraits of the Kurfürsts, and is perfect in every detail. The light which falls from the dome illuminates every corner.

This extraordinary radiance has a divine effect, and the method of lighting should be adopted by other churches.

The four squares round the church are adorned with huge fountains, ornamented by the most bold and splendid figures. We went into the Abbey of St. Peter from here, where Michael Haydn resided. This, too, is a beautiful church. Here stands, as you know, the monument to M. Haydn. It is quite good, but placed in too remote a corner. The placards arranged round it have rather childish inscriptions. In the urn his head rests, and, I thought to myself, thy peaceful spirit, dear Haydn, speaks to me from thy tomb, and if I cannot be as placid and clear as thou art, no one on earth reverences thee so deeply as I do. (Tears came into my eyes and we passed on.) We lunched at Herr Pauernfeind's, and as the weather allowed us to go out, we climbed the not very lofty but beautiful Nonnenberg, from which we had the loveliest view of the outlying part of Salzburg. It is almost impossible to describe the beauty of the valley. Picture to yourself a garden of several miles in circumference in which are endless castles and estates seen between the trees ; picture a river winding in all manner of fantastic curves through meadows and cornfields, a magic carpet of brilliant colour ; picture interminable avenues of gigantic trees, and the whole enclosed by the loftiest mountains, which seem to be the watchmen of this exquisite valley, and you will be able to form some feeble idea of its unspeakable beauty. Other things relating to Salzburg sights which I shall see on my way back shall be related in chronological order."

The continuation of this letter followed on September 21st, dated from Steyr:

" You will see by the date of this letter that several days have gone by since we had to leave Gmunden for Steyr. Thus, to go on with the description (which I begin to repent undertaking), of my journey, I must go back to the day that followed.

The next morning was the most beautiful day the world can ever have known. The Untersberg gleamed and flashed with its smaller satellites among the peaks in or rather next the sun. We made our way through the valley I have described to you. I felt as if we were in Elysium or Paradise, except that we drove in a charming, comfortable carriage, a luxury which Adam and Eve never enjoyed. Instead of meeting savage, wild animals we met ever so many pretty girls. I ought not to make such wretched jokes in such a heavenly neighbourhood, but there is something in the air to-day which prevents my being serious. So we drove on, steeped in bliss, through the glorious day and still more glorious scenery and came to a pretty, dainty little castle called 'Monatschlöschen,' because a Kurfürst had it built for his fair one in a single month. Everyone knows the story here, but no one takes objection to it. Commendable toleration! This small building, too, contributes its charms to the glorifying of the valley. Some hours later we arrived in the remarkable but extremely dirty and uncanny town of Hallein. The inhabitants all look like ghosts, pale, hollow-eyed and thin as threadpaper. This frightful contrast made a fatal impression on me : it was as if one had dropped from heaven on to a manure heap, or as if after Mozartian music one listened to a piece of the immortal A. ——. Salzburg and Salzburg sights could not move Vogl to desist from pushing forward to Gastein for his gout. We went on therefore through Golling, where we came to the first really insurmountable mountains, beyond the terrifying ravines of which lies the Pass of Lueg. After we had crawled slowly up a great mountain, with other frightful mountains rising in front of our noses and on either side, we reached the highest point, and looked down into a bottomless gorge which at first made one's heart stand still. When one had recovered a little from the first shock one became aware of a stupendous wall of rock which seemed at a little distance to close us in as if in a blind alley, so that it looked as if there were no way of getting out.

In this terror-inspiring work of Nature man had sought to commemorate a deed of terrible bestiality. For it was here that the frightful massacre was perpetrated by the Tyrolese hiding in the rocky caves firing down on the Bavarians, who wanted to gain the Pass, so that the latter were hurled into the abyss, in the deepest depths of which rushes the roaring Salzach, without knowing where the shots came from. This bloody work continued for days and weeks. On the Bavarian side stands a memorial in the form of a chapel and on the Tyrolean a red cross planted on the mountain. These sacred symbols are intended partly to commemorate and partly to expiate a horrible crime. Oh, dear Christ, to how many deeds of shame must Thou lend Thy countenance? Of Him who in Himself is the most convincing testimony to human wickedness, they erect an image everywhere in wood and stone, as much as to say, ' See here, we have trampled under our profane feet the most perfect creation of the great God. What shall hinder us then in annihilating easily the rest of ordinary mankind ? '

But we turned our eyes to less depressing objects and set our mind to finding a way out of the trap. After descending a while between the ever-narrowing walls of rock, where path and river often were hardly two fathoms in width, the road here, where one would least expect it, under overhanging cliffs and alongside the wrathfully boiling Salzach, becomes, to the relief of the traveller and his agreeable surprise, wider and more even, though still shut in between mountains soaring into the sky on either side. At midday we came to Werffen, a market town with an important fortress, built by the Salzburger Kurfürsts, and since renovated by the Kaiser. On our return journey we climbed up to this and found it rather too high, but the view of the glorious valley, guarded by the gigantic Werffner Mountains on one side, which are visible as far as Gastein, was worth it. Heavens! Description of travel is ghastly. I can't go on, but when I arrive in Vienna, early in October, I'll hand over to you this scribble in person and add the rest by word of mouth."

It was not till the autumn, in the beginning of October, 1825, that Schubert, in the company of Josef Gaḥy, whom he had met in Linz, hired a one-horse carriage and drove in three days from Linz back to Vienna. Vogl went on to Italy for his health.

Let us turn now to the artistic products of Schubert's visit to Upper Austria. As we have learned from the master's letters, there were the songs dedicated to Countess Sophie von Weissenwolf from Walter Scott's " Lady of the Lake " ; these had been finished more or less before he started on his travels. Among lyrics were : " Das Grablied der Frauen und Mädchen," " Coronach," the sacred " Ave Maria," " Heimweh," " Norman's Song " and " Allmacht," after poems by Ladislau Pyrker, whom Schubert had met in Gastein ; " Die junge Nonne," " Ellen's Second Song," " Jäger, ruhe von der Jagd." Further, there were among compositions for the piano the wonderful A Major Sonata, with the beautiful andante and romantic scherzo, and the lost Gastein Symphony, which had been designed for the Society of Music Friends.

In Vienna Schubert's return was made the occasion by his friends for festive meetings. Schober had come from Breslau and Kupelwieser from Rome, to the master's infinite delight. " Schubert is back," wrote Bauernfeld in October, 1825, in his diary. " Friends assemble with him in guest or coffee house, and often stay till 2 or 3 in the morning." Schubertiades were held by Schober, and in " Mondschein " House by Schwind, and at the actress', Sophie Müller. " Jenger brought the Freiburger singer and his superb flutist with him this evening," notes the sentimental star of the Burgtheater in her diary. " Schubert came too, and so we had music till half-past ten. An overture for four hands from Schubert's opera and his last compositions from Scott's ' Lady of the Lake ' delighted me."

Anton Ottenwald again posted up Pepi Spaun, who was still in Lemberg : " There is really nothing new to tell you about Schubert ; genius as always reveals itself in his works ; he creates divinely through the affections with a vivid, all-absorbing sensuousness, and he has the true temperament for friendship. He is at present happy and, I hope, well."

At " New Year " the Schubertians gave a joyous party at Schober's. Bauernfeld wrote a priceless parody on the Schubert circle, which was read aloud at Schober's New Year banquet.

" Silvester Night at Schober's without Schubert, who was ill," wrote Bauernfeld in his diary. " Dramatic parody concerning friends and lady friends there assembled, and read aloud with great applause at midnight. Moriz (Schwind) figures in it as Harlequin, Netty (Hönig) as Columbine, Schober as Pantaloon, Schubert, Pierrot. Moriz and I slept at Schober's, and I stayed with him over midday."

At the beginning of the New Year several performances took place of the new D Minor Quartet (with variations on " Der Tod und das Mädchen "), which Schubert had just finished, under the conductorship of the composer, to the score printed by the brothers Karl and Franz Hacker in the Schönlaterngasse No. 675, and by Josef Barth and Franz Lachner in the Landstrasse. In February the composer went to a morning concert with Bauernfeld in the great " Redoutensaal," where he listened with enthusiasm to Beethoven's D Major Symphony and " Egmont." On the afternoon of the same day he went with the poet to Schuppanzigh's, where quartets of Haydn and Beethoven and a quintet of Mozart's were played.

" Everything glorious ; Grillparzer was present," noted Bauernfeld in his diary. Ever more frequently were Schubert's songs being sung now in the houses of Viennese musical citizens and at the Society of Music Friends' concerts. His works were on sale in all the most important Vienna music and art shops, especially in Leidesdorf's and Sauer's, in the Kärntnerstrasse, at A. Pennauer, Cappi & Co., both in the " Graben." Matthias Artaria, in the Kohlmarkt, gave the tone-poet for his D Sonata (opus 55) and the " Divertissement à la Hongroise " (opus 54) an honorarium of 500 florins, which honorarium was paid by Anton Diabelli in Graben. A proof of growing local fame was that reproductions of Schubert's portrait, painted by Reider and engraved by Passini, were exhibited for sale in all the Vienna art shops. The art publishers, Cappi, in the Graben, had the following advertisement put in the *Wiener Zeitung* on December 9th, 1825 :

" The art-dealers, Cappi & Compagnie, at Graben No. 1134, are showing a very successful portrait of the composer, Franz Schubert, reproduced by Herr Passini from the original painting by Rieder, price 3 florins. The talented composer, whose music, especially his vocal compositions, have so often delighted distinguished audiences, appears in this picture to the life. It is a most speaking likeness, and we are sure that the numerous friends and admirers of Schubert will find it an acceptable gift."

In those days an opportunity again offered itself to the master for applying for an important musical post. The vacancy in the conductorship of the Imperial Court Orchestra, on the death of Salieri, had been filled by Eybler, thus leaving the post of Vice-conductor free. Schubert, who had once been a chorister in the Imperial Court Choir, sent in his application with the following letter, dated April 7th, 1826 :

" YOUR MAJESTY AND GRACIOUS EMPEROR,—

In deepest respect the undersigned craves the favour of being granted the post of Vice-conductor of your Imperial Court Orchestra, and supports his application with the following points :

1. The applicant is a native of Vienna, the son of a schoolmaster. He is 29 years of age.

2. He enjoyed the high honour when a pupil at the Konvikt of singing as a chorister in the choir of your Imperial Majesty's Chapel.

3. He received a perfected education in composition from the at that time Court Conductor, Anton Salieri, which qualifies him to undertake the conductorship of any orchestra in the world.

4. His name, through his composition of both vocal and instrumental music, is well known in the whole of Germany.

5. Five masses by him have been already performed in various churches in Vienna, and are in preparation for small or large orchestras.

6. He has never, so far, filled any post, and hopes by this means to achieve the object of his artistic ambition.

Should he be appointed to the post he will ever strive to fill it to the best of his ability.

> Your humble servant,
>
> FRANZ SCHUBERT."

Our master went at this time to the newly-appointed Court Conductor, Eybler, taking him one of his masses, with the object of its being produced, with what success Schubert himself relates :

" Eybler, when he heard my name, said that he had not hitherto heard any of my compositions. I am not conceited, but I certainly should have thought that by this time the Court Conductor of Vienna might have heard of me and my work. When I came a few weeks later to inquire the fate of my child, Eybler said that the mass was good, but not composed in the style which the Kaiser liked. I took my leave at once and thought to myself : ' So I am not fortunate enough to be able to compose according to the style His Imperial Majesty approves ! ' "

Thus his wish to be of use in the Hofkappele, where he had gained his first great musical impressions, was doomed to disappointment. In this connection a report made by the musical Count Karl Harrach to the Hofmeister Prince Ferdinand Trautmansdorff is of interest :

" The applicants for the appointment of Vice-Court Conductor regarded as competent were—

1. Ignaz Ritter v. Seyfried.
2. Adalbert Gyrowetz.
3. Franz Schubert.
4. Konradin Kreutzer.
5. Joachim Hofmann.
6. Anselm Hüttenbrenner.
7. Wenzel Würfel.
8. Franz Gläser.

There is not the least question that all these applicants are worthy men, and that many of them have considerable qualifications.

Franz Schubert rests his claim on his first-rate record as chorister and on a testimonial from the deceased Salieri, from whom he received instruction in composition. He also sets forth that he has completed five masses for small or large orchestra, and that these have been performed in various churches. Notwithstanding these very considerable attainments on the part of this candidate and the others, I am of opinion, in my official capacity, that in present circumstances economy must be practised, and the problem of the filling of the Vice-conductorship will be best solved by appointing an individual who has grown up in the service of the Court, so as to avoid imposing a new burden on the Imperial expenditure. I, therefore, feel bound to name for the post the well-known conductor, Josef Weigl, whose appointment I here strongly recommend. . . ."

Thus this new effort on the part of Schubert to obtain a regular position failed, as it had done in the case of Laibach. The post was conferred on Josef Weigl, the popular composer of the " Schweizerfamilie."

" I wish I could have got this post," Schubert said to Spaun, " but as it has been given to one so worthy to fill it as Weigl, I must not complain."

According to Josef Hüttenbrenner, intrigues soon after prevented Schubert getting a very good appointment as Conductor at the Kärntnertortheater. A year before he had refused the offer made him by Count von Dietrichstein of a post as second organist in the Court Chapel, in spite of the advice of his friend, Schwind, who wrote to him : " All you've got to do, to be a made man, is to improvise on a theme for the organ. . . . Here in Gmunden an organ to practise on is at your disposal."

Towards the summer of 1826 the circle of Schubertians began to thin. Some went into the country : for instance, Bauernfeld, who was busy on an opera-text for Schubert, " Der Graf von Gleichen," accompanied Mayrhofer from Grünbühel to Kärnten. Schubert went with his friends, Schober and Schwind, to the lovely village of Währing, with its vineyards and flower gardens. In this idyllic landscape he wrote in ten days, in a burst of creative genius, his last string quartet, the great G Major, which sparkles with brilliance and passion. Countless charming songs flowed, too, from his indefatigable pen. It was now that he wrote the music

to Shakespeare's verse in " Cymbeline," " Hark the Lark." One
version of the story goes that, through Schubert coming to fetch
Schwind for a walk, and finding him too deeply engaged in his
painting to leave it, Schwind, to prevent his going away, told him
to compose something till he was ready, whereupon, with music
paper that he ruled himself and the first book he could lay hands
on, Shakespeare's " Cymbeline," he composed the delightful song
in a few minutes. Franz Doppler says, however, that the song was
composed at the inn " Zum Biersack " at Währing one Sunday,
when the party of friends, on coming back from an expedition to
Pötzleinsdorf, stopped to rest at the inn, and found Friend Tieze
sitting there on a table with a book before him. Schubert took
the book from him and began turning over the leaves. Suddenly
he exclaimed, pointing to the poem, " If only I had music paper
here! A beautiful melody has come to me!" Doppler then
drew the necessary lines on the back of a menu card, and in the
middle of harp-playing, clash of billiard balls and waiters hurrying
to and fro, and all the bustle of Sunday business, the song came into
being.

Several letters give evidence that the friends who had gone
far away from Vienna did not forget Schubert this summer.
Bauernfeld and Mayrhofer wrote humorously from Villach to the
master : ". . . Here you can't get decent wine—Italian stuff that
tastes more of mustiness than wine. Greet your boon companions, Rieder, Perfetta, and the rest. What is Bocklet doing?
I can't forget his playing and I long for him. Just think of it,
I haven't found any piano except in the Klagenfurt coffee-house.
I have composed and sung most of the numbers to ' Graf v.
Gleichen.' The following description will give you some idea
of our manner of life :

THE MERRY MEN OF VELLACH

Saturday began the fable,
And we still are wandering on,
With the lengthy measuring table,
That from place to place has gone.
Sunday we with many others
Did a country trip begin,
Playing greasy cards, we brothers,
In a dirty country inn.

Monday came the land surveyor,
And we sketched in open fields.
Good things, even though evil weather,
Tuesday's dinner-table yields.
Manager, he came on Wednesday,
Such a change improves the view,
For the Huntsman and the Keeper
Seemed on Thursday strange and new.

Friday was a pretty mix-up
With the bonny girls on leave,
Miracles were said to happen,
Which we gladly would believe.
Saturday we spurned temptation
And returned to duty's steep,
Much affected by our virtue,
For the snow lay fairly deep.

So this pleasure and the other
Hand in hand the day reveals,
In the end one knows no longer
If one's standing head or heels.
Wine and cards, manager, Pater,
For our blood refreshing food.
Leave the Viennese their Prater,
Villach, Vellach—there 'tis good.

Or the end like this :

Guzzling, gobbling—Holy Pater,
Manager—anything worse to show !
Viennese, where is your Prater ?
Villach, Vellach—Oh, oh, oh !

I greet you over and over again, and will, if possible, do what
I told you. At any rate, I would like the Linz and Kremsmünster
addresses.

Your BUFELD.

Something more. Two beautiful girls of 16 and 17 were here
last year. About six months ago they both died. They were the
daughters of the Châtelaine of the Castle here. Is that not
devilish sad ?

B."

" DEAR SCHUBERT,—

Bauernfeld hasn't left me much room, but here goes : Come by all means out of your Viennese foxhole. Felbel will be pleased. Anyhow, address me here. Schober will give you the proper address. I am as well as a lover out of a job can be. My work distracts me and my companion amuses me, so that I often forget a wider gulf exists between Ober-Vellach and the Trattnerhofe than between Grinzig and Nussdorf. Write now if you like, but better wait till I am quite alone, when I shall appreciate it all the more. Adieu.

Your MAYRHOFER."

Schubert's answer was :

" DEAR BAUERNFELD,—
DEAR MAYRHOFER,—

It's good news that you've done the opera. I only wish I had it before me. My opera books have been asked for here, to see what can be done with them. If your book is ready one could submit this and get its value (of which I've no doubt) recognised. For God's sake, do this with it or send it to Milder in Berlin. Mlle. Schechner has appeared here in the ' Schweizerfamilie ' and is greatly liked. As she resembles Milder, she may be useful to us. Don't stay away much longer ; it is very dull and wretched here— *ennui* has made too much way. From Schober and Schwind one hears nothing but lamentations, more pathetic than anything we heard on Good Friday. I've scarcely been once to Grinzing since you've been away. Schwind I haven't seen at all. From all this you may judge of the sum total of my lively doings. The ' Zauberflöte ' was very well done at the Theater-an-der-Wien, but ' Frieschütz ' at the Kärntnertor very badly. Herr Jakob and Frau Baberl at the Leopoldstadt inimitable. Your poem, which has been printed in the *Modezeitung*, is lovely, but I like still better the one in your last letter. The sustained good spirits and the comical sublimity, especially that cry of anguish at the end wherein you make masterly play on the word Villach—ach—ach, seems to me to be among the most delicious things of the kind I know. I am not working at all. The weather here is really dreadful ; the Almighty seems to have deserted us completely and forbidden the sun to shine. Fancy not being able to sit out in a garden in May. Terrible! Horrible !! Frightful !!! The cruellest deprivation for me imaginable! Schwind and I hope to go to Linz with Spaun in June. Either there or in Gmunden we may arrange a rendezvous. Only let us know for certain—as soon as possible—not after two months have elapsed!

Farewell."

Nothing came of the journey to Upper Austria indicated in this letter. The master's plans were once more frustrated by lack of funds, a lack from which he and his friends chronically suffered.

" I can't possibly come to Gmunden or anywhere else," he wrote on July 10th, 1826, to Bauernfeld. " I have no money; besides I am not at all well. But I don't let myself be cast down—in fact, I am very lively. All the same, come as soon as you can to Vienna, because Duport wants an opera from me, but doesn't like any of the books I've submitted, and it would be splendid if yours was favourably considered. Then we should at least have money, if not honour. Schwind is, in respect to Nettel, quite out of hand! Schober is doing private business. Vogl has married!!! I entreat you to come as soon as you can because of the opera. In Linz you've only to mention my name and you will be well received.

Your SCHUBERT."

After his summer change of air at Währing the composer set to work in Vienna with renewed vigour. Beautiful new *lieder*, after verses by a friend, J. G. Seidl, streamed from the never-exhausted fount of his fantasy, such as " Der Wanderer an den Mond," " Das Zügenglöcklein," " Die Unterscheidung," " Bei dir allein," " Die Männer sind méchant," " Irdisches Glück," " Wiegenlied," the magnificent chorus for men's voices, " Mondenschein," by Schober, and " Grab und Mond," by Seidl. As a climax to the creations of this richly productive year came the Sonata in C Major dedicated to his friend Spaun, the A Minor Rondo for piano and violin, and the piano trio in B Major.

It seemed as if Fortune were inclined at last to cast a ray of light on the lot of the always industrious composer, ever waiting for recognition, when a Swiss publisher, Georg Nägeli, in Zurich, asked him to write a sonata for a collection of miscellaneous compositions for the piano. The poor musician, suffering acutely from want of money, asked to be paid in advance an honorarium of 120 florins, a request which evidently offended the publisher, for he took no notice. Schubert never heard from him again. Conscious that his name was becoming known abroad, and discouraged at home by the shabby remuneration of Viennese publishers and absence of the necessary propaganda for his works, Schubert endeavoured again to do business with Breitkopf and Härtel of Leipzig, also with the firm of Probst. A letter to the former publishing house, dated August 12th, 1826, runs as follows :

" DEAR SIR,—

In the hope that my name is not quite unknown to you, I venture respectfully to ask if you would not be disposed to accept some of my compositions for publication in exchange for a small honorarium, as I am extremely anxious to become as well known in Germany as possible. I could send you a selection consisting of songs with pianoforte accompaniment, quartets for strings, and pianoforte sonatas and duets. I have also written an octet. In any case, I should regard it as a special honour to be connected with such a famous firm as yours.

Awaiting an early reply,
I remain, with expressions of my highest esteem,
Your humble servant,
FRANZ SCHUBERT."

The answer from the firm is dated September 7th, 1826 :

" It would give us great pleasure to come to some arrangement with you to our mutual advantage, and we are indebted to you for your suggestion. But as we are, so far, quite unacquainted with the market value of your compositions and therefore are unable to make you a definite pecuniary offer (which the publisher could only fix according to the success of the work undertaken), we leave it to you to consider whether you would not be inclined to inaugurate what may prove the opening of a lasting and satisfactory connection by accepting in return for publication a certain number of presentation copies instead of payment. We do not doubt your acceptance of this proposal, and suggest that you should first submit to us one or two pieces only for the piano, either solos or duets. If, with these, our hopes of success are at all realised, we shall be happy to offer for future works financial remuneration on a satisfactory basis.

With highest esteem,
Yours obediently,
BREITKOPF AND HÄRTEL."

After this there was no further communication between Schubert and the world-renowned firm of publishers. Also with the publishing house of Probst Schubert had no luck. The latter replied on August 26th, 1826, to his letter :

" Though I thank you heartily for your confidence and assure you that I should be pleased to do my utmost to extend your reputation as an artist, I must confess that the somewhat unique expression of your genius and of your creations has interfered with their being generally understood and appreciated by our public, and I would ask you to bear this in mind in sending me your manuscripts. A few songs, not too difficult, pianoforte compositions for two and four hands, of an agreeable and tuneful character, would be the most suitable items for the attainment of your object and mine. If once a successful start is made, it will be easy to follow it up, but in the beginning one has to humour the public. . . ."

When Schubert sent the manuscripts the publisher returned them with the remark that, in the first place, the desired honorarium of 80 florins was too high for a single volume, and that, in the second, the firm was bringing out a collected edition of the works of Kalkbrenner, and so for the present it must deny itself the pleasure of publishing Schubert's.

But a pleasant little surprise was to brighten the year that had been so unfortunate for the artist. It came from the Society of Music Friends, to whom the master had offered to dedicate a symphony (probably the lost Gastein Symphony). At the instigation of the Secretary, Josef v. Sonnleithner, the Society, without reference to Schubert's offer, granted him a remuneration of 100 florins. " You have," said the letter in which the sum was sent to Schubert on October 22nd, 1826, " given the Society of Music Friends in the Austrian capital repeated proof of your sympathy, and your distinguished talent has been used to the best advantage in our service and that of the Conservatorium.

In that they know how to appreciate your remarkable powers as a composer, they wish to show you a mark of their gratitude and esteem, and would have you regard the sum they ask you to accept not as an honorarium, but as a proof of how much the Society feel they are indebted to you and owe you thanks and recognition."

In earlier years Schubert had been closely connected with the Society of Music Friends. Perhaps the first time was when the favourite tenor, August von Gymnich, sang the " Erlkönig " at one of their evening entertainments. Afterwards many evenings were devoted to his compositions, and the leading artists and amateurs of musical Vienna took part in their production. A proof of how, as years went on, the tone-poet was increasingly valued and admired in this exclusive musical circle is to be found in the fact that when the Committee of the Society were considering the publication of a series of biographies of famous composers it was decided, at the suggestion of Leopold Sonnleithner, to issue a biography of Schubert, and the Schubertian Jenger was entrusted with the task of writing it. It is true that as far as Schubert was concerned the idea ended in smoke, for Jenger never seriously worked on a biography of Schubert. A year later, however, the Society of Music Friends elected him a member " of their representative body," for which honour Schubert, on June 12th, 1827, expressed his thanks in the following letter :

" The Society of Music Friends in the Imperial City having done me the honour of electing me a member of their body, it gives me great pleasure to say that I feel extremely flattered and I hope that I may fulfil the duties of my membership worthily."

To return to the autumn of 1826. If we find Schubert, as in earlier years, devoting all his days to work, we see him in the evenings nearly always in the convivial company of his intimate friends. The diaries of two young students from Linz, Franz and Fritz v. Hartmann, newcomers among the Schubertians, give a lively account of these meetings. Thus Franz von Hartmann writes, under December 15th, 1826 :

" I went to Spaun's to a great ' Schubertiade.' Fritz was already there, and he and von Haas introduced me. It was a huge party. There were present several married couples of a miscellaneous description, the mother of the Court official and State Secretary Witteczek, the wife of Dr. Watteroth, Betty Wanderer, the painter Kupelwieser and his wife, Grillparzer, Schober, Schwind, Mayrhofer, and his landlord Huber, Bauernfeld, Gahy (who played duets with Schubert splendidly), Vogl, who sang nearly 30 beautiful songs, Baron Schlechta, and several other secretaries and people about the Court were there. The trio of the fifth March, which always reminds me of my good mother, moved me almost to tears. When the music was over we had animated conversation and dancing. But I wasn't much inclined for courting. I danced with Betty and once with each of the matrons von Witteczek, Kurzrock and Pompe. At half-past twelve, after a hearty leave-taking from Spaun, I saw Betty home and went on to the ' Anker ' where I found Schober, Schubert, Schwind, Derffel and Bauernfeld. Home and to bed at 1 o'clock in very lively spirits."

A painful event in the musical life of Vienna was the death of Beethoven in the following spring.

It may seem surprising that though the two great masters of music in the same city were, of course, personally acquainted, there was little intercourse between them. This may be accounted for partly by the fact that it was only in the last years of Beethoven's life, when the master was cut off from nearly all society by his deafness and so difficult of access, that the name and work of the younger Schubert became well-known in the musical world. Also it may have been because, with his usual modesty, Schubert, who from his boyhood had looked up to Beethoven with reverence as a sublimity, was in too great awe of him to seek his society and to become more intimately acquainted. It is true that Schubert often met the master in musical circles and at the theatre, and sometimes saw him at the publisher's Tobias Haslinger, or in a beer or wine cellar, some haunt of Schubert and his friends, where the mighty and deaf tone-poet would be sitting in solitude at a little table, smoking his pipe and lost in meditation. And often he crossed Beethoven's path on the green Bastions and near the Stubentor, or would meet him on his wanderings outside the town in the outlying Döbling, Heiligenstadt or Grinzing. Once the young composer was prevailed on by his friends to take his courage in both hands and present Beethoven in person with the pianoforte variation for four hands which he had dedicated to him. According to one account, it was said that he had not found the master at home and had left the music at his house. But, on the other hand, Anton Schindler, Beethoven's factotum, refers to Schubert's visit to Beethoven thus : " It fared badly with Franz Schubert when in 1822 he brought his variations with four hands with his dedication to the master. Although he was accompanied by Diabelli as interpreter, his shyness and taciturnity hindered his expressing his feelings for the master as he had intended, and he played a very unfortunate *rôle* at the interview. The courage which had sustained him as far as the house entirely deserted him in the majestic presence of the artist. When Beethoven expressed the wish that Schubert himself should write down the answers to his questions, his hand seemed chained to his side. Beethoven ran through the copy and lighted upon an inaccuracy in harmony. Gently he drew the young man's attention to it, adding at once that the mistake was no deadly sin. Schubert, perhaps because of this mild, reassuring remark, completely lost his composure. Only when he was out of the house did he pull himself together and curse himself for his awkwardness. He never again had the courage to present himself to the master." Schindler brought certain compositions of Schubert's to the notice of the master shortly before his death.

"When Beethoven's illness, after four months' agony, took a temporary turn for the better, his mental condition was such that it was impossible for him to resume his usual brain work, and we had to think of something that would be a congenial distraction to occupy his mind. So it came about that I brought him a collection of Schubert's *lieder*, about 60 altogether, many of them still in manuscript. I did this not only to provide him with something to do, but to give him an opportunity of getting more than a cursory knowledge of Schubert's artistic creations and so win from Beethoven a favourable opinion of his talent."

The great master, who before had known scarcely five of Schubert's songs, marvelled at the number of these, and wouldn't believe that Schubert up to that time (February, 1827) had written over 500. But if he was astonished at the number he was still more so when he learnt their quality. His amazement knew no bounds, and for several days he could not be torn away from the songs, and devoted hours to their perusal. The " Iphigenie " monologue, the " Grenzen der Menschheit," " Die junge Nonne," " Viola," the " Müllerlieder," and many more, filled him with delight and enthusiasm. " Truly this Schubert has the divine spark," he exclaimed. " If I had come across this poem I should have set it to music too." Not once but many times he said this, and could not praise enough the material, the contents and Schubert's original treatment of them. He thought it extraordinary that Schubert was able to make a song so long that it seemed to contain in it ten other songs. In short, Beethoven's admiration for Schubert's talent became so intense that he asked to see some of his operas and pianoforte works ; only his illness prevented this wish being gratified. But he spoke often of Schubert and prophesied that he would soon excite much notice in the world. And in Beethoven's last illness Schubert did visit him again, if Anselm Hüttenbrenner is to be believed. The latter wrote : " Professor Schindler, Schubert and I, about eight days before Beethoven's death, came to see him. Schindler announced us and asked which of us Beethoven would see first, and he said, ' Let Schubert come.' " And, according to Josef Hüttenbrunner, Anselm's brother, Schubert was with the painter Teltscher, who went to make a sketch of Beethoven in pencil before he died. " Beethoven fixed on them glazed eyes and made incomprehensible signs with his hand, whereupon Schubert, deeply moved, with his companion, left the room."

In a terrific storm of thunder and lightning the mighty hero of music gave up the ghost on March 26th, 1827. On the day of the funeral Schubert, with his friends, went once more to the Schwarz-spanierhaus to pay the master their last respects. At Bauernfeld's side, behind Grillparzer, Lenau and Raimund, he walked beside the coffin as if in a dream, with his modest head bowed, in the great procession of Vienna's famous men, carrying a draped torch, and he heard, moved to profound emotion, the graveside oration written by Grillparzer and spoken by the Court actor Anschütz in powerful ringing tones :

" He withdrew from the world and so they called him misanthropic, and because he avoided sentiment, unfeeling." After the funeral Schubert, Schwind, Bauernfeld and Schober met at the inn " Zum Schloss Eisenstadt," where till midnight they remained in earnest conversation over Beethoven and his work.

" To him whom we have just seen buried ! " exclaimed Schubert with the first glass of wine; and with the second he said, smiling sadly, " To him who is to be the next," perhaps with a clairvoyant presentiment that he himself was to be the chosen one of Fate.

Thus the two great tone-poets lived for quarter of a century in the same city without coming into much personal relationship. It was not till after his own death, which soon followed Beethoven's burial, that Schubert in the old Währinger Cemetery was brought into near neighbourhood to the great master whom he so admired and reverenced. In those days Schubert, whose life was again clouded by melancholy, began the magnificent song cycle from poems of Wilhelm Müller, the " Winterreise," in which he soared to the highest summit of his lyrical creation. " That he chose the ' Winterreise,' " wrote Mayrhofer, " is proof that he had become graver. He had been for long very ill, had had many depressing experiences; life had lost for him its roseate hue; for him winter had set in. . . ." And Spaun tells us; " Schubert had for some time appeared altered and depressed, and on my inquiries as to what was the matter he only replied : ' You will soon know and understand.' One day he said to me : ' Come to Schober's to-day and I will sing you a set of songs that will make you shiver ; I am anxious to know what you'll think of them.' They touched me more deeply than any other songs I've ever heard. He sang in a voice vibrating with emotion the whole of the ' Winterreise.' The tragic and passionate tone of these songs took us aback. Schober said that the only one he liked was ' Der Lindenbaum.' Schubert said, ' I am more pleased with these songs than with any others in the world, and you will get to like them too.' He was right ; we were soon mad about those songs, with their yearning pathos, when Vogl sang them in his masterly manner." No joyous echoes of this life gushed forth from Schubert's melodious soul in the cycle; the songs were deep, heart-harrowing chords from the other side ; they were resounds from the dusky aisles of eternity.

At first the young Schubertians had not responded to the immortal call. It was only when the great singer Vogl with his colossal voice lent the songs brilliance and soul that the friends listened enthralled and became drowned in the sweet sadness and melancholy longing of the Schubertian music.

One of the most beautiful and happy episodes in Schubert's life was the journey undertaken in this year to the emerald-green Styrian land, the last before his death. Once more his soul, always disposed to sadness, was to be ravished by the beauties of Nature, and to delight in hearty hospitality and sympathy extended to him by good and art-loving people. The invitation came from the Advocate, Dr. Karl Pachler, whose house was famous for its music. Frau Marie Pachler, a brilliant pianist, who had been often in friendly intercourse with Beethoven, was interested in Schubert's compositions, and her attention had been called to them particularly by Anselm Hüttenbrenner. She invited Johann Baptist Jenger, who had a post in the Ministry of War in Vienna, and whom Schubert counted among his friends, to come during his leave to her house in Graz, and to bring with him the master.

On January 12th, 1827, Jenger wrote to Frau Pachler: " . . . Schubert kisses your hand, *gnädige Frau*, and will be pleased to make the acquaintance of so warm an admirer of Beethoven's creations. God grant that our hearty desire to come to Graz this year will be fulfilled."

And on May 5th another note from Jenger was despatched to Graz:

". . . I think it will be best to fix the journey to Graz for the beginning of September. Certainly I shall be sure to bring Schubert with me this time, and probably a second friend, the lithographer Teltscher." And on August 30th Jenger announced that they were setting out on their journey.

On Sunday, September 2nd, the express post-chaise, containing Schubert and Jenger, rolled over the plain of Wiener-Neustadt and the Semmering, then by Mürzzenschlag and Bruck-an-der-Mur to the Styrian capital, where, after twenty hours' posting, the musician and his friend arrived safely. Graz was then still an ancient Mediæval city. Renaissance palaces in an Italian style of architecture stood cheek by jowl with old German burgher-houses with painted gables. The courts and alleys were quaint and crooked, full of picturesque corners, such as the "Murbräu-stubel" and the "Krebsenkeller," and numerous Gothic wine-houses wreathed in vines. The town-tower and the old clock-tower sent down from the bastions a friendly welcome to the traveller, the latter booming the hours in deep tones through the green valley. Cheerful greenery and gay flower gardens rose in terraces on the slope of the mountain on which stood the castle.

The reception accorded Schubert by the Pachler pair was unusually hearty. He was soon introduced to the most musical and cultivated residents in the town, who were all at home in the Pachler household. He met there, of course, the brothers Hütten-brenner, his faithful Joseph and the musically-gifted Anselm. There was much music and dancing. All the artistic families in the town gathered together in the hospitable house, and listened full of reverence to Schubert's playing. The master composed specially for the gay evening entertainments the Grätzer Gallops and Waltzes, the original Styrian dances and the "Valse nobles." Once Schubert took part in a concert of the Steiermärkische Musikverein, of which he was an honorary member, in the city Playhouse, where he played the accompaniment to "Norman's Song" from Walter Scott's "Lady of the Lake," and where his vocal quartet "Geist der Liebe," by Matthisson, was produced. The master, with his friends, also visited the Graz Theatre to see

Meyerbeer's opera " Crociato," of which, however, they formed
no very favourable opinion.

The days passed in cheerful society. Picnics were given in the
beautiful neighbourhood of the Styrian city of flowers. There
were walks on the Schlossberg, whence Schubert, the lover of
Nature, revelled in the glorious view of the valley, with its chains
of blue mountains, extending almost as far as the Mountains of the
Krain.

They drove to the little toy Haller Castle at the foot of the Ruckerl-
berg, belonging to Dr. Haring, surrounded by its romantic
park, comparable to the Garden of the Hesperides. The roof
was crowned with a tower over the door, and two smaller towers
flanked the building. The big garden, with terraces ornamented
by statues of gods, by urns and sundials, was full of flowers and
fruit, and the branches of mighty beeches made a cool, pleasant
shade. Here *al fresco* " Schubertiades " took place ; there was
dancing, singing and acting. " Der Fussfall im Hallerschlössel "
was the title of an amusing little piece, in which Schubert took a
part. In the old courtyard of the building a tablet, put there in
1885, informs those who still wander to-day in the green park of
the dainty little castle, in letters of gold, that Franz Schubert, in
September, 1827, passed happy hours here with his lively friends.
" In Lasting Remembrance of the *Lieder* King " the inscription
runs. Another idyllic spot in green Styria connected with
Schubert's visit to Graz was the Wildbach estate, which belonged
to a widowed aunt of Dr. Pachler's, a Frau Anna Massegg. The
party drove thither in separate carriages—Schubert with his
friends, Jenger and Hüttenbrenner, in one, and the Pachler family
in another. They bowled along white roads, up hill and down
dale, through the verdant landscape, passing woods and fields,
mills and farms and fruitful vineyards, till they came to a narrow
valley thickly bordered by dark woods, where in an opening
Frau Massegg's small castle gleamed a friendly welcome to the
visitors. Here in a sunny corner, in the very midst of forest and
mountain, the Pachlers' *tante* had brought up six fair, graceful
daughters. In Wildbach, with the tutor Fuchs—also a fine
musician, father of the well-known Viennese composers and
conductors, Johann and Professor Robert Fuchs—and with his
friends, Schubert passed many a merry day in the society of the
six lively and beautiful girls. There was music in the forest and

strolls on the mountains, and under the exhilarating influence of the excellent Schilcher wine many mad pranks were played. Days and nights devoted to the dance and music passed like a dream. Homage was paid to Bacchus, and the impetuous boy Eros gave wings to time, yet there were quiet hours in which Schubert sometimes communed alone in secret with the muse.

In Graz, besides the Grätzer dances, the song " Heimliche Liebe," and the old Scotch ballad "Edward," from Herder's " Stimmen der Völker in Liedern," were composed. At the same time Schubert felt inspired to begin other compositions, and set to music various verses by the Styrian poet, Leitner. These were " Weinen," " Winterabend," " Sterne " and " Der Kreuzzug." But all too soon the delightful days in Graz came to an end, days in which Schubert, surrounded by glorious Nature, admired and adored by joyous, natural, artistically receptive people, had drunk deep in the goblet of happiness and joy.

On September 20th the two friends left the hospitable house in Graz and drove through the green country back to Vienna, not without pausing on the way to look up friends and acquaintances of Jenger's.

Jenger wrote on September 27th, with regard to his joint journey with Schubert in Styria, to Frau Pachler as follows :

" Through Josef Hüttenbrenner, who is lucky enough to be going back to Graz, we, Friend Schwammerl (nickname for Schubert in Graz) and myself, thank you, dear gracious lady, most heartily for all your kindness and friendship, which neither of us will ever forget as long as we live. Seldom have Schubert and I enjoyed such glorious times as in Graz and its surroundings, and we shall always remember Wildbach, with its dear inhabitants, as the crowning delight. . . . A brief description of our return journey may not be without interest to you, *liebe, gnädige Frau.* . . . In Fürstenfeld we were very cordially received by my good old friend, Frau Bürgemeisterin Fritzi Wittmann. We spent the morning in seeing what there is to see in the town, and at 3 the same afternoon resumed our journey, and got to Hartberg (at 8 that evening), where we found very comfortable quarters for the night. On the 22nd we ordered our carriage at 5 in the morning. It was a glorious day and we had a perfect drive to Friedberg, where we arrived and breakfasted at 10.30. From there we went by foot to the top of the Eselberg, whence we got a splendid view over Styria and Hungary as far as Austria. When we stood on the frontier we took off our caps and sent a message of thanks on the wings of the wind, with greetings, for all the hospitality and kindness shown us by the dear people in Styria, and we made a resolution to come there again as soon as possible. . . . We spent Sunday and Monday till 3 in the afternoon in Schleinz with a lively party—Viennese acquaintances of our landlord, the merchant Stehman—and then started on the journey to Vienna, which we reached at 10.30 in the evening, alighting under the lamp of the 'Blaue Igel,' where Schubert put up. So here we parted."

After the beautiful and happy days in Styria, Schubert found it difficult to accustom himself to taking up life again in Vienna. His thoughts constantly flew back to Graz, and he wished himself once more in the bosom of the genial, hospitable and artistic Pachler family.

As a token of his gratitude for his hospitable reception there, the master dedicated to Frau Pachler the songs " An Sylvia " and " Heimliches Lieben," and composed for her husband's birthday a march for four hands, with which she and his son, Faust, were to present him as a surprise.

In Vienna Schubert's life again became devoted to his artistic creations, his imagination increased in creative strength, and from the master's overflowing heart streamed one intoxicating melody after another. In the rich harvest of this year were the chorale for eight voices, " Schlachtlied," from Klopstock, the solemn quartet "Nachtgesang im Walde," the comic terzet, " Die Hochzeits-braten " (Schober's words), a cantata on the recovery from illness of Irene Kiesewetter, the *lieder* " Lied der Anne Lyle," " Gesang der Norna," " Das Lied im Grünen," " Der Hirt auf dem Felsen." Also a poem of Grillparzer's, " Ständchen," beginning with the verse " Zögernd leise in des Dunkels nächt'ger Stille," was set to music at this time by Schubert. This came about through the agency of Anna Fröhlich, Professor of Singing at the Vienna Conservatorium.

Other fruits of those richly productive days was the much-sung " Deutsche Messe," a simple, religiously-inspired vocal work with organ accompaniment composed for the pupils of the Vienna Polytechnic to the text of Johann Philipp Neumann. For the piano came now from the treasure-trove of his genius those costly

Jenger, Hüttenbrenner and Schubert
By Josef Teltscher

The " Mondschein " House
By Moriz von Schwind
(Vienna State Museum)

little gems, "Moments Musicals" and the "Impromptues,"
miniatures in tones, music for quiet, holy hours, in which an inner
radiance of beauty shines from some blue, magic heaven. Chamber
music Schubert enriched with the magnificent E Major Trio,
(opus 100), for piano, violin and violoncello, with its affecting
andante *con moto*, full of melody, and the scherzo bubbling over
with racy humour.

At that time Moriz von Schwind, the master's *intimus*, made up
his mind to migrate to Munich to carry on there his studies in
painting. He was working busily on an oil painting, " Spaziergang
vor dem Stadttor," in which he immortalised members of the
Schubert circle. The picture speaks of the young artist's sadness
at the thought of so soon parting from the Viennese circle of
Schubertians. Also Schubert was to feel acutely the loss of
his best friend; it seemed to him like a farewell to the careless
joyousness of youth. " Schubertiades " were now few and far
between; the lively, high-spirited boys had matured into the
dignity of manhood. Some of them developed into eccentric
recluses, who withdrew themselves altogether from gay society,
such as the poets Mayrhofer and Sauter, who had always been
rather inclined to melancholy brooding. Several entered the state
of holy matrimony. The portrait-painter Kriehuber married;
Spaun took to wife Franziska Roner; Kupelwieser led his Johanna
Lutz to the altar; and even the elderly singer Vogl had gone late
a-wooing, and had married his pupil, Kunigunde Rosa. But there
were many delightful farewell festivities. Schubert played for
the dancers at Kriehuber's wedding; they sang, polkaed and
swore eternal friendship. Only when the party broke up and the
friends dispersed, Schubert, the poor musician, was left more and
more alone with his loneliness. His heart, sick with the longing
of unrequited love, overflowed with melodies in which the note
of sadness became ever more distinctly heard. The master wandered through the great gay city, with no companions except
poverty and care. If a few groschen found their way into his
pocket from the stingy publishers, with whom, in consequence of
his eternal financial necessity, he was constantly in correspondence,
he would solace himself in a wine-shop with the costly juice of
Bacchus. Then, for a short time, his troubles would be forgotten,
the creative fire stimulated anew, and the hours would fly by like a
rosy, blissful dream. But this detachment from earth and its

cares was only temporary. Soon he was a prey again to the petty
worries, the soul-deadening anxieties of prosaic everyday life.
Some way had to be sought and found to conquer the depression
caused by poverty.

" You are progressing," he said at that time, on meeting
Bauernfeld, who had got an appointment in the service of the
State. " I foresee you becoming a Hofrat and a famous writer of
comedies. But myself ? What is to become of the poor musician ?
In my old age I shall be like Goethe's Harpist, going round begging
my bread at the doors of the rich." " You are a genius, but a
fool ! " was the friend's answer to the melancholy musician,
" *nullum magnum ingenium sine aliqua mixtura dementiae fuit* . . .
rouse yourself to make an effort ; get the better of your laziness ;
give a concert next winter of your compositions. Vogl will, of
course, support you with pleasure. *Virtuosi* like Bocklet, Böhm
and Linke would think it an honour to put themselves at the
service of such a *maestro* as you. The public would scramble for
tickets, and even if you don't with one blow become a Crœsus, you
will at least rake in enough to cover your expenses and over for
a whole year at least. A repetition of such a successful evening
would be called for every year, and if the novelties, as I fully expect,
cause a *furore*, then you may snap your fingers at your Diabelli's,
Artaria's and Haslinger's with their paltry honorariums. A
concert, then. Follow my advice ! "

And finally Schubert was prevailed upon by his friends to bring
his compositions before the public at a concert. It took place on
March 26th, 1828, at 7 o'clock in the evening in the concert hall
of the Austrian *Musikverein*. The programme consisted chiefly
of his more recent works : the *lieder* " Der Kreuzzug " and " Die
Sterne," by Leitner, " Der Wanderer an den Mond," by Seidl,
fragments from Æschylus, " Die Allmacht," by Ladislaus Pyrker
(all sung by Vogl), " Auf dem Strome," by Rellstab, choruses such
as Grillparzer's " Ständchen," given by Josefine Fröhlich and pupils
of the Conservatorium, Klopstock's " Schlachtgesang," the G
Sharp Major Trio (opus 100), the first movement of a new violin
quartet. Admission tickets cost 5 florins, and were to be obtained
at the music shops, Haslinger, Diabelli and Leidesdorf. The
concert hall was filled to overflowing, the applause tremendous,
and the takings 800 florins, for that time a considerable sum.
After the concert the Schubertians met at the " Schnecke," where

the master and his success were commemorated with liquid festiveness. The newspaper critics were not altogether favourable :

" Herr Franz Schubert gave a private concert at which only his own compositions were performed," wrote the Vienna correspondent of the *Berliner Allgemeinen musikalischen Zeitung.* " Mostly songs—a *genre* in which he excels. The numerous audience of friends applauded frantically every item, and many songs had to be repeated." " There is only one voice to listen to within our walls," declared the *Dresdner Abendzeitung* " and this cries : ' Hear Paganini. . . .' It is only natural that in comparison with him, all other musical artists should be put in the shade. But many, nevertheless, are content if in that shade they can earn a few guldens, and so it comes about that besides his concerts, a number of others given by musical academies and societies are announced. *Multum clamoris, parum lanae !*

I will only mention a private concert given by the favourite composer, Schubert. . . . All the singers and everything they sang were more or less clapped to excess. There was, it can't be disputed, much that was good, but, of course, the lesser stars in the musical sky pale inevitably before the brilliance of the great comet which has arisen there (Paganini)."

Bauernfeld, under March, 1828, makes the following entry in his diary :

" Schwind has won the hand of Netty (Hönig) in spite of a hole in his tail coat. Betrothal feast. . . . Schubert's concert was on the 26th. Huge applause ; good takings." Another Schubertian, Franz von Hartmann, wrote in his diary : " Went with Louis and son-in-law to Schubert's concert. How magnificent it was ! I shall never forget it. After, we went to the ' Schnecke,' where we rejoiced till 12 o'clock. . . . "

The artistic success of this concert was the last bright spot in Schubert's life, which was destined to last only a few months longer. The not inconsiderable profits of 800 guldens for the most part served to pay off old debts, and did not contribute in any way to an improvement in the master's economic position. He continued poor. " Dame Care " was his inseparable companion. He was now, as it were, famous in a way ; honoured and beloved, at least in the circle of his numerous friends and admirers, who adored and understood him. But the almighty wealthy parvenues who set the fashion showed no disposition to patronise the new genius.

His colleagues, too, in the musical profession, who themselves had won success only with more or less painful effort, were too proud and taken up with their own achievement to trouble about Schubert's. So the rich clinked the gold in their pockets, and were undisturbed in their luxurious living by the thought that again there was a poor musician roaming about the streets of their city who, like Mozart, created immortal things, but lived in abject poverty.

The leading critics, whose opinion carried weight, took no serious notice of Schubert's music, because of its unusualness and freedom from the old laws and traditions. Their gods were Rossini, who flooded the world with brilliant fireworks, and Paganini, who with his magic fiddle bewitched the hearts of men and women. The work of the poor, struggling Viennese master was either ignored altogether or only mentioned with slighting remarks or sneers, such as " *The numerous friends and patrons were not slow in supplying vigorous applause,*" or " *The lesser stars pale before the brilliance of the comet in the musical heaven (Paganini).*"

Schubert met with little encouragement from his Vienna publishers, who were very backward in the payment of honorariums. It is true that in time he came into connection with three firms in Germany : Probst, who has been mentioned before, published the Trio (opus 100). The firms of Schott in Mayence, and of Bruggemann in Halberstadt, asked for manuscripts, which they generally returned, of a " light and brilliant character, not too difficult and likely to be popular ! " The scanty honorariums which now and again came in were just sufficient to cover the cost of a lively evening with friends at an inn. So it was inevitable that the master should incur fresh debts. His irregular life, full of cares and anxieties, was often lacking in the meals necessary to existence. He lived chiefly on coffee and rolls at the Café Bogner, or as Bauernfeld tells us in his diary, on " Apples and fritters for supper . . . well that no one can see into the inside of his soul and empty purse."

Friends helped him out, and sometimes the beggared composer who had raised for the world immortal fabrics of tones, would slink in secret to his step-mother in Lichtenthal and say : " Now *Frau* Mother, just look in your stocking and see if you can spare me a few twenty kreutzer-pieces, so that I may have a good meal this afternoon ! "

A post as conductor, which would have meant a living, in spite of the exertions of his friends, Schubert never succeeded in obtaining. The State required the services of no new talent. For giving lessons, as Mozart had done, Schubert had neither the gift nor patience. His bitter experience in youth as a schoolmaster put him off trying this method of bringing grist to the mill. Rather starve and be free to dream, to sing and compose as an independent artist! Poverty and want only belonged to his outward circumstances. Schubert was still in the spring-time of life, and could have afforded to wait till Fortune and Fame showered on him their favours in abundance. There was no sign of the vast inner store of beauty which flowed from his heart being exhausted. On the contrary, more generously and lavishly than ever his fantasy found expression in new beauties, piled picture upon picture, wonder upon wonder, and brought forth from the master's soul in an intoxicated fever of creation the most costly and exquisite treasures. So within a few months, or even weeks, came the great C major symphony, Schubert's most magnificent composition for orchestra, full of radiant life and inexhaustible wealth of imagination, perfect in the art of instrumentation and rich in tone-painting; the powerful mass in E sharp major, in the solemn sanctus of which, with its Hosanna fugue, effects are reached equal to those in Beethoven's great mass and in Bach's mass in H minor; the, in its way, quite original string quintet in C major (opus 163), in which Schubert, with the use of two 'cellos, brought out an extra strength of tone in the delicate magic melody; several original piano pieces for four hands, his three last sonatas for piano, priceless pearls in which he reached the same level of brilliance, depth and solemnity as his great prototype Beethoven. Also his lyrical muse inspired the master to the composition of a group of songs of incomparable beauty; for instance "Mirjams Siegesgesang," from Grillparzer, for soprano solo with chorus and piano accompaniment, that with its reminiscence of Händel's heroic manner makes a striking impression; the cantata "Glaube, Hoffnung und Liebe," the 92nd Psalm for baritone solo and choir, a Tantum Ergo, an Offertorium, the famous "Hymne" for male chorus.

In the summer of 1828 he received invitations to Graz from the Pachlers, and to Gmunden from Ferdinand Traweger. The latter wrote on May 19th: " Zierer tells me that you would like to visit Gmunden again, and that he was to ask me what I charge for board and lodging, and to let you know. Really you put me in a quandary. If I didn't know you so well and your frank way of thinking, I might be afraid that you wouldn't come because I should not charge you anything. But in order that you mayn't worry yourself with the thought that you are going to be a burden, and so can stay as long as you like, listen to this : for your room, breakfast, dinner and evening meal, I'll charge you 50 kreuzer, and for what you drink you can pay me extra. I must close, or I shall miss the post. Write and tell me at once whether my proposal suits you.

Your sincere friend
FERDINAND TRAWEGER."

Schubert accepted neither of these invitations, and a letter to Frau Pachler from Jenger explains why. His financial needs were so pressing that he was unable to muster sufficient money for the journey. Added to his material anxieties, his health, owing to insufficient nourishment and irregular hours, grew worse from day to day. His mind became clouded with presentiments of death ; he heard the black wings of the pale angel rustling not far off. He was haunted by the thought that now it was high time to complete his life's work and to give the world the last deep treasures of his bleeding heart. Thus another invitation had no results. It came from his friend Franz Lachner, who asked him to come to Budapest to attend the first performance of his opera, " Die Bürgschaft " through Anton Schindler, Beethoven's factotum, who wrote in the most cordial tone :

" Our friend Lachner is so much occupied with the preparations for his opera that he has deputed me to ask you to come and be present at the great event, which takes place on the 25th or 27th, and I and my sister add thereto our invitation to you to take up your quarters with us. There is room under our roof and at our table for a friend we so honour and admire as yourself. We hope most sincerely that you will soon be in our midst without further demur. You can take the express on the 22nd, and we shall expect you here on the 24th, if you give us two days' notice. Now for a second proposal. Your name is so well known, and your work appreciated here, that we think you should, when you come, give a private concert. As I know how timid you are of any such under-taking, I can assure you in advance that people here will be glad to arrange for you all the business details. You must, however, do a little yourself *ecquidem*—get six letters of introduction from noble houses in Vienna. Lachner suggests Count Esterházy. A word to our friend Pinterics will procure you some of his princes. Anyhow, you should get a good letter written to the Countess Tölöky, who is the great patroness of art here. Don't let yourself be damped by imaginary difficulties. All you've got to do is to deliver the letters if it turns out to be necessary, and so *basta*! A few 100 guldens in your pocket by such simple means is not to be despised, and other advantages may come of it. . . . You will be well supported, and we have a young amateur tenor here who sings your songs and sings them really well. That is by the way. My sister will accompany. . . . So we will expect you and give you a hearty welcome in the land of the *mustachios*."

Schubert only left Vienna again for three days, when at the beginning of October he made an excursion with his brother Ferdinand and two friends to Eisenstadt and visited Haydn's tomb. On the advice of his doctor, Schubert had given up living in Schober's house, and, to be nearer fresh air, had gone to his brother Ferdinand in the Vorstadt Neue Wieden, Firmiansgasse (to-day Kettenbrückengasse No. 6). Here he still worked with feverish ardour, possessed by a demon of artistic creativeness, with new ideas and melodies flowing in a never-ending stream into and from a soul drugged with beauty.

It was with him, as with Mozart, a restless striving for the highest—the tragedy of a man literally working himself to death for the sake of art. It gave the world masterpieces of inestimable value, but brought Schubert all too early to the grave. The swansong of his genius before it sank into eternal night was that group of exquisite *lieder* inspired by words of Rellstab, Heine and Seidl. The music which Schubert gave to the verses of these poets, specially to Heine's " Atlas," " Ihr Bild," " Das Fischermädchen," " Die Stadt," " Am Meer," was distinguished by all the power of expression, all the wealth of tone-imagery which the master's genius had at command ; once more and for the last time all the joy and sadness and passionate yearning of the artist's romantic soul was poured out in divine song.

Towards the end of October a change for the worse in Schubert's condition set in. At the inn " Zum roten Kreuz," in Himmelpfortgrund, where he, with his brother Ferdinand and some friends were lunching, he ate fish which brought on a serious stomach disorder. From this time his exhausted physique would not permit of his taking anything except medicines. But he still went for walks in the open air. Early on the morning of the 3rd of November he wandered as far as Hernals to hear in the parish church there a requiem composed by his brother Ferdinand. It was the last music to fall on his ears. The next morning he entered himself with Josef Lanz as pupil for fugue composition at Simon Sechter, intending to combine these lessons with a study of a treatise on the fugue by Friedrich Wilhelm Marpurg. But on November 11th he was so overcome with weakness that he had to stay in bed. On the 12th he wrote to his friend Schober: "I am ill; I have not eaten anything for eleven days or drunk anything. I stagger reeling from armchair to bed and back. I am in Rinna's hands. If I take anything, I cannot keep it down. Come to my rescue in this desperate plight by being so good as to lend me books. I have been reading Cooper: 'The Last of the Mohicans,' 'The Spy' and 'The Hermit.' If you have any others of his, I beseech you to leave them for me with Frau von Bogner at the Café. My brother who is conscientiousness itself, will conscientiously fetch them for me . . . or any other books.

Your friend

SCHUBERT."

He corrected for the publishers the proof of the second part of the "Winterreise," and then sank into a condition of absolute exhaustion. The physicians, Josef von Vering and Johann Wisgrill, held a consultation at his bedside on November 16th, and decided that he was suffering from a severe nervous fever. Some of his friends visited him once more. To Lachner he spoke of great plans for the future, and looked forward to his recovery to finish " Der Graf von Gleichen." Spaun he tried to reassure with the remark : " There's really nothing the matter with me, except that I am so weak I feel as if I should fall through the bed."

Bauernfeld relates in his reminiscences that he found him in depths of depression. " The last time I visited Schubert—it was on the 17th of November—he lay stretched out, complained of extreme weakness and heat in the head. Yet in the afternoon he was quite conscious and showed no signs of delirium, though my friend's depressed mood filled me with the worse fears. . . . Only a week before he had spoken with great energy about the opera, and how splendidly he was going to orchestrate it. His brain was full of new harmonies and rhythms, he assured me, and with that he dozed off."

In the evening of November 17th he began to be delirious, and on the following day he could only with difficulty be kept in bed. He whispered mysteriously into his brother Ferdinand's ear : " Tell me, what is happening to me ? " And when his brother tried to calm him, he answered in his fever : " No, it is not Beethoven who is lying here ! " When the doctor came soon after, he stared at him and said, pointing to the wall, very slowly and earnestly : " This is my end."

On November 19th, 1828, at 3 o'clock in the afternoon, he died. His friends were deeply moved. Under November 20th, Bauernfeld wrote in his diary : " Yesterday afternoon Schubert died. Monday I was talking to him, Tuesday he improvised, Wednesday he was dead. I can hardly believe it. It is iike a dream. The most honest of souls, the truest of friends. I wish I lay there instead of him. He leaves the earth with fame." Schubert's father formally announced his son's death to the composer's friends in the following words :

" Yesterday, Wednesday afternoon, at 3 o'clock, my dearly-loved son, Franz Schubert, tone-artist and composer, fell asleep to awake in a better life, after a short illness and receiving the Blessed Sacrament, in the 32nd year of his age. My family wish to inform friends and acquaintances that the funeral will take place on Friday, the 21st, at half-past two in the afternoon, from the house No. 694, Neu Wieden. The body will be carried to the parish church of St. Joseph in Margarethten and there consecrated. Vienna, November 20th, 1828. *Franz Schubert, Schoolmaster in Rossau.*"

In the habit of a hermit, a crucifix in the folded hands, with features serene and transfigured, the young master lay in his coffin. It was a grey, rainy November day. The faithful Schubertians followed their beloved genius to the Währinger cemetery, where, separated by only three graves from Beethoven, he was laid to rest. So Schubert died at thirty-one—poor as he had been born and lived. He left behind a few personal possessions, old music books and instruments, of so little value that the whole fetched scarcely 63 guldens. But he left posterity the fifty-nine folio volumes, immortal works of art, among them stacks of unpublished manuscripts, treasures which only after decades have gradually been unearthed. There was hardly enough to cover the expenses of his illness and funeral. The cost of the erection of a tombstone after a design of Schober's had to be defrayed by subscriptions raised among the circle of his friends. Anna Fröhlich gave, for this object, two concerts. Grillparzer composed for the gravestone the words which excited so much controversy :

" Here the Art of Music has buried a rich possession, but still greater hopes."

" Still greater hopes." Yes, to what still greater heights might the genius of Schubert have soared, with what an infinite wealth of musical treasures might he not yet have endowed humanity ! We may curse the cruel strokes of Fate which cut off the divine Mozart in the flower of his youth, afflicted Beethoven with deafness, and ended so prematurely the life of Vienna's greatest genius. Yet we may take comfort from the thought that it is only the master's outer covering that lies turned to dust in the grave. The spirit of his genius has risen untrammelled above all earthly cares and sorrow, and lives for the world to-day in imperishable works of divine song and heavenly beauty.

The Artist and his Work

IF the genius of Schubert as an artist was of a grandeur and prodigality unexampled in the history of music, as a man he was not without many weaknesses and failings. It would seem as if his person merely served as a medium by which his almost somnambulistic creative power as an artist conveyed its inspiration from the spiritual world to earth.

According to the testimony of contemporaries, there was little that was attractive in his outer man. He was short, his face round, fat and puffy—" Schwammerl " his friends nicknamed him. His forehead was low, his nose of the snub variety, his dark hair extremely curly, which gave him a somewhat nigger-like appearance. He always wore eyeglasses even in the night, so as to be ready to compose directly he woke in the morning. His expression was, as a whole, neither intellectual, distinguished, nor genial. Only when he was composing, did his face change and become interesting, almost demoniac. Then his eyes would flash with the fire of genius. " Those who knew Schubert intimately," relates his friend Josef von Spaun, " saw how intensely his creations moved him, and how they were often born in pain. When one beheld him in the morning at work, with flashing eyes and glowing cheeks, another being altogether from his usual self, one received an impression not easily forgotten." ⌒ ε of his acquaintances, Dr. G. F. Eckel, draws a picture of his outward appearance, faithful in detail if perhaps rather exaggerated. " His figure was small and muscular," he writes, " with strongly developed bones and muscles rounded without angles. Chest and shoulders broad and beautifully formed. Small hands and feet ; a quick, strong footstep. His rather large, round skull was thatched with a wealth of thick, brown, curly hair. His face, in which both forehead and chin were more strikingly developed than the rest of his features, was much more expressive than handsome. His eyes, light brown, if I am not mistaken, in colour, lit up when he was excited under heavy lids and bushy eyebrows. The habit of knitting his brows as if short-sighted made his eyes appear smaller than they were. His nose was short and turned up, with wide nostrils; his lips full and generally firmly closed. A so-called beauty dimple adorned his chin. His complexion was pale, but, as is generally the case with genius, changeable. The play of his features, the soft fire of his eyes, the laughing mouth, were expressive of the genius within him." And many other contemporaries, friends, poets, musicians and painters, have told us in their recollections much about Schubert's appearance, habits and character—much that is true and much that is fiction.

He was painted, drawn and lithographed countless times, but from most of the accounts and portraits it is to be gathered that Schubert was an ordinary everyday-looking person in appearance, looking just as any other assistant schoolmaster in the suburbs might look. There was nothing striking about him; nothing to attract attention, like Beethoven's Jupiter head, which betrayed at a glance the unusual character of the man as he dashed, hat in hand, over the Bastions, with his hair floating in the wind, lost in thought. Schubert's exterior had nothing in common with the popular conception of the man of genius. The spirit within left no marks on the outer covering, but remained hidden. What was wonderful about this man—his heart of gold, his profound temperament—was invisible. From the secret recesses of his being poured the God-given stream of inspiration; there lay the root of the mysterious power which blossomed forth so abundantly. His was no commanding, imperious nature; on the contrary, it was dreamy, clinging, deeply introspective. Admirably in his easy verse, Grillparzer characterises the mentality of the Viennese tone-poet in lines beginning "*Schubert heiss ich, Schubert bin ich und als Solchen geb' ich mich. . . .*"

However much contemporary descriptions of Schubert's outward person may differ, all who knew him are agreed with regard to his sincerity and unaffectedness in social intercourse. Käthi Frölich, Grillparzer's friend, expressed it thus :

"His was a wonderful disposition. He was never envious and captious, as so many I could mention. On the contrary, he was always delighted to hear anything beautiful in music. He would fold his hands and rest his chin upon them and sit entranced. The innocence and guilelessness of his mind were beyond all description." A peculiar modesty which was almost shamefacedness was characteristic of him. We remember how, as a boy, he confided to his friend Spaun that he thought sometimes in secret that he might " do something one day," and added, " but who would dare try, after Beethoven." Once, when he had already produced masterpieces and was asked for a composition, he answered, " As I have nothing finished for a whole orchestra that I could send conscientiously out into the world, and as there are so many pieces available by great masters, for instance, Beethoven's overtures ' Prometheus,' ' Coriolanus,' ' Egmont,' etc., I must ask you to excuse my sending anything, for if I sent a mediocre composition it would injure my reputation." When once at a party many of his songs were being sung, Anna Fröhlich relates that he exclaimed, " That's enough ! I am beginning to be bored." At a concert in the drawing-room of the Princess Karoline von Kinsky, when Schubert was accompanying his own songs, everyone was enraptured with the singer Baron Schönstein, and none of the audience took any notice of the composer. Only the hostess, Princess Kinsky, tried, as Spaun tells us, " to make amends for this neglect, and overwhelmed Schubert with praise, as if she wished him to overlook the listeners having been so enchanted with the singer that they had forgotten to thank the accompanist and composer of the songs. Schubert answered that he was grateful to the Princess, but begged her not to concern herself about him, he was used to being overlooked, and really preferred to be left to himself." He used to hold up his hands in protest if his compositions were praised to his face, and once, on hearing something he had composed a long time before and forgotten, he was astonished and delighted, and declared that he had no idea he had ever written anything so beautiful ! Thus Schubert lived in the world unrecognised in his real greatness ; all push and self-advertisement were repugnant to his modest nature. He had neither the energy nor the self-confidence of the imperious Beethoven, who, conscious of his genius, understood how effectually to bite a way through for his work. Schubert valued above all things being free to go his own way quietly ; anything like appeals for sympathy and *réclame* he avoided with his true Viennese nonchalance. Artistic vanity was foreign to his straightforward, simple character, and if admirers of his music came to burn incense at his shrine he withdrew all the more into his shell. The young German poet, Hoffmann von Fallersleben, an ardent admirer of the composer, gives an instance of this :

" Often and often I had expressed the wish to Panofka to make
the acquaintance of Franz Schubert. ' Very well,' answered
Panofka, ' we'll go out to Dornbach, where Schubert is often to be
found during the summer, and it will be better to visit him there.'
So we went one evening by the coach to Dornbach, and our first
question on descending at the ' Kaiserin von Österriech,' was
to ask whether Schubert was there. ' He hasn't been to Dornbach
on Sunday for a long time, but may be here to-morrow,' we
were told, and we built our hopes on Monday. The next morning we wandered about in the woods, lay on the grass, had
breakfast and returned to our ' Kaiserin ' to find no Schubert.
We had dinner and went back by the coach the way we had
come. We then thought of another method of running him
to earth, and sent him a friendly invitation to dine with us at the
' Weissen Wolf.' A place was laid for him and a bottle of wine
waited. He didn't come, so we drank the wine. A fortnight later, on Ascension Day, when the library was closed at
2 o'clock, I again drove off in the coach with Panofka, this time
to Nussdorf. Our inquiries for Schubert were vain. We went on
to Heiligenstadt, then to Grinzing, into the heart of the village.
The wine was bad, but there was a nice garden to sit in, with an old
fiddler playing in it. Suddenly Panofka exclaimed, ' There he
is ! ' and he hurried up to Schubert, who, with several friends, was
looking for a place. Panofka brought him to me. In great
delight, I greeted him warmly, referred *en passant* to the trouble
we had taken to find him, and expressed my pleasure at meeting
him at last. Schubert stood before me in great embarrassment,
not knowing what to say, and after a few conventional words
asked to be excused and left us, and we saw nothing more of
him. ' That is really a little too much,' I said to Panofka. ' I feel
now that I would rather never have seen him. I should never have
dreamed that the creator of such divine melodies could be such
an indifferent, ordinary, not to say discourteous person. And,
even apart from his conduct to us, there is nothing about him
different from any other man in Vienna : his accent is *wienerisch*, he
has a clean shirt, a well-cut coat, a polished hat, like any other
Viennese, and in his face and his whole bearing there is nothing
that in the least resembles *my* Schubert.' "

Occasionally, however, Schubert could throw off the mask of
modesty and assert his pride as an artist and make the standpoint

of genius clear. So, at any rate, Bauernfeld relates, giving an account of an incident at the Café Bogner. The Schubertians were assembled there, and some members of the Kärntnertor Orchestra, who were present, began giving expression to their disgust at the master having refused to supply a solo piece for their concert. They were artists as good as he was, they said, and there were none better in Vienna. " Artists ! Artists ! " thundered Schubert. " *You* call yourselves artists. One of you bites between his teeth a wooden tube, the other blows out his cheeks playing the bugle ! Do you call that art ? It's just a piece of mechanical trickery that brings in pence. Fiddlers, wind-blowers ! that's what you all are. Nothing else. But I am an artist. I ! I am Schubert—Franz Schubert, whom all the world knows, who has done things that are great, beautiful ; things of which you have no conception ; and I shall do more beautiful things. . . . For I am not just a mere bungling country composer, as the stupid newspapers think. Let the fools talk as they like. . . ."

There were heights and depths in Schubert's life. His temperament was divided between the transitory pleasures of this world and the divinity of another. He could be in as gay and exuberant spirits as a child one minute and the next as downcast and depressed as any hypochondriac on the earth.

As Bauernfeld says, there slumbered in the tone-poet a twofold nature. " The Austrian element, sensuous and rough, came perhaps too boisterously to the surface during Schubert's bouts with his associates when his spirits were at their highest, but always in the background the demon of melancholy hovered with its dark wings. No evil spirit truly, because under its influence, in the hours consecrated to it, the most beautiful songs, full of exquisite pathos, were produced." It was the mysterious and the tragic in his genius which burst forth explosively in his artistic creation, if not with the titanic force of a Beethoven, yet in its more gentle form far more deeply moving. It was the same tragical note which we meet in other creative men of genius, in Mozart, Kleist, Hugo Wolf, and it proceeds from the depth of the soul of genius, where the mysterious demon reigns. While Schubert's spirit struggled and wrestled for the highest, he was fettered to a life of poverty. His gentle character made it possible for him to contemplate existence with the calm vision of the fatalist ; he raised no complaints, did not rebel ; he seemed resigned to having been chosen by Fate to wander through this mortal life only in the shadow of happiness. It may be that he who had no abiding home, no musical position, who was poor and unrecognised by the majority during his short life, learnt earlier than most of us the perishableness of all earthly benefits. When very young he had felt the shuddering presentiment of the human tragedy ; when still little more than a boy he had sounded the abyss in all its depths almost as far as the gates of death itself. And this melancholy oppressed him, and it was only by his passion for creation that he could free himsel from the demonic element. Often in his lonely hours melancholy made a poet of him in words as well as tones. There was the verse " Mein Gebet," which he wrote in the year 1825, when illness threatened to cloud his life. Or he would, as we have seen, confide to his diary the emotions caused by melancholy : " No one understands another's pain or another's joy. We think we are together, but are far apart. Oh, torment for those who find this out ! " Or he would pour out his heart to a friend, as in the letter that he wrote to the painter, Kupelwieser, in Rome, from which we have already quoted the significant passage : " I am the unhappiest, most miserable man in the world. Think what it is to know that one's health is so bad it will never be better. Think what it is to have seen one's most brilliant hopes wrecked. Happiness, love and friendship contain for me nothing but pain." But it is in his music that the melancholy of his soul, the wistful longing for the solution of the mystery beyond the veil, is most eloquently expressed. How it grips the heart in the " Winterreise," in the melody " *Einen Weiser seh ich stehen, unverrückt vor meinem Blick.*" . . . " *Krähe lass mich Endlich sehen Treue bis zum Grabe,*" and so on. But it was not always that the master set his vision on the dark side of life. Schubert wrestled with and overcame the crisis of his soul through art. Then he would cast from him all depression, and again, by hurrying to his beloved friends, quaff the cup of pleasure. The quick, gay Viennese blood awoke in his veins, the virile nature of the Viennese, of the easy-going Austrian, came into evidence, as the following verse of Bauernfeld shows :

> " *Doch früher hast du gelebt—und nicht*
> *Als Musikgelehrter als bleicher,*
> *Voll war und rund der Bösewicht,*
> *Ein behaglicher Osterreicher.*"

An artist young in years, he required, as did all creative spirits in light-hearted Vienna, the relaxation which, when enjoyed in peace and harmony, stimulates to higher efforts. Spheres of joyous amusement he sought and found among his beloved and ·devoted friends. A Spaun, a Schober, a Schwind, the brothers Hüttenbrenner, Mayrhofer, Bauernfeld, Kupelwieser, Jenger and Lachner—all valued the friendship of Schubert, who possessed nothing but his Heaven-born genius, with which he knew how to ennoble and elevate their lives. The lively intercourse with these loyal friends was for the composer a blessed recreation and release from the exhausting artistic work on which he poured out his heart's blood ; it was flight from the world, in which, while he created, the demon held him enthralled. It afforded the refreshment of change of scene, and excursions into the green country, to Grinzing or Dornbach ; or an evening's enjoyment of Bacchus in a smoke-ridden Vienna beerhouse or wine-shop in the midst of his young friends, smoking their pipes, dispelled all sadness in innocent merriment and laughter. Or there were those joyous Schubertiades in the houses of citizens, where men and women thronged round him, loving and admiring him as their brother. He played for them, and they danced, joked and flirted, and Schubert made music for the gay, careless revellers out of the melancholy stillness of his soul.

Next to friendship, joy in the beauty of Nature was the bright spot in Schubert's existence. The profound love of Nature so magnificently expressed in his songs, symphonies and quartets drew him as it drew Beethoven from the narrow confinement of the town into the country. Change of air, exercise in the freedom of Nature, were to him, the romanticist, a necessity of his being. In the cathedral-like stillness of the forest, in the fragrance of old flower gardens, his muse gathered impressions, poetic and ineradicable. Perhaps to no other Austrian artist can Grillparzer's often-quoted lines be applied with more aptness :

" *Hast Du vom Kahlenberg das Land dir rings besehen,*
So wirst du, was ich schrieb und was ich bin, verstehen."

If we would understand completely what Schubert the man and musician was, his creation and work, we must also learn to know intimately the Viennese landscape, for which " Friend Schwammerl " cherished a love and admiration only second to Beethoven's. But he did not find in it, in the same way as the Titan, a source of musical inspiration; he was not a daily wanderer in the fields and lanes, with his hands behind his back, tearing along, the wind blowing his hair into wild confusion, seeking a refuge from his fellow-men in Nature. Schubert, on the contrary, inclined to peaceful enjoyment, liked best to visit the country in the congenial company of his friends. "In summer he went regularly out of the town," Spaun relates, "and it would happen sometimes that on a fine evening he would forget in convivial society an engage-ment in some distinguished house, and this would give offence, about which he troubled himself little. Evil tongues said of him, because he liked to drink a glass of wine in good company at some country inn, that he was a roysterer and drunkard. Whereas he was very moderate, and never, even when merry, consumed more than a reasonable quantity."

Instinctively Schubert listened to the voice of Nature, and the slightest contact with her stirred the harpstrings of his soul, and they sang of all that he saw, heard and felt in the Viennese landscape : the sunny, cheerful meadows and gardens, the mysterious murmur of the forest, the rushing streams, the distant city seen in the glow of evening, the fluttering weather-cocks, the post-horn echoing through the village main street, the dogs barking in the courtyards. And the organ-grinder was there, too, going from house to house, turning the handle of his hurdy-gurdy and holding out a plate for coins. Between meadowland and wood meandered the silver, singing brook, in which the trout flashed backwards and forwards quick as lightning, and by the well before the door stood the old linden tree. The son of the Lichtentaler schoolmaster, whom life treated generally in such a stepmotherly fashion, was in his element when, on balmy spring or summer evenings, he sat dreaming over a glass of wine in a garden full of the scent of pinks, lavender and briar-roses in Grinzing, Nussdorf, Dornbach, or Salmannsdorf. From near and far sounded the sob of fiddles and tinkling guitars ; Viennese folk music in rhythmical three-four time. And Schubert, born of the people and grown up in their midst, felt as if he heard his own voice speaking to him. He would sit quietly there medi-tating, and, lifted on the wings of wine, would spin new melodies. In such hours he would have changed places with nobody; he was conscious of being, by the grace of God, an artist with a mine of wealth within him and the power to bestow it on the world.

The Schubert landscape began directly behind the house in

which the composer was born in Lichtental, close to the Nuss-
dorfer and Döblinger high road, where, behind small Biedermeier
houses, were fruit and flower gardens and flourishing vines.
" For the first time after many months, I again took a walk," wrote
the young master once in his diary. " Anything more agreeable
can hardly be conceived than in the evening after a hot summer
day to walk in the green fields between Währing and Döbling.
They seem made for the purpose of strolling. It was in the twilight,
and I was with my brother Karl. I felt so happy that I constantly
stood still and exclaimed, ' How beautiful this is ! ' " And the
Schubert landscape continued to where the road dips into the
Heiligenstadt Valley, there where to-day the little house still
stands in which Therese Krones lived, and the Raimund song,
" Brüderlein fein, Brüderlein fein," seems to echo from it as if in
a dream. It goes on, past the house in which once Beethoven
and the young Grillparzer spent a summer together, through the
Grinzing avenue to the village of Grinzing, where the low buff
houses have imposing entrance gates, and the courtyards
resound with merry folk-music and have walls covered with
ivy and vines. Near these is the little Square and the tiny Gothic
parish church, with its delicate baroque tower, which Schwind
has immortalised in a picture, showing Schubert, Bauernfeld
and Lachner drinking each other's health in an arbour at
" Heurige " time. Then through terraces of vines the way wound
up the mountain-side to the great green shady beech-wood,
which, in its cathedral-like stillness and silence, seemed endless.
And to Schubert's landscape belonged, too, the path on which
Beethoven had composed his idyll, " The Pastoral Symphony,"
and the vineyards, meadows and valleys round the Kahlenberg,
and the Schafberg, where the little dreamy wine villages in spring
are pink with peach blossom.

The master often made pilgrimages to Mödling and its neighbourhood. Here was Schubert's chosen world, a world full of flowers,
grapes, music and song. Here there came to him a happiness which is
only known by the favourites of the gods ; here he experienced that
creative ecstasy which leads the way to Heaven from the troubles and
sorrows of this suffering life. Here Schubert's music was born—
those immortal melodies which ring into our souls from the "Müllerlieder," the " Winterreise," the piano sonatas, the Schubert dances,
and from hundreds of themes in the string quartets and symphonies.

But Schubert's wanderings, as we know, were not confined to the country round Vienna. He made those delightful trips, real "sentimental journeys," into Upper Austria, the land of woods and streams and orchards round Bruckner's home, of beautiful churches and monasteries in the baroque style of architecture. He went to Mozartian Salzburg, and climbed the majestic Alps of Styria. What profound appreciation of Nature, what romantic sentiment fill the descriptive letters written to his brother Ferdinand while he was travelling with the singer Vogl we have already seen.

It was only the man Schubert who was poor, not the artist who had within him a source of joy and creative riches, of which no outward cares could rob him. Music was in him—that music which is set alight by all that is beautiful; music deeper and greater than any pleasure and pain, music that transformed his whole existence into a vast "Sursum Corda."

His life was lived apart from everyday events. He was essentially a worker absorbed in his work. He laboured in all seriousness with an unceasing industry which his friend, Moritz von Schwind, characterised as inhuman. He began to serve his muse early in the morning, and she did not leave him till the afternoon, never without leaving behind some costly gift. It would have been impossible for an artist, even one of genius, to have accomplished what Schubert gave the world, an output only comparable to Mozart's in extent and richness, in the short span of life allotted to him, if he had not possessed that rare moral energy, delight in work and joy in creation. His life was a perpetual battling with the flood of ideas, an earnest yearning for perfection. He worked with every fibre of his being; he dedicated himself wholly to spirit and feeling, and sacrificed his strength and health on the altar of art. When he was creating, the world was forgotten; his spirit received wings and soared away as if in the grip of some unearthly power. Let us review briefly his life's work; let us consider the relative position of Schubert and his creations in the history of music. As a master of sheer tone, Schubert belongs to the category of great musicians known as the Viennese classics. His work is within the period which starts with Gluck, continues with Haydn and Mozart, and reaches its highest point in Beethoven.

Schubert carried on and supplemented the work of his predecessors; he was a sort of reformer who struck out on new lines and sounded new depths of tone, so that his works, like those of Haydn, Mozart and Beethoven, have lost nothing even till the present day of their significance and charm.

As far as musical education goes, Schubert's was built upon by no means such important and thorough foundations as Mozart's, whose father was a musician of unusual culture and attainments, and proved the boy's strict and most admirable teacher, training him and preparing him to the best advantage for his *début* as a prodigy in the cultivated circles of the highest aristocracy. Nor had Schubert the advantages of the young Beethoven, who, in the Bonn organist, Neefe, and the Austrians, Schenk and Albrechts-berger, found invaluable musical " bear-leaders." Certainly the orchestra and choir of the Imperial Court at Vienna provided the boy Schubert with an excellent training. Yet chiefly it was the instincts of his own genius apart from the romantic influences of the " Zeitgeist " by means of which the precocious child educated and advanced himself. The instruction Schubert received from Salieri was of short duration, and, as it was based on traditions of the old school, with its conventional and dry methods, it exercised small influence on the growing youth, who was so strongly inclined to romance.

Thus Schubert, as a performing musician, remained in a certain respect an *amateur* genius as it were, a naturalist in his art. He never achieved sufficient mastery of any instrument to count as a *virtuoso*, like Mozart and Beethoven, who were among the most famous pianists of their time. Under his hands, nevertheless, the notes became singing voices. " He wasn't an elegant, but a very accurate and fluent piano-player," Anselm Hüttenbrenner informs us. " He accompanied his songs splendidly, always in correct time, and he could play with ease like old Salieri from a score. With his short, fat fingers, he mastered the most difficult intricacies of his sonatas." As a conductor, also, Schubert did not distinguish him-self like Gluck, who was famous as Conductor of the Court Orchestra, and Haydn, who conducted in the chapel of the princely house of Esterházy. All his life he never attained to any position as an executant in his art, and never filled any musical post.

With regard to general culture, he had not the lofty intellect and cultivated mind of Beethoven, who took the liveliest interest in all cultural and artistic movements, especially in contemporary literature. Schubert was exclusively a musician, and as such was a first-rate judge of music. " He invariably," as Anselm Hüitten-brenner says, " hit the right nail on the head. In this he resembled Beethoven, who also was a caustic critic." He cherished the profoundest admiration for Beethoven, Mozart and Handel. His favourite works were Beethoven's symphonies, especially his C Minor, Mozart's " Don Juan " and his Requiem, Handel's " Messiah." As a homely schoolmaster's assistant, he had sought to improve himself by omnivorous and often indiscriminate reading of books by modern authors, and through associating with his cultivated friends. His genius, and the clairvoyance it gave him, raised him above all the shortcomings in his education to the heights of a transcendental world which is only open to a few choice spirits.

As every creative artist, whatever his gifts may be, is in some way or other dependent on the culture and art of the past, and also on that of the contemporary world, so Schubert's creations were in many respects influenced by his predecessors and con-temporaries. He went to school with the old masters, Handel, Gluck, Haydn, Mozart, and held firmly to the old musical forms of the sonata, the symphony, the fugue and variations of the theme—in short, the old forms which, through the overflowing wealth of his fantasy he understood how to invest with new and romantic interest. Beethoven, more than any other of the artists of his day, had the most powerful influence on the young com-poser. No one else had so steeped himself in the dæmonic element of the great master. No one had felt and grasped the majesty of his music to the same degree as Schubert, for whom Beethoven was ever the ideal before his eyes, leading him on to become his gentler, more graceful and feminine counterpart.

" Who dare attempt anything after Beethoven ? " he had said to his boyhood's friend, Spaun, in the Konvikt. And once when he was hurrying home from school and saw the announcement of a performance of " Fidelio " at the Kärntnertortheater, he sold some of his books at an old curiosity shop to buy a ticket. When he succeeded in acquiring a manuscript in the master's handwriting of the song " Ich liebe dich so wie du mich," he wrote on the fly-leaf : " The immortal Beethoven's handwriting came into my possession August 14th, 1817," and on a blank page he composed a composition inspired by reverence for the master. " He can do everything," he said once to the author, K. J. Braun, of Braunthal,

in speaking with enthusiasm of Beethoven, " but we cannot understand everything, and much water will be carried away by the
waves of the Danube before people arrive at a complete understanding of what this man has created. Not only is he the most
sublime and prolific of all composers, but he is the most courageous.
He is equally strong in dramatic as in epical music, in lyrical as in
the prosaic; in short, there's nothing he cannot do."

No wonder, then, that Schubert felt he must hear over and over
again all Beethoven's most important works. No wonder that the
young disciple strove to émulate the older master with all his might.
And it was thus that his genius in the domain of the symphony,
chamber music and pianoforte sonatas sometimes approached the
Titan's gigantic achievement, and in the *genre* of the musical lyric
and song even surpassed him. The stimulus which Schubert
received from Beethoven's work was enormous, and what is said
of Beethoven's relations to the muse of his predecessors, Haydn
and Mozart, is true of Schubert's to Beethoven. The influence of
the latter on Schubert's artistic development was of infinite
importance; although the nature of the two artists was of an
opposite character, and their aim took different directions, Schubert's
method was modelled on Beethoven's. Beethoven was a fighter,
and his heroic music unfolded itself to greatest effect on a grand
scale; his province was the symphony; whereas Schubert, on the
contrary, exercised his gift to most advantage in the field of the
lyric, the *lied*, the pianoforte-fantasia, and chamber music.

There may occur often echoes in Schubert's music of the older
master; nevertheless, he was as much an original genius as Beethoven. His marvellous inventive faculty enabled him to apply any
suggestions that he may unconsciously have received, or theme
that in his passion for creation he had perhaps transferred to his
own original uses, in such a unique manner that they became in
the transit absolutely Schubertian. As a rule, the tremendous
wealth of his own ideas far outweighed any motives that might
have come to him from another source.

When Schubert first saw the light, Mozart had already passed
through the shadow of death, Haydn had achieved his greatest
triumphs, Beethoven's genius was still under the incentive of his
iron will and mighty brain, storming unexplored heights in music.
Instrumental music had undergone a complete evolution in style
when, in the place of Handel and Bach—who had used the out-

going forms to great effect—Haydn, Mozart and Beethoven stepped into the breach and conquered with their new creative methods. In the province of the theatre, the operetta and the *opéra bouffe*, through Gluck and Mozart, had reached classical perfection. Only one child of the musical muse still waited for artistic development in order to blossom into full beauty, and that was the musical lyric or *lied*.

The development of the German choral play, and the discovery of the mine of poetic riches that existed in the *Volkslieder* for literary purposes, struck out a new way of release for the German song of an artistic kind from the old formation of earlier times.

In the art of poetry it was Herder who first drew the attention of poets to the wonders of the folk-poesie; then Bürger, Hölty and Stolberg sought to use Herder's ideas in their ballads and songs; and finally the genius of Goethe raised the German *lied* to heights hitherto unreached in the art of song.

First Peter Schulz, in his famous collection, " Lieder in Volkston " (Berlin, 1782), followed the new line indicated by Herder, with music. Next Johann Friedrich Reichardt was the most fertile composer of *lieder*. He expended great care on the choice of the text, and, instead of using the unpretentious poetry of the Göttingen coterie, he selected lyrics of Goethe and Schiller for the subject of his song compositions. His example was followed by Karl Friedrich Zelter, who was Goethe's musical adviser and whose poems and ballads, as those of Johann Rudolf Zumsteeg, who was the original creator of the ballad composition, had a stimulating effect on the two masters of the ballad, Schubert and Löwe.

In Austria, especially in the Alpine regions, there had flourished from time immemorial a *Volkslied* saturated with music which greatly enriched the music of the Viennese school and its songs.

The development of the artistic form of song began chiefly with the National Choral Play Society, which, under Kaiser Josef II., in the year 1778, was inaugurated with Umlauff's " Bergknappen." Now there began a lively producing of song compositions. Admirable services in this art were rendered by Anton Steffan in his " Sammlung deutscher Lieder für das Klavier," by the musicians Hofmann, Friberth and Rupprecht, Holzer, Schubert's teacher, and others. " Three new types of song were the outcome of this movement," writes Wilhelm Krabbe. " The sentimental aria, out of which later was evolved the great operatic aria and the ariette. Steffan, whose songs were strongly supported by instrumental elements, turned his attention particularly to the accompaniment. Holzer is a first-rate melodist, while Rupprecht is remarkable for a considerable talent in lyrical songs of sentiment."

With regard to the Viennese classics, Haydn, Mozart and Beethoven, their song texts exhibit often a tendency to adhere to the old artistic form of the aria and cantata style, the recitative giving the sense of the verse in declamation, with the poetical rhythm accompanied by corresponding musical rhythm. Thus Haydn's songs are for the most part influenced by the opera aria, such as his "Treue," "Genügsamkeit" and "Sympathie." The genuine *lied* characteristics come out in his "Ständchen," or in the beautiful melody "An die Freundschaft"; above all in his oratorios, "The Creation," and "Jahreszeiten" and in the Austrian National Anthem. Mozart played a greater part than Haydn in the development of the Viennese *lied*. Many of his *lieder*—for example, the music he composed to Goethe's "Veilchen," or the beautiful "Abendstimmung"—are forerunners of Schubert's romantic lyrics. Beethoven's first songs are in form purely strophic, and somewhat of the type of the eighteenth-century ode, such as Goethe's "Mailied." Belonging to the Viennese *Stimmungslyrik* category is the mature song-creation of Beethoven, strongly influenced by Mozart—"Adelaide," to words of Matthisson, and the six Gellert *lieder*, which are of the nature of religious hymns. He reaches his highest point in his song composition in settings to Goethe's poems, above all in the "Liederkreis an die ferne Geliebte," which in their romantic feeling come near Schubert's the *lieder* epoch.

Through their creative activity, all the tone-poets of the Berlin and Vienna schools we have named, succeeded in giving to the song the romance, and the ballad, a corresponding musical style. They retain the melody of the words in notes, and render the spirit of the poem, by means of a harmonious accompaniment and delicate tone-pictures, as faithfully as possible. Schubert was destined to follow in the steps of these composers along the way which led to the highest perfection of the German song in art, and to find in it the great task of his mission.

Schubert's activity as a composer coincided with the flowering time of German romanticism. In Germany it was poesie which first showed and smoothed the way for the other arts, as has in all times been the case, and lent them the power of romantic expression. Hölderlin's sympathetic writings were filled with dreams of longing for human unity with Nature, such as this poet of genius imagined he had found in the world of Hellas. The brothers Schlegel and Tieck chose as the subject of their artistic delineation the weird and supernatural, and fantasy was the queen of the boundless realm of their poetry. The refined, delicate youth Novalis thought to conquer the world anew with the spirit of poesie in defiance of all history, sciences and earthly circumstances.

To many of the German romanticists the Vienna of that time, palpitating with music, seemed the Mecca of their dreams. They trooped into the city of Mozart and Beethoven, and among the pilgrims were Clemens Brentano, Friedrich Schlegel and his wife Dorothea, Zacharias Werner, Adam Müller, the painter Overbeck, and the two Veits. And the young student Eichendorff, seeing life in the light of a yearning emotionalism, also seized the pilgrim's staff and drew near the Imperial city with a heart beating high with enthusiasm. Here he met the leaders of the romantic movement, and ripened into the wonderful poet whose soul long afterwards would be filled sometimes with infinite longing for the place where in his youth the genius in him was awakened.

> " . . . *Wolken da wie Türme prangen*
> *Als sah'ich im Duft mein Wien*
> *Und die Donau hell ergangen*
> *Zwischen Burgen durch das Grün.*
> *Doch wie fern sind Strom und Türme*
> *Wer da wohnt, denkt mein noch kaum*
> *Herbstlich rauschen schon die Stürme*
> *Und ich stehe wie in Traum.*"

The day of romanticism had dawned for Vienna, and the magic blue flower, the moonlit faerie nights about which Tieck, Schlegel, Novalis and Eichendorff raved and sang, became with Schubert music, and was coloured and pictured in tones.

In early boyhood Schubert had betaken his muse to the fount which is the source of all musical art, to song, to the *lied*. He was only fourteen when, with the instinct of genius, he set to music any poem he came across, and produced the ballad-like dramatic songs of " Hagar's Klage," " Der Vatermörder " and " Leichenfantasie." At fifteen he created his first purely lyrical composition, " Das

Klagelied." He was still then under the sway of the transmitted style which reigned in the lyrics of Haydn and Mozart, and in the songs in stanzas of Riechardt and Zelter ; but soon the personal note began to be heard. His soul, filled with the romantic spirit of the time, sought new methods of expression, struggled to invest the melody with meaning and to achieve a richer and finer elaboration of the accompaniment. New land was explored, golden gates sprang open, melody upon melody streamed out of the secret mystic well of his soul. The limitless capability of music to paint in tones was discovered and the right form for the romantic sentiment found. The melody grew out of the rhythm of the poem, declamation and song melted into each other ; and so what the symphony was to Beethoven, the opera to Mozart, the musical drama to Wagner, the song was to Schubert. It formed the crowning summit of his artistic creativeness, and was what one may term the kernel and turning-point in the whole history of song. As he adapted much from the legacy of his predecessors in the musical lyric, Schulz, Neefe, Reichardt, Zelter, and, starting from the Viennese school of Mozart and Beethoven, found new methods of applying harmony from the inspiration of the words, so his *lied* was a fruitful forcing-ground for the lyrical creation of his successors ; for, without Schubert, what Schumann, Brahms, Liszt and Hugo Wolf accomplished in this line would be unthinkable. It was Schubert who led the way and forestalled all others in declamation, melody and harmony in the accompaniment and the freeing of the aria from recitative. Everything that comes under the head of the new and newest in song construction was either demonstrated or indicated by Schubert.

There was and is something unique in Schubert's melody. If in the beginning there were reminiscences in it of his forerunners and contemporaries, very soon Schubert's characteristics alone came into the foreground. It does not allow of historic explanation ; a certain school and tradition may have helped to form it, the style of the time have influenced its structure and variety, but the fascination of its grace, its sweetness, its abundant fullness of feeling, its picturesqueness, that is Schubert's unique possession— in that consists the true greatness of Schubert's genius. His melody is so original that everywhere it can be recognised at once as Schubertian. And it is so extraordinarily rich in invention, now light and sparkling, as the thoughts stream forth, then growing in an elemental force and power till it reaches the sublimity of tragic might and immortal grandeur. Schubert surpasses in sheer melody all those masters who have gone before and have come after him ; his song is more many-sided, more lavishly rich than that of the greatest—Beethoven, Mozart and Bruckner. The root of his melody, which appears to us to be the spiritual glorification and harmonious union of Nature and art, lies in the music of the people, the *lied* and the dance. From these elements he created it and lifted it with the sensuous grace of his natural *naïveté* and the creative force of his genius to the highest intellectual eminence. Like the writings of Raimund, the dance measures of Lanner and Strauss, Schubert's melody was born out of the soul of the Austrian people. It speaks the language of the Austrian home, it is purely *urwie-nerisch ;* it has the light, swaying dance element, the divinely gay, but at the same time melancholy Viennese atmosphere. As no other musician (unless it is Hugo Wolf), Schubert possessed the gift of getting inside the text that he was illustrating in tones. If the poem appealed to his fancy and temperament, at once there was let loose in him an elemental impulse to find the fitting expression, a musical and rhythmic association of ideas which explains the extraordinary capacity Schubert possessed of living in and feeling the poetry of the most widely differing poets, and the power of suiting himself to them musically and giving them individual shape.

In his accompaniments, as well as in his melody, Schubert transcended all who had gone before him. Here, too, he is unique. For though the polyphonic construction of the Schubertian piano-forte accompaniment owes something to Beethoven, the combination of the piano-polyphonic harmony with the melody of the song is Schubert's own original work. Both dovetail closely into each other ; one without the other is inconceivable. The art of illustrating vividly the text in tones was brought by Schubert to the highest pitch of perfection. The whirl of the spinning wheel, the babbling of the brook, the fluttering of flags in the breeze, the ripple of waves, the sighing of the wind—for every sound, every mood, every word, whether it be the rushing river, the shining sea, the melancholy of the evening twilight, the rustling of the trees in the forest, the flashes of summer lightning in the starry sky—the fantasy of the tone-poet knows exactly how to find the characteristic expression, and often by the introduction of a single, striking motive he can characterise a poem as a whole as well as in detail. A case in point is the " Winterreise."

A glance at the poems into which Schubert breathed the music of his soul testifies to the universality of the master's understanding of lyrical poesie. The range of the poems he set to music comprises the whole of the lyrical output from the middle of the eighteenth century to Schubert's death ; thus extending from Utz, Matthisson, Hölty, Kosegarten, Schubart, Klopstock, Herder, Ossian, Stolberg, Schlegel, Körner, Claudius to Goethe, Schiller, Rückert, Uhland, and Heine. The greater space in Schubert's numerous lyrical compositions is accorded to Goethe, Schiller, Wilhelm Müller and Mayrhofer. No matter whether the poets selected by Schubert were on the lofty peaks of Parnassus, like Matthisson, Schiller, Klopstock, Hölty, and Ossian, or merely dwellers in the humbler poetic plains, the very moment any subject charmed Schubert musically he, in the rapture of creation, crowned it with a garland of exquisite tones.

The names of many of these poets are forgotten to-day, but their works, through Schubert's genius, have become immortal. As one example from many, we may take the name of that Schmidt of Lübeck, author of the " Der Wanderer." Who has heard of him to-day ? But the genius of Schubert has glorified in music his poem, which he came across by chance in an old pocket-book (where it had been printed privately in 1808 and afterwards appeared in a published collection in 1815). " Der Wanderer " is one of the most famous songs of all times, and has been sung all over the world.

Of course it was the Weimar prince of poets, Goethe, who took the first place in Schubert's artistic creations. Although he himself had no particular understanding or love for music—he once took lessons on the 'cello in Strassburg, and had an ordinary appreciation of the best when he heard it—his lyrics inspired all the German composers of songs, from Reichardt, Zelter, Mozart, Beethoven, Schumann, Mendelssohn, Löwe to Brahms, Liszt and Hugo Wolf. The reason of this may be the extraordinary musical quality of his poetry. With regard to rhythm and melody, without any effort at highly-coloured effects, his lyrics fired the imagination of all musicians. Goethe was for Schubert the decisive poetic influence, as later Heine and Eichendorff were for Schumann, and Mörike for Hugo Wolf. The universality of the Goethean lyrical genius found its most congenial musical exponent in Schubert, who captured the poet's intention and sentiment in the shortest and simplest song as well as in the majestic great hymns, and could give musical shape to the smallest poetical details as well as following a dithyrambic outburst with the glowing fury of passion. We find among the various poems of Goethe's set to tones by Schubert, *lieder*, ballads, romances, songs of Nature, religious and philosophic verses. The famous series opens with the song " Gretchen am Spinnrad," which the boy of seventeen composed on October 14th, 1814. Even this first song was a work of genius— the very first modern song with an artistic accompaniment, thus inaugurating a new epoch in the history of the musical lyric. The motion of the spinning-wheel is the motive of the accompaniment, above the humming rhythm of which the singing voice rises from the heart of the poem, reaching heights of pathos and passion with the words " *sein Händedruck und ach ! sein Kuss !* "

The second great triumph which the young master owed to the poet was the composition of the " Erlkönig " in 1816. Here Schubert's power of expression showed itself with still greater force ; the rhythm and harmony are of the richest character. The luxuriant picture composition of the piano accompaniment brings out all the dæmonic elements in the Goethean ballad : the racing triplets, the ghostly ride through the storm in wind and mist, the shrill discords, the torment, horror and cries of the frightened boy—all combine to produce a masterly effect, ending with the moving and dramatic recitative telling of the arrival of the father at the inn with the child dead in his arms. Schubert in this composition has transcended every limit hitherto known and created something entirely novel and fresh. Also in other poems of Goethe—in the " Heidenröslein," (the popularity of which has made it a *Volkslied*), " Wonne der Wehmut," " Nähe des Geliebten," " Trost in Thränen," " An Mignon," " Meeresstille," " Rastlose Liebe," " Schäfers Klagelied "—he understood exactly how, in the piano accompaniment by expressive melody and artistic form, to nuance the sentiment of every one of the poet's words. It may seem extraordinary that Goethe never recognised his sympathetic interpreter in music, although the friends of Schubert were not backwards in sending the poet examples of his composition, and especially strange was it that he had no understanding for the stupendous music of the " Erlkönig." But Goethe's musical taste and limited knowledge of music were satisfied with the compositions of his contemporaries, Reichardt and Zelter, who to-day count for little. The complete recasting of the poem treated into a new musical work of art, in which the poem has become inseparably united with and merged in the music, was beyond his comprehension, and he was accustomed to having his poems set to music by every new composer who cropped up. Only once in later years, when Wilhelmine Schröder-Devrient performed for him the " Erlkönig " in masterly fashion (April, 1830), the aged poet was moved to the somewhat cool remark : " I have heard this composition once before and it did not impress me, but as you have given it the whole stands out as a really complete picture."

Schubert also wrote music to poems of Schiller, for whom he cherished a great love and reverence, being attracted in Schiller to an idealism similar to his own. Nevertheless, the reflective character of Schiller's lyrical genius made it less responsive to the melodious rhythm which suited Goethe's poesie wonderfully. Schubert's genius, which was capable of finding a way of entering into the feelings of poets of every description, and, in fact, had set to music a whole century of lyrics, also discovered for Schiller a fitting characteristic musical style. The great dramatist, without having any special gift for music himself, had a finer feeling for the art than Goethe. He had written much that was beautiful on the subject of his relations to music in the essay, " Uber Charakter-stellung in der Musik," and in his famous letter of December 29th, 1797, to Goethe, he speaks of his tendency to regard the opera " with confidence " as a means, " like the Bacchanalian choruses, of giving a nobler form to tragedy, and, through the power of music, stimulating the senses to a more perfect receptivity." Schubert endeavoured earnestly to master the reflective elements in Schiller's poetry, so as to give it a dramatic style in music corresponding with the poet's temperament. He recognised the difficulty of the task, in consequence of the enormous extent and length of Schiller's poems. He set to music altogether forty-one of these, and accounted for their proving less popular than many of the songs he had composed to less (in comparison) significant texts by their unusual length, which rendered it difficult to give them a compact, unified form. In spite of this, there are some rare pearls of Schubert's art among his Schiller settings. For example, " Gruppe aus dem Tartarus," " Elysium," and the beautiful romances " Das

Mädchens Klage," " Das Mädchen aus dem Fremde," the ballads " Ritter Toggenburg," " Der Alpenjäger," the lyrics " Sehnsucht," " An der Frühling, " Die Entzückung an Laura," and others. The classical poetry of Herder and Klopstock also gave inspiration to Schubert's muse. The former's " Die Verklärung," in its artistic form and mature treatment, belongs to some of the most successful of Schubert's earlier songs. Into Klopstock's love-song " Rosenband " (" Im Frühlings Garten fand ich sie ") is infused the whole tenderness and sweetness of the Schubertian melody. Elegies which are among the best lyrical work of Klopstock were set by Schubert to appropriately melancholy airs ; also his great religious hymns were reverently interpreted into music with sublime effect. Among older poets who inspired Schubert were Schubart, (whose " Forelle " has become one of the master's most popular songs) the two poets of the " Hainbund," Stolberg and Hölty, and further, Matthisson, Ossian, Kosegarten and Claudius.

In the first years of his composing, Schubert occupied himself chiefly with setting Matthisson's verses to music. It was not only the gay and playful Anacreontic songs, " Abend " and " Lied der Liebe," and the much-sung evening song, " Geist der Liebe," that he composed with the most finished artistry, but the more serious elegiac poems like " Geisternähe," " Totenopfer," and " Adelaide." For the songs of Ossian, the poetic sentiment of which had once exercised on the classic writers Klopstock, Herder and Goethe great influence, Schubert created a specially characteristic melody. He knew how to represent all the sublimity of the poetic pictures and the intensity of the poet's feeling for Nature and the fantastic character of his poesie. Famous above all is " Kolmas Klage," and the wonderful rhapsodic songs, " Cronnan " and " Die Nacht."

A masterpiece of song is " Auf dem Wasser zu singen," the words by Leopold Graf Stolberg, a poet of the *Sturm und Drang* period, and his charming " An die Natur " and " Daphne am Bach."

From the temperamental poet, Matthias Claudius, the master selected twelve *lieder* for composition in his first period ; they were nearly all composed in November, 1816. The most celebrated are " Der Tod und das Mädchen," a masterly song which is reproduced in the D Minor quartet in the form of a Mozartian ariä, " Am Grabe Anselmos," dedicated to the singer Vogl, the declama-

tory " Bei dem Grabe meines Vaters," the " Abendlied " and
" Wiegenlied," and the gay and graceful " An die Nachtigall."

To the year 1815, that particularly productive year in Schubert's
first period, belong the twenty songs to the words of Kosegarten,
of whom personally little or nothing is known. The music to these
was the work of a few days, and came forth in a positively volcanic
eruption of the creative spirit. Among them are the pathetic " An
die Untergehende Sonne," the solemn " Nachtgesang," which
paints the dying autumn, the sad " Das Sehnen," " Die Mond-
nacht," and others filled with a gentle erotic sentiment, " Huldi-
gung," " Die Täuschung," " Alles um Liebe."

The highest point in Schubert's lyrical work is reached in his
setting of the songs of Wilhelm Müller, of Dessau, the romanticist
and enthusiast for the " antique world." Next to Goethe's
poems, they play the most important part in Schubert's composition
of songs. Two song cycles—the idea of a cycle of songs may
have come to him from Beethoven's *lieder-kreis* " An die ferne
Geliebte "—were set to music by Schubert from poems by Wilhelm Müller in 1822 and 1825. The cycle of " Die schöne Müllerin " consists of twenty songs in four parts. The introduction
contains numbers 1 to 4. This brings the miller apprentice on to
the high road, along which he wanders till he comes to the mill
and enters its service. He is soon in love with the miller's daughter.
His thoughts are always flying to her. He holds converse with the
flowers and stars, and asks them whether she loves him. He sings
her a morning greeting, and sends her a nosegay which shall speak
for him. But his courtship remains uncertain, and all love's
yearning and suffering fill his heart. At last he gets a hearing and
his pain turns to rapture. But it lasts only a short time, this happiness of love described in numbers 11 to 13. Then the huntsman appears, and his entry breeds jealousy and resentment in
the poor youth's soul. He is broken-hearted, and the story ends
with the death of the young lover. The ripples of the same stream
which lured him to the miller's beautiful daughter sing his death
knell.

The opening number, the well-known " Das Wandern ist des
Müllers Lust," has apparently nothing directly to do with the
story related in the cycles. It is not characteristic of Schubert's
style, or that of any other composer ; it is one of those vagabond
songs which is reserved in the mouths of the people for joyful

marches and wandering adventures, songs which are common property and, unwritten, are handed down from generation to generation. It is open to doubt whether Schubert invented this melody himself or adapted it from songs he had heard often sung on the high road by wandering tramps. It is a chorus song, pretty in its rusticity, and, whether original or not, admirably suited to fix in the mind a picture of the young apprentice at the moment that he starts on his wanderings, singing to himself, hopeful and in good humour.

His figure shows itself first in more detail in the second song, when he turns off the road and follows the brook, with which he holds a conversation. Schubert's intention to depict him as a simple, ingenuous youth is shown in the words " *Ich weiss nicht wie mir wurde, noch wer den Rat mir gab,*" and here there is no fore-shadowing of coming pathos, which is perhaps rather too obviously avoided. Remarkable from a musical point of view is the expression of fantastic elements in the singing water rendered by a subdued bass melody.

Among the songs in this cycle, which lose in significance when sung separately and not in a sequence, is the third number. If one doesn't know what has gone before, its beginning in sixteen-time, dancing demi-semi-tones on the piano excites astonished curiosity. But in connection with the gaily gliding play of the ripples in the previous song, it gives splendid expression to the surprise of the young wanderer when he suddenly sees the stately mill rising before his eyes. For the next few moments his surprise increases as one fresh object after another reveals itself. The melodious declamation of the singing part is full of childlike delight ; the youthful miller rejoices at the sight of the house, its shining windows and the bright sunshine. The little stream laughs in the piano bass as if at a good joke. This is one of the liveliest and friendliest of all Schubert's numbers, whether taken in the context or not. The fourth number gives for the first time a clearly defined impression of the miller youth's bashful nature in " Die Danksagung an den Bach." The mixture of pleasure and timidity with which he regards the miller's daughter is a true Schubertian touch.

In the " Feierabend " we see him in the mill itself, and here he comes before us for the first time as a manly character. There is power in the way in which he wishes he had " a thousand arms,"

A Schubert Evening
Oil sketch by Moriz von Schwind
(Schubert Museum, Vienna)

and in contrast all the more effective is the fervid simplicity and warmth of heart expressed in the melody by the words " *dass die Müllerin merkte meinen, treuen Sinn.*" This number is great and full of touches of genius ; by the simplest method the scene is enlarged and figures are portrayed in a few strong strokes. Few notes are devoted to the master of the mill and his daughter, but they serve to make them known to us. The change from minor to major, the poetry of the end, when the poor, tired youth seems to be sinking into the earth from weariness, yet, as if in a dream, babbles, about his beautiful " Müllerin "—all is a story in music. In the following five numbers the young miller's love affair becomes a serious matter. The best known of them is " Ungeduld," a masterpiece as big as it is short. It contains fever and recovery, tempestuous weather and the broad rays of the sun, and, in conclusion, " Dein ist mein Herz."

This expression of an inward haste, of an unmanned emotion, reoccurs in other numbers of the Müller cycle : in " Jäger," and somewhat more faintly in " Eifersucht und Stolz," in the bright and radiant " Mein." This kind of nervous nuance suits very well the gentle suffering temperament. The nature of the young miller would be too girlishly tender without these strong outbursts of psychic emotion, and it is only when we have learnt to know this side of him that we find his softer mood so winning. " Ungeduld " stands out in contrast to the other songs in the courting phase, in that it is the only one in which hope and courage live in the breast of the youth. The others are filled with a touching spirit of resignation and sadness, which is attributable to Schubert's own conception of the miller's story. On a first reading he was struck overwhelmingly with its pathos, and so it comes that in his musical setting the tragic *dénouement* is never left out of sight, and the hearers are constantly reminded of it. This element calling for our sympathy even makes itself felt in the stage of the history at which the miller is supposed to be happy and the poet lets him enjoy his happiness. In the humorous " Mein " Schubert has introduced on his own initiative a little melancholy episode ; it is to be found in the words " *Ach ! so muss ich ganz allein.*" And still more distinctly this inclination to sadness is heard in the " Pause " in a voice too deeply tuned for the psychic organ of this quite simple creature. There can be no doubt that in the course of composition Schubert lost sight, somewhat, of the miller boy, and went beyond the limits of his class. At the end of the verse, for instance, " Des Müller's Blumen," makes a touching and attractive termination, but is too serious and too exalted for the situation. We find in this part of the work other passages which scarcely fit the simple miller tone. Only at the very end of the whole cycle he recaptures the quiet, noble sentiment, and unites it with the son of the people's modesty and reserve.

The most beautiful parts of the whole cycle are the numbers from 15 to 18. What a wonderful representation is here of the sufferings of a noble man's heart that has received its death wound, yet clings to love for the woman who has dealt the wound! A heart which even when dying is jubilant at the thought that she who has broken it may remember: " *Und wenn sie wandelt am Hügel vorbei und denkt im Herzen, der meint es treu ! dann, Blümlein alle, heraus, heraus ! "*

What a burst of spring music, what a glorified apotheosis of the poor miller! And even now the composer does not spare the poor heart yet another last struggle. The youth, in despairing hope, turns to the brook and calls " Turn back ! " Then he is seized with bitter irony when, in the broken tones of the lower octave, he says " *Mein Schatz hat's Grün so gern* " (" My love is so fond of green "). In the " Bösen Farbe " the first bars of the piano are full of grim wrath ; then he sings in lively tones, " *Ich möchte ziehen in die Welt hinaus*," but one knows that this outburst of joyous spirits is only gallows-humour, turning into a wild cry of pain. In number 19 he sings with the serenity of a soul who has done with life. Now the brook breaks out again with a heavenly, comradely song, and the poem ends with a simple quiet lullaby, from the even rhythm of which sounds a beautiful grave-side oration of sorrow and consolation.

Nearly four years after " Die schöne Müllerin " came the other great song-cycle, " Die Winterreise." Again the poet draws a wanderer and endows him with a natural mode of expression in the healthy language of the people. But this wanderer sets forth in the winter in ice and snow. His footstep lags and is tired ; he is sorrowing for the love he has lost. The pale phantom-like figure is staggering along the road of Calvary to the grave. The motive of the music, mostly in a subdued minor key, is melancholy. It sounds in plaintive airs of wild pain, cries out and groans in despair, in glorified resignation, reaching at last a plasticity of mystic vision far removed from the earth. There is a great advance in maturity of artistic development since the " Müllerlied," in musical expression, in the tone-painting of moods, in the soulful depth of the melody, which is no longer simply *Volkslied* melody, but rises to the highest ideal of the song in art. A new world of music opens its doors. It is a work of a man who has matured, who has gazed shuddering into the deep, and seen all that is vain and worthless in this life ; who is tired of living, and feels that he is drawing near the valley of the shadow of death.

The cycle includes twenty-four songs. Schubert finished the first part in the early months of the year 1827, the second in the late autumn after his Graz journey. A short connected melody opens the cycle. The wanderer's " Gute Nacht " sounds forth in a stream of harmony, tremulous and sad . . . and as the wind stirs the flag flying from the roof so the low plaintive melody stirs our heart-strings. Pain sobs on in the petrified sorrow of frozen tears, which fall without relieving the heart of its grief. And often one hears the complaint becoming fainter, the melancholy spirit softened and consoled, and the voice of the wanderer seems to sing an old *Volkslied* as he comes to the fountain before the door, where stands the linden tree. Then comes, like a ghostly apparition, the dream of spring, the spring-like magic melody, which, in the middle of winter, sings of gay flowers and green meadows. But there are the ice flowers still on the window panes, and the dream of spring fades. And now the post-horn sounds, depressing instead of enlivening the sick heart, whose last hope has died with the autumn leaves. Ever new tone-pictures in a minor key arise one after the other. There is the stream, ice-bound, tired like the heart of the wanderer, the sky dark with the flight of crows, which are his uncanny companions, and the flutter of whose wings is heard in the piano accompaniment ; there is night in the village, the magnificent picture of the stormy dawn, the signpost with its outstretched hand pointing always to the goal and awakening a last flickering ray of hope that one may yet be master of one's fate, and once more in cheerful and merry mood fare into the world. And then, most touching of all, the organ-grinder ; from the deep bass of the bagpipes rises the melancholy melody of the song of the organ-grinder, with his empty plate—the picture of Schubert's own life, moving, simple and deeply pathetic. " *Wunderlicher Alter, soll ich mit dir geh'n, willst du zu meinen Liedern deine Leier drehn?* "

By the side of these two song-cycles, in which Schubert reached the highest peak of his lyrical creation, ranks worthily as swansong his well-known cycle of songs from the text of Rellstab, Seidl and Heine—in all fourteen songs, none of which have any connection with each other. It begins with seven songs by Rellstab, among which is the " Ständchen," with its immortal melody and accompaniment written as if it were meant for the guitar. The six songs which Schubert composed to words of Heine belong to the most beautiful inspiration of his muse. He discovered them in the then just published " Buch der Lieder," and, charmed with their poetic quality, he at once set them to music. The original quite subjective character of these poems led Schubert to make a new departure in order to find a fitting musical medium in which to paint the Heine poesie. He made use of a freer, more recitative, dramatic style, almost approaching that of the speaking song. The rhythm of " Atlas," with its gloomy, rolling accompaniment, its moving melody and change of expression, achieves a colossal effect. The modulation in " Ihr Bild " is simpler. The singing voice glides into unison with the accompaniment, and the " picture," which once was radiant in life, hovers like a mysterious vision over the chords, conjured up by the memory, to sink once more into the dark shadow of the harmony. The charming melody of the " Fischermädchen " has a light swaying rhythm with chords that swing like a barcarolle, and this marks the older style of the song. In " Die Stadt " Schubert gives a wonderful impressionist picture in tones of a town seen in the glamour of the evening twilight, with its towers rising against the horizon.

Equal in dramatic boldness of effect is the musical colour in ' Am Meer." After the mysterious harmonies of the short introduction, the melodious song begins in unison with the accompaniment. Solemn chords paint the picture of a wide shining sea, aglow in the last rays of the setting sun, then the scene changes with the rising of the mist, the swelling of the waves, the flight of the gulls, and sounds which come before a storm. Uncanny is the rushing, tremulous piano accompaniment, above which the song in melodious recitative rises thrillingly. The same majestic chords with which the *lied* began close the dramatic tone-picture. Perhaps even grander is the power of musical expression in " Doppelgänger," where the emotion reaches the heights of passion. Above the solemn, gloomy chords of the accompaniment sounds the emotional tone-painting of the ethereal moonlight, and the despair in the love-song of the wanderer, who, to his horror, sees the reflection of his own image as in the mirror of the picture. The suggestion of the dramatic painting is increased by the recitative style of the song. Schubert has here developed a form of expression that he had often made use of before, and has so intensified the tone-painting, both in the accompaniment and in the declamation of the singing voice, that it led the way to a new epoch in lyrical music, and was later further elaborated by the masters who followed in his footsteps, more particularly by Hugo Wolf.

The sojourn of leaders of the romanticist movement in Vienna, where they excited much attention, naturally led to Schubert setting some of their poems to music. Not, strange to say, Tieck, Brentano and Eichendorff, but the brothers Schlegel, Novalis and La Motte Fouqué. He set three of Wilhelm Schlegel's sonnets, translated from the Italian, one of which was the expressive " Lob der Tränen " ; of the younger Schlegel, Friedrich, he composed music to sixteen poems.

Novalis, the mystical, lyrical poet and great leader of the early romanticists, inspired Schubert's muse with many beautiful subjects—notably the famous hymns, including the communion hymn " Wenige wissen das Geheimniss der Liebe," and " Ich sehe dich in tausend Bildern, Maria."

From the works of Ludwig Uhland, head of the Swabian school, whose musical interpreter was Konradin Kreutzer, Schubert chose only one poem, " Frühlingsglaube." This was one of the master's most popular songs, full of longing and joyous springtime sentiment. Also Rückert and Platen inspired some fine creations of Schubert's. From the former he took " Sei mir gegrüsst," the artistically perfect in harmony and feeling " Du bist die Ruh," and the delicious " Lachen und Weinen." Platen supplied him with " Du liebst mich nicht " and " Die Liebe hat gelogen."

A poet with whom the master associated personally, and who had encouraged him to devote himself entirely to music, was Theodore Körner, the poet of the War of Freedom and Burgtheater dramatist. Schubert was introduced to him by his friend Spaun, and he composed music to twelve of his poems. They belong to his very early period, and are, for the most part, written in the simple, straightforward strophic style.

With regard to the Austrian poets, the greatest lyricist of them all, Nikolaus Lenau, came into prominence only after Schubert's death ; and Grillparzer's lyrics lacked the specific musical character for being set to notes, though the master composed at least one effective song to his text, " Bertas Lied in der Nacht " (from the " Ahnfrau "). A more important *rôle* in his compositions was played by the poetry of Schubert's intimate friends. Their names do not adorn any history of literature, the poems were mostly amateur attempts, yet many of their verses have been immortalised by Schubert's genius. Of the poetising Schubertians, Franz Schober supplied the master with a dozen poems, the splendid " Schiffers Scheidelied," " Viola," " Am Bach im Frühling," " Vergissmein-nicht," the lovely hymn " An die Musik," etc. From Spaun he set " Der Jüngling und der Tod," and " Schwanengesang." From Bauernfeld, " Der Vater mit dem Kind " ; and many other poems by Senn, Stadler and Baron Schlechta. But undoubtedly his friend Mayrhofer was the most lyrically gifted of the Schubertians, and for him the master set forty-seven poems to music. Mayrhofer's thoughtful and often melancholy lyrics had a great attraction for Schubert, and during the time that they lived together exercised a considerable influence on his development. Among Schubert's compositions to texts by Mayrhofer are to be found many pearls of music. They form, with Goethe's and Müller's songs, the zenith of Schubert's lyrical achievement ; and they are, besides, a memorial of a noble friendship. Their period falls between the years 1814 and 1824. The years 1814 to 1816 brought forth the first Mayrhofer songs in simpler form, such as " Am See," " Liane," " Abschied," " Liebesend," " Der Hirt," " Geheimniss," " Abendlied der Fürstin." The first of the really great Mayrhofer songs belong to the year 1817, and these include the beautiful, serious " Philoktet," " Fahrt zum Hades," " Antigone und Œdip," the powerful " Memnon," dedicated to the singer Vogl, " Uraniens Flucht," " Iphigenia," the exquisite tone-pictures " Auf der Donau," " Nach einem Gewitter," " Am Strome," and " Wie Ulfru fischt." The years 1818 to 1820 saw a new departure in Schubert's setting of Mayrhofer poems in the songs " An die Freunde," " Beim Winde," " Sternennächte," " Orest auf Tauris " and " Der zürnenden Diana." After a pause, the friends collaborated again in 1822 to 1824, and once more Schubert crowned his comrade's verse with enchanting melody. This was the third and last Mayrhofer group, and comprised the romantic "Nachtviolen," the solemn "Sieg," the "Heliopolis-Gesänge," the profoundly psychic "Abendstern," and "Auflösung," and, above all, the celebrated "Gondelfahrer" for four voices.

Worthy of mention among other Austrian poets who inspired Schubert's muse was the talented Johann Gabriel Seidl, from whose poems the master in 1826 and 1828 composed in all ten pieces: the emotional "Der Wanderer an den Mond," the "Zügenglöcklein," the charming melodious refrain songs, "Die Unterscheidung," "Bei dir Allein," the beautiful "Wiegenlied," and the romantic chorus for men's voices and horns, "Nachtgesang im Walde." From the dramatist, Matthäus von Collin, he drew the magnificent ballad, "Der Zwerg," composed during an afternoon's walk with friend Randhartinger, and the *lieder* overflowing with melodious melancholy, "Wehmut" and "Nacht und Träume." The celebrated Austrian authoress of popular romances of the Biedermeier time, Karoline Pichler, is represented in Schubert's lyrics in the year 1816 by "Der Sänger am Felsen" and "Der Unglückliche." Among the German writers of texts for songs are numerous small, insignificant poets whose names have only come down to posterity through Schubert's genius, such as Georg Schmidt, of Lübeck, whose "Wanderer" is one of the composer's most inspired productions. It is not to be wondered at, considering the universality of Schubert's lyrical creations, that foreign texts were utilised by him. We have already mentioned the songs and ballads of Ossian. From ancient Greece come "So wird der Mann, der sonder Zwang gerecht ist" (translated from Æschylus by Mayrhofer), and "An die Leier" (translated by Bruchmann). Of Italian sonnets there were translations by Schlegel of Dante and Petrarch, an arietta from Goldoni, various songs of Metastasio. Among these are three written for the opera singer Lablache, whom Schubert had got acquainted with at reunions in the house of Hofrat Kiesewetter. Famous creations of the master are Shakespeare's "Hark the Lark" from "Cymbeline," and "To Sylvia" from "The Two Gentlemen of Verona," and songs from Scott's "Lady of the Lake."

In songs on a more ambitious scale—chorus part-songs for men's voices—Schubert was successful, and composed much which was of great value. He may have been attracted to writing for several voices by the possibility offered by this form of intensifying his tone-painting and musically in developing still more the interpretation of the poem. Here he made use of, besides the piano, other instrumentation. Schubert has rightly been called the Master of the Song, and, with equal justice, the classic of literature for men's chorus. From his earliest youth he had occupied himself with compositions of the kind, and continued to do so till the end of his life. Works for special occasions were among these creations, as, for instance, the chorus for the celebration of his teacher Salieri's jubilee. One of the most beautiful things he ever composed in the lyrical line was " Gesang der Geister über den Wassern," from Goethe, for eight voices, with viola, 'cello and double bass accompaniment. After several re-writings it was performed on March 7th, 1821, at a concert given at the Kärntnertortheater, with the " Erlkönig," which was received with enthusiasm, whereas the beautiful part-song completely failed to elicit any applause. " Herr Schubert's chorus for eight voices," wrote the critic of the *Allgemeine Musikalischezeitung*, " appeared to the audience to be an accumulation of musical modulations without rhyme or reason. The composer resembles in this sort of effort a chariot-driver whose team of eight horses swerve first to the right and then to the left without making any progress along the road." To-day this song numbers with other compositions for several voices—for example, " Die Nachthelle," " Grab und Mond," " Das Dörfchen," " Sehnsucht," Klopstock's powerful " Schlachtlied," the romantic " Nachtgesang im Walde " for four men's voices with four horns, the splendid " Hymn " for eight male voices, " Ruhe, schönstes Gluck der Erde," to the finest achievements of every choir for men's voices in the world. Schubert lifted the part-song from mere commonplace sing-song to the level of sublime art—and the theatre continued to draw him always like a magnet. Our master never abandoned hope that some time or other his music would conquer the stage. Undaunted by rebuffs, he worked at one musical play after another, and opera after opera—a bitter Calvary in his artistic career, for all his efforts in this direction proved vain. Even if something was produced it never met with the expected success. He knocked at the doors of theatre directors, and generally they remained obdurately closed, as was only likely at a period when Rossini ruled the opera repertory. Schubert was no dramatist; he did not possess the fiery theatrical glow of a Mozart or Richard Wagner and he had no idea of stage routine. The libretti placed at his service by Madame von Chezy, Schober, Castelli and

Josef Kupelwieser were so poor, that they did not meet the require-
ments of the most ordinary stage technique. The many lyrical
beauties with which the charm of his music invested these literary
patchworks, the delightful *entr'actes* and ballet music, could not
compensate for lack of dramatic movement, the absence of an
erotic element and exciting situations. But even from Schubert's
unsuccessful operatic creations his successors derived valuable
stimulus. Here, too, was a phase of development in German
music not to be undervalued. The elements of German romanticism are to be found in his operas, though not in a definite unity
of form. The material he put to music was essentially romantic;
one has only to think of " Des Teufel's Lustschloss," with its vivid
ghost scenes, the Spanish story of " Fernando," " Die beiden
Freunde von Salamanka," " Alfonso und Estrella," the use made
of the " Song of Roland " in " Fierrabras," the scene of which is laid
in the time of the Crusades; and romantic is the music in its colour-
ful instrumentation and bold harmony, and its ample application of
the chorus, especially men's chorus.

Liszt, in writing on Schubert's " Alfonso und Estrella," says:
" Schubert possessed the gift in the highest degree of dramatising
lyrical inspirations, but what he found beyond his power was the
scene. His sublime muse, with gaze fixed ever in the clouds, preferred to cast her azure mantle over asphodel fields, woods and
mountains, and was unversed in the artificial raiment in which the
dramatic muse moves cautiously between curtain and footlights.
His winged strophes took alarm at the rattle of machinery and
revolving wheels. He is to be rather compared with the mountain
stream, which breaks loose from the snowy peaks and in a foaming
torrent descends, veiling the rocks with a network of sparkling
iridescent drops, than to the majestic rolling river that waters the
plain. . . ."

Nevertheless, Schubert exercised an influence on the development of the opera and its style which cannot be overlooked. The
way in which, by harmonic declamation, he made of a song or a
ballad a little musical drama in itself, enhanced by tone-painting
of often the deepest pathos, opened up new paths for coming
artists in opera. Through the introduction of a *leit-motiv*, which
runs organically through the whole song and fixes its style, as, for
instance, the whir of the spinning-wheel in " Gretchen am Spinnrad," and in many songs in the " Winterreise," Schubert, with

the boldness of genius, indicates the road which led to the style of the Wagnerian music drama.

In the department of the symphony and chamber music, Schubert's creations are priceless. Here his genius spreads its wings with mighty strokes, and his fantasy pours forth its treasures in rich abundance. As a composer for instruments, Schubert is the worthy follower of Beethoven. In certain respects he struck out a new and original line in the symphony, as he had originated new æsthetic laws for the song. While Beethoven in his powerful musical epics speaks to us in ever new ways of the mysteries of existence and the gigantic sovereign might of the human mind in bidding defiance to fate, Schubert, the romanticist, finds expression for every lyrical emotion which his fantasy evokes in beautiful tone-pictures ; he reproduces the creations of his fantasy for us glorified by music. As Hugo Riemann truly says, the first lyricalist among symphony composers, Schubert, with his almost unconscious leaning to picturesqueness, increases the capability of music to create in our imagination pictures of a world of wonder and romance. His music is not, like Haydn's, Mozart's, Beethoven's, an exclusive and purely subjective expression of feeling, but he has always something to portray, to paint, even when he is developing a theme.

Entirely influenced, as romanticist, by *Stimmung*, Schubert as a symphony composer was impressionist. Thoughts succeeded thoughts, melody followed melody ; it was an outpouring of tones in a multitude of motives running concurrently ; his works in their symphonic form resemble those we meet with again later in Anton Bruckner. The Schubertian themes exist for themselves alone and are self-contained, so that they are little adapted for thematical treatment in the style of the old masters. Thus Schubert's symphonies apparently are wanting often in the strictly logical form of the older classical writers, and have not the classic unity of Beethoven's. Neither do they reflect those impassioned conflicts which the Titan Beethoven fought to the bitter end in tones. They are frequently full of heavenly *longueurs* ; they breathe the romantic spirit, testify to the inexhaustible wealth of melody within him. They are the tone-paintings of youth, and are full of the spring of the Viennese landscape, the fragrance of apple blossom and lilac, the rustling of the woods, the singing of the stream.

If we count the lost " Gastein Symphony," Schubert wrote in all

nine symphonies.   Most of them belong to his early years, when
the tone-poet played in the amateur orchestra at the Konvikt
establishment and had every opportunity of experimenting with
instrumental composition.   He was sixteen when he finished his
first symphony, in D, on October 28th, 1813, written for the
birthday celebration of the Director of the school, Innocenz Lang.
It was played by the Konvikt Orchestra.   The work is of the old
school, reminiscent of Haydn, Mozart, and the young Beethoven ;
the melody is clear and cheerful, the instrumentation simple and
transparent.   The year 1815, so rich in his creations, produced
two symphonies.   The second, in B, finished on March 24th, has
a slow introduction leading to the largo, which contains the chief
theme, with solemn rhythm for wind.   Schubert built his themes
now after the pattern of the Viennese classical composers.
Mozartian fervour characterises the second movement, Haydn
is the model for the minuet, the finale is filled with the rhythms of
Viennese folk music.   His third symphony, in D, finished a few
months later, is genuinely Schubertian and *wienerisch*.   In the
minuet the grace of the Vienna *Vorstadt* invites you, fiddling
alluringly, to join in the dance.   If these three creations were
tentative efforts on the part of the young master, the fourth
symphony, in C minor, which followed in the year 1816, the
so-called " Tragic," is a remarkable advance.   Beethoven's C
Minor Symphony was a favourite of Schubert's, and may have
served him as a model.   But the young Schubert was not tragic
in Beethoven's sense ;   he did not thunder with his fist on the
portals of Fate ;   he felt no violent rebellion against the gods.
The suffering of the lyrical poet-composer finds vent here in an
overwhelming expression of sadness and resignation.   The first
movement begins with an *adagio molto,* and above the accompaniment of the strings rises plaintively a yearning melody.   Then
follows the *allegro vivace,* full of passion, which, from the depths,
struggles stormily for light and beauty.   Lyrical and truly
Schubertian is the singing *andante.*   In the finale, again, the
tragedy of the human soul is heard, and the latter is led by yearning
from the drabness of everyday life to the bright heights of dream-
land.   In this symphony Schubert has in many respects found
himself.   He follows no longer in the footsteps of his classical
forerunners ;   the romanticist who paints feelings and moods in
tones is awakened.   In the autumn of the same year the master

began his fifth symphony, in B, which, simply orchestrated without trumpet or drum, seems to have been composed for an
amateur band. Herein the Schubert who loves life, rather than
the tragic Schubert, is in evidence; especially are the trio of the
minuet and the closing movement remarkable for fresh inventive-
ness and *wienerisch* joyous melody. In the year 1817 followed the
sixth symphony, in D. The first movement is again introduced
with an *adagio*. The leading motive displays Schubertian
melody ; the instrumentation is somewhat thin, as if intended for
a small orchestra. In the third movement, with its dance rhythm,
the composer, following the example of Beethoven, has written
for the first time " *scherzo* " instead of " minuet." At this point
came a pause of four years in the composition of Schubert's
symphonies. He practised his talent and creative power in
chamber music, and not till 1822 did he launch a new symphonic
work, having been recently occupied with a sketch of one,
the so-called E major, which never, however, got further. It
was his seventh symphony, the famous " Unfinished," the finest
of Schubert's masterpieces in this domain. The work consists
of only two movements, *allegro moderato* and *andante con moto*.
For the third movement, which was to have been a *scherzo* only,
a sketch exists, and in the original score only a page of this is
orchestrated. It is not known why the tone-poet left this symphony
unfinished. Was it because pressure of other work prevented
his going on with it ? Did the work seem to him sufficient in two
movements ? Or was he not satisfied with his sketch of the third ?
These questions are really futile, because the two movements of
the " Unfinished " Symphony are regarded by posterity as so
perfect in themselves that they are rightly ranked among the most
magnificent creations of the whole orchestral literature of the
world. In hardly any other work of the master is the magic
charm of Schubert's muse in all its melody and grace so triumphant ;
perhaps it is the most Schubertian of all Schubert's works.

" When after the introductory bars of the allegro," wrote
Hanslik on the subject of this symphony, " clarinets and oboes
chant their sweet song above the soft murmur of the violins,
every child knows who the composer is, and the half-suppressed
exclamation ' Schubert ! ' is whispered through the concert-hall.
He has scarcely made his entry, but one knows the sound of his
footstep and his way of opening the door. Now when there

sounds above the minor song the contrasting G major theme on the 'cellos, a charming *lied* movement of almost rural domesticity, there is a thrill of rejoicing in every breast; we feel he is standing there, after a long absence, in our midst. The whole of this movement is a stream of sweetest melody; the power of genius has made it so crystal clear that one can see every little pebble on the ground. And warmth and radiance is over all; one can almost hear the leaves rustling in the golden sunshine. The *andante* gains in width and grandeur as it unfolds. Tones of sorrow and of wrath are rare in this song of fervid happiness and serene contentment. The storms of passion are more musically effective than dangerous. It seems as if the composer could not tear himself from this sweet air, for the end of the *adagio* is long, perhaps too long, drawn out. . . . At the close of the *andante* his flight of inspiration loses itself in the invisible, but we still hear the beat of its wings."

Like the first movement, the *andante con moto* has no concise form, according to rules laid down by the classical writers of symphonies. It is a flood of Schubertian melodies which flow side by side, an abundance of thoughts in sound that playfully join hands. The instruments are like voices coming from the human breast, and sung by human lips. It is a naïve, primitive art springing straight from the soul without any collaboration of the intellect, untrammelled by premeditation.

The composer never heard a performance of the symphony. It is possible that he may have entertained the idea of producing it at one of the Society of Music Friends concerts. But, according to the rules of the Society, only the works of amateur members, and not of professional musicians, could be given by the Society. In 1825 he sent the score to the Styrian Music Society, of which he was an honorary member, through Anselm Hütten-brenner, in the hope of its being performed in Graz. Extra-ordinarily enough, Hüttenbrenner received the symphony and kept its possession a secret for years. It was not till May 1st, 1865, that the Viennese Court Orchestra conductor, Johann Harbeck, discovered it in Graz, and soon after it was performed for the first time.

In the last years of his life Schubert wrote his symphonic master-piece, the C Major Symphony. Again a long pause had elapsed since his last symphonic work. Standing in the shadow of the

giant Beethoven, the young composer, with his irresistible ambition
to approach the heights the older master had reached, waited till,
through ceaseless labour and artistic maturity, he should have
acquired, by his creations in chamber music, technical perfection
as well as experience in gathering together his thoughts into a
symmetrical apotheosis.   Again there rushed on him an avalanche
of sublime ideas, one giving birth to the other, so rapidly and with
such volume that they were difficult to control and build into a
structure of surpassing grandeur and beauty.   A solemn and
romantic *andante* for horns and wind instruments introduces the
first movement.   Soon the strings dominate, but gradually give
place, as in the triolet motive, to the brass, the oboes and bassoons,
to the flutes and clarinets.   The melody floats through various
combinations of chords, and its play on change of harmony
begins ever afresh, first gliding from major to minor, till in a jubilant
coda all chords and harmonies mingle and fill the whole orchestra
in the solemn-sounding C major theme of the opening.

The *andante con moto* is rich in beautiful motives.   The bassoons
begin in folk style and rhythm; above the oboe sings its
plaintive melody and the clarinets follow.   The motive leaps
from A minor to A major, and the melody breathes a true German
fervour.   It rises in impetuous passion, the strings burst into a
romantic dance movement, and again clarinets and bassoon begin
to accent the theme.   The A minor motive sounds more distinct,
the orchestra becomes more emotional, the oboe sobs forth its
melancholy song, the flood of various melodies sweeps by once
more.   And now a sub-theme begins, played by the 'cello, and is
taken over by the oboe.   The movement glides from F major to
A major.   In conclusion, the harmonies swing back once more
into the original A minor theme, and the movement dies away in
resignation.

The *scherzo*, bubbling with joy in life, reminds us of Bruckner's
famous *scherzo* in its blissful melodiousness.   It wakes the
orchestra to new stormy soarings.   A motive full of fiery rhythm
comes next, and then a countrified air from the Austrian mountains, wonderfully transformed, rising coquettishly on high notes,
to descend again in swaying undulations.   The trio, a broad
terzet melody, is the yearning in song of the romanticist who
has drained the blissful cup of inspiration to the dregs.

The finale is a Dionysian feast of musical tone-painting.   Triolets romp in Bacchanalian tumult, melodies of joy rush through the orchestra, driven by the demon of passion, in an exultant frenzy of divine harmony.

Schubert never experienced the joy of hearing this masterpiece of all his masterpieces performed. He offered it also to the Society of Music Friends, but this time it was refused on the ground of its being too difficult and complicated. Ten years later Schumann came to Vienna and found the symphony at Ferdinand Schubert's. After a visit to the graves of Schubert and Beethoven in the Währinger cemetery, the German musician visited brother Ferdinand, who told him many things about our master, and showed him the relics he had left behind. " To end with," Schumann relates, " he allowed me to look at the treasures of Franz Schubert's compositions which had been left in his hands. The wealth thus revealed to my eyes made me shiver with ecstasy. Where to begin, where to leave off! Among other things he showed me the scores of many symphonies, several of which had never been heard, because they were said to be either too difficult or too complicated for performance. Who knows how much longer the symphonies of which I am speaking would have remained hidden there covered with dust if I had not at once come to an understanding with Ferdinand Schubert and asked leave to send them to the directors of the Leipzig Gewandhaus Concerts, or to the artist himself who conducted the concerts, whose discernment and insight not the tiniest unfolding spark of talent ever escaped, much less anything so brilliant and masterly as these unknown creations of a full-blown genius. So all was settled. The symphonies came to Leipzig, were heard, understood, heard again and again with delight and almost universally admired. The enterprising firm, Breitkopf and Härtel, purchased the works and their rights, and so they lie now before us, and the scores will soon be, as we wished, at the service of the world. . . . The symphonies have had an effect on us here only second to Beethoven's. All artists and friends of art are at one in singing their praises, and from the conductor who made such a careful study of their production, so that it was an unadulterated pleasure to listen to them, I heard a remark which I should have liked to have repeated to Schubert as a message of joy. ' Years may still pass before these works become recognised in Germany as essentially a living element in German music, but there can be no fear of

them being overlooked or forgotten ; they bear within them the
impress of eternal youth.' So my pilgrimage to the graves of the
two departed masters brought me double good fortune, for besides
being reminded of the relative of the one, I found on the grave of
Beethoven a steel pen, which I greatly treasure. Only on a festive
occasion like the present do I use it ; may all that is pleasant flow
therefrom. . . .''

We now come to a consideration of Schubert's chamber music.
He cherished for it, as for the *lied*, a particular partiality.

In this branch of music he had been brought up. At home,
as well as in the town Konvikt School, he played in quartets, and
so from his earliest years he had the opportunity of hearing and
taking part in chamber music. And one can truly say that in his
career as a composer he had done everything there was to be done
in this line. The number of his string quartets is fifteen, in addition
to which there are a piano quintet, a quintet for strings, an octet,
two piano trios, a string trio, a nocturne for piano, violin and
violoncello, a funeral march for nine wind instruments, and several
smaller chamber music works. What a tremendous span in the
master's artistic development exists between the three quartets in
" various keys," composed when he was fifteen, and the string
quintet (opus 165) belonging to his last years ? At first he followed
the old Viennese school ; then he modelled himself on Beethoven
chamber music, developing it on his own strenuous lines, always
pushing forward indefatigably, ripened by years of life's manifold
changes and suffering till here, too, he struck out a path, which
opened the way to a new art, stretching far into the future. Inexhaustible in Schubert's chamber music as elsewhere is the flow
of melody. As in creations of the master in other branches of
the art of tones, the themes he adopted in his chamber music are
of a romantic spirit ; they are sweet and lovely and genuinely
Schubertian, derived from the music of the people. They paint
in tones pictures and impressions that have been stored in the
memory. The variety and grace in their treatment is amazing,
and, as is often the way with Schubert, the joyousness of the
themes and lively *tempo* are emphasised by repetition, and he
lingers on them lovingly ; and these *longueurs* constantly contain
some of his most happy inspirations.

Let us consider now some of these works singly. In the quartets
belonging to his youthful period, between the years 1812 and 1815,

though composed under the influence of Haydn and Mozart, the personal note often breaks through in the *crescendo* of the melody. The string quartets in E flat major and E major of the year 1818 are Schubertian in their sensuous joyousness, and more mature in their original style. The first wholly characteristic of Schubert is the so-called *Forelle* quintet, a perfect picture painted in exquisite tones of the Austrian landscape. The themes in the first movement are full of romance and grace ; the *andante* sings the dream of a beautiful summer in the Austrian mountains ; the *scherzo* breathes the gay Viennese waltz spirit. Then come the variations on the *Forelle* Song (Song of the Trout). The strings begin the theme with a four-part movement, and in the variations the separate instruments, especially the piano, come into prominence and sing the melody one after the other. The fiery finale closes this gay musical picture of the beauty and joy of Nature.

The transition from the youthful to the mature masterpieces of Schubert is marked by the string quartet movement in C minor belonging to the year 1820. Here we notice the striving after a more original form of expression, and more vivid tone-painting in a higher degree than hitherto. The theme begins on the G string of the first violin and is taken up by the other strings. It rises phantom-like from the deep, and, swelling mightily in volume, reaches a grandiose height. It is full of passion, and opens the gates to a new and lovelier world, to which Schubert, led by his genius, ascends in a furious joy of creation.

Schubert's three masterpieces of quartet compositions, which place him in the same rank as his prototypes, Haydn, Mozart and Beethoven, are the string quartets in A minor, D minor and G major. The first-named belongs to the year 1824 and was composed during his summer visit to Zselesz. Its lovely and elegantly proportioned themes commemorate his enjoyment of the beauties of country life. " The score," writes Oscar Bie, " resembles a peaceful picture. It is like a landscape, the basses forming sturdy tree-trunks, the medium voices branches, and the high voices blossom, so that one can hardly distinguish between upper and lower, but find in the reflection of the motive a unity which includes all Nature's music."

The sweet, dreamy melody of the first violin rises above the striking rhythm of the viola and the 'cellos and the slightly swaying accompaniments of the second violin. Here again we meet the change from minor to major so beloved by Schubert. A triolet form connects the first theme with the friendly second in C major; a short *coda* forms the expressive dying away of the movement. Schubert uses for the *andante* a melodious motive in slow dance rhythm from " Rosamunde," which, in ever novel changes, hurries from voice to voice, first diving into the deep and then flying upwards in the beautiful play of harmonies. As if a fugitive from the friendly, sunny Viennese landscape, the minuet dances on in swift and joyful rhythm, and the finale, coloured by the Hungarian folk music which Schubert had absorbed in the idyllic country scenes of Zselesz, swells to a warmly temperamental conclusion.

The second famous quartet (in D minor) dates from the year 1826. At that time severe depression, illness and the struggle for existence weighed heavily on Schubert's soul. By his art alone he cast off what threatened to become chronic melancholia, and he created this masterpiece. The rhythmic triolet motive, often called the " Fate Motive," reminiscent of Beethoven's in the C Minor Symphony, introduces the first movement. This sonorous theme, which paints the power of inexorable fate, is met by a long-drawn melody on the violins, blossoming into colour. The variations of the second movement deal with the thought of death, which so often occupied Schubert, and utilises the partly-transformed melody of the touching song, " Der Tod und das Mädchen." Of course the master draws a wide bow over the simple, mild air of the song. A tone-picture comes into being, equal in its grandeur to Holbein's "Dance of Death." A *scherzo* follows this movement, with its vivid religious solemnity, in sharp rhythmical cadences, announcing a return to life. Freed from all melancholy reflection, with a sighing aspiration to the highest good obtainable in this earthly existence, the finale flows along in stormy, passionate *joie de vivre*.

The last string quartette (in G major) was written by Schubert in the almost incredibly short time of ten days at Währing in the year 1826. It surpasses in loveliness of melody and in depth of feeling all that preceded it. The first movement opens with calm resignation, expressive of the present mood of the artist matured through joy and sorrow. It scintillates with orchestral brilliance. There is an outburst of wild passion which is soon calmed by the soothing voice of the 'cello, and the movement ends as it began,

with longing and resignation. The *andante con moto* introduces
the soft, sweet melody on the violoncello in E minor, and then this
is interrupted with runs of tumultuous chords. The themes change
into new combinations and the movement dies solemnly away in
a sad, plaintive melody. The *scherzo* changes from a cheerful
country-dance rhythm to a weird, ghostly motive. The finale
rushes along stormily, the passionate themes hurry from instrument
to instrument, spinning all the time new tangles of sound till the
play of harmony at last breathes exhausted a low *pianissimo*, and
then strikes two powerful chords with which it ends.

Other pearls of Schubert's chamber music are the two piano
trios in B (opus 99) and in E flat (opus 100) for piano and violins
and violoncello, as well as the octet in F major for two violins, viola,
'cello, double-bass, clarinet, horn and bassoon. The piano trio in
B belongs to the year 1826, which was so productive in chamber
music, the year in which were created the two masterly quartets
in D minor and G major. The first movement begins with the
theme played by violin and 'cello in unison, rhythmically accompanied by the piano. The theme gets the bit between its teeth,
runs from instrument to instrument, till the piano, accompanied by
the strings, leads the melody on to new glories in sound. In the
andante the piano starts the rocking chorus of themes, which is
taken up by the 'cello, played through and then passed on to the
violin, accompanied by a swinging rhythm on the piano, till this,
lending new colour brilliance to the melody, undertakes the further
development of the theme. The *scherzo* is full of exuberant tones,
and its trio in Viennese dance rhythm—folk melodies idealised by
Schubert's art—flash through the *rondo*, which concludes the work,
with sparkling brilliance.

The piano trio in E flat major was composed by the master after
the completion of the song cycle " Die Winterreise " in November,
1827. It is, in contrast to the more lyrical, feminine B major trio,
as Schumann says, manly and dramatic. Here also Schubert reveals
himself as a master of a technical means of expression, of a never-
exhausted series of inspirations, and in the discovery of new colour
in harmony and in the artistic elaboration of folk lore subjects.
An energetic, masculine rhythm gives character to the first movement. Tender and graceful is the mood of the elegiac *andante con
moto*, of which, it is said, a Swedish folk air is the underlying
theme. The *scherzo* is again a Viennese dance rhythm, speaking

the native dialect; the fragrance of Austrian earth pervades the last movement, which concludes with flaming *élan*.

Under the influence of Beethoven's famous septet, Schubert composed in 1824 his octet. It consists of six successive movements in suite form. The first begins with an *adagio*. The chief theme starts in an ecstatic *allegro*, now the wind instruments lead, then the strings, producing a graceful, luminous tone-painting, full of novel modulations, played by eight instruments. Dreamily beautiful sounds the *andante*, in which the lovely soft melody of the clarinet floats, singing above the strings. Their voices follow the other instruments which, first alone and then together, emulate each other in investing the theme with divine harmonies. The *scherzo* races along with lively humour. A variation movement follows on an *andante* theme and gives the instruments alone and together an opportunity of shining. The minuet moves in a pleasant dance rhythm. The concluding movement, after a serious slow introduction leading to a joyous *allegro*, lends itself to manifold combinations of beautiful harmonious motives for both strings and wind.

The first performance of the octet took place in the salon of Count Ferdinand von Troyer, who had ordered it. He played the clarinet on this occasion, Ignaz Schuppanzigh playing the first violin. The latter three years later produced the work for a second time at a subscription concert. Then for several years it remained in obscurity, till in 1861 the Vienna Helmesberger Quartet produced it with success, and it has ever since been one of the master's most popular works.

A worthy termination to Schubert's chamber music is the string quintet (opus 165), which he composed shortly before his death for two violins, viola and two violoncellos. It goes far beyond, in volume of sound, the usual chamber music, and has almost the character of a symphony. By the use of two violins Schubert understood how to invest the work with an unusually rich and romantic tone-painting. In the first movement, which begins with a majestic C major chord, the violin starts the motive. The play of the instruments is first high and then deep, till the 'cellos make their true Schubertian contribution, which is adopted by violins and viola, and loses itself in new combinations and beauty of sound. The *adagio*, a striking melody, reminding one of Bruckner in its grandeur and solemnity, leads us with the abundance of its magic harmonies into the wonder world of the German romantics, full of moonlight magic, longing and love-sickness. The *scherzo* is characterised by stormy passion, its restless movement interrupted by a slow serious trio, an *andante* of solemn sublimity. The finale is saturated with Hungarian folk music and ends in a passionate climax.

This masterpiece shared the fate of the great C Major Symphony. Schubert was destined never to hear it. Nearly two decades had to pass before the world of music discovered this one of the sublimest creations in the art of tones.

In his compositions for the piano, as well as in his songs and chamber music, Schubert used his own original musical expression, leaving behind his forerunners, Haydn, Mozart, Beethoven. As Robert Schumann writes professionally in this connection : " Schubert's compositions for the piano in some respects are in advance of Beethoven's, wonderful and admirable as these are (heard, on account of his deafness only in his imagination). . . . Schubert understood how to instrumentalise, as it were, the piano, in that he makes everything come direct from its heart, whereas in the case of Beethoven we have to borrow its colour from the horn, the oboe, etc. If we were to add something on the inner nature of his creations in general it would be this : He found tones to express the very finest and most delicate sentiments, thoughts and conditions of life. As there are a thousandfold varying illustrations of habits and dress in men, so it is in the Schubertian music. What he looks at with his eyes or touches with his hand is converted into music; from the stone that he throws into the water spring, like Deucalion and Pyrrha, living human figures. After Beethoven, he was the most distinguished of all who, as the deadly enemy of all Philistinism, practised, in the highest sense of the word, the art of music."

Schubert, who was not a masterly performer on the piano himself, like Mozart and Beethoven, considered less in his piano compositions the demands of technique and virtuosity than satisfying harmonies and sweet sounds. They are wrung from the soul, are intimate, dreamy, romantic and inward. Simplicity and noble construction, combined with the brilliance of tone-painting, render them musical miracles such as only proceed from the heart of genius. Schubert's piano compositions are not suited to the great concert halls, where the *virtuosi* in technique seek to dazzle cosmopolitan audiences, but their proper *milieu* is the home, the quiet room, where a circle of sympathetic listeners are gathered together to delight in this most wonderful music which speaks to the soul. Compositions for the piano occupy an extensive space in Schubert's creations. They are written sometimes for two, sometimes for four hands. Among them are sonatas, variations, fantasias, *moments musicaux, divertissements,* marches, polonaises, rondos, dances, waltzes and *écossaises.* A special *genre* in Schubert's piano works are the six *moments musicaux* and the impromptus (opera 90 and 142). The master followed here somewhat in the steps of his predecessors who were the inventors of the lyrical pianoforte piece, like Rameau, Scarlatti, Philip Emanuel Bach, Field, etc., and his musical " Stimmungsbilder " anticipate Schumann's " Kinderscenen " and " Albumblättern, " Mendelssohn's " Lieder ohne Worte " ; Chopin's ballades and nocturnes.

They are beautiful miniatures in music—tone-poems, intimate confidences from Schubert's innermost soul ; melodies in chords, elaborated with a delicate filagree of runs and flights of harmony that bring us straight into the blessed sphere of romance. With regard to the impromptus, it is often thought that these were fragments of a Schubertian sonata. On this subject Robert Schumann has written as follows : " Now that he has long been at rest, we are carefully collecting and annotating all that he left behind. There is nothing among it that is not pervaded with his spirit ; in few works by others is the zeal of the creator so clearly impressed as in his. Thus in the two first impromptus, every bar whispers ' Franz Schubert ' ; as we know him in his inexhaustible humours and varying moods, as he charms and disappoints, and again fascinates, we find him again. Yet I can hardly believe that Schubert really wrote the title ' Impromptu ' over these pieces ; the first is so obviously the first movement of a sonata, so perfectly rounded and finished, it leaves no doubt in my mind. The second impromptu I believe to be the second movement of the same sonata ; in character and method it resembles the foregoing closely. What has become of the last movements, or whether Schubert ever finished the sonata his friends must know. One might perhaps regard the fourth impromptu as the finale, if the sketchiness of the treatment were not rather against the supposition. However, only a glance at the original manuscript can clear the matter up. . . . If one plays the two first impromptus one after the other, and runs on as a finish the fourth, there is, if not a complete sonata, one more beautiful remembrance of him. A sonata is such a beautiful ornament in the crown of a composer's work that I would gladly attribute another to Schubert, nay, twenty more. . . . "

Numerous were the sonatas which Schubert composed. They generally adhere strictly in form to the four-movement sonata type. The first two sonatas date from the year 1815; the spiritual relationship of the master to his admired and reverenced prototype, Beethoven, is very marked in their contents.

The sonata in E flat major composed in 1817 shows a great step forwards. The tone-poet has begun to go his own way. Quite Schubertian is the *andante* steeped in pathetic resignation, and graceful and *wienerisch* is the gay minuet. A still further advance is to be remarked in the romantic sonatas in F flat major (opus 147) and A minor (opus 164), belonging to the same year. A melodious song of romantic longing is the beautiful sonata in A minor (opus 145), of the year 1825. The dreamy *andante* sings of fairy legends and lore, of love and pain, and the closing movement tells in chivalric fashion of noble deeds of achievement and happiness. A high-water mark was reached in Schubert's piano compositions with the sonatas of the year 1825 in A major (opus 120), A minor (opus 42), D major (opus 53), and the unfinished C major, known as the " Reliquie." In the last Schubert has reached to Beethoven's heights.

He had steeped himself in Beethoven's sonatas, but in his own he is no imitator; his inspiration comes from his muse alone, and he originates a new art in sonata-writing. His lyrical nature divulges a stream of romantic melodies, which are conjured out of the keys of the pianoforte as if by magic. All is a vast song from the depths of his soul. The tone-painting is luxuriant, the modulations bold, the harmony novel. The first movement of the A minor sonata begins like a *Volkslied;* its magnificent chords and rich imagery are repeated in a variety of colour effects, it glides through changes of key back into A minor in the closing *coda.* The theme of the *andante* has manifold variations, in which Schubert's wealth of ideas is splendidly used, first mystic, then gracefully elegant, and it ends in tragedy. The *scherzo* dances along with a swing, alternately in major and minor. The *rondo* of the last movement in *vivace* time whirls and romps to a merry conclusion, more or less characteristic of the whole. The great D major sonata (opus 55) reminds us of Beethoven's most beautiful sonatas. The deepest and most impressive movement is the slow, famous *andante con moto*, a song that thrills with its exalted message of profound peace and happiness. The unfinished sonata in G major is no less remarkable for richness of conception and boldness in execution. Here the solemn *andante* is again a witness of the inexhaustible and overwhelming flow of Schubert's genius. And worthy to rank with these masterpieces are the three sonatas in C minor, A major and B major, composed in September, 1828, shortly before his death. The last, in B major, indeed, was completed only seven weeks before he lay on his death-bed. It is full of Schubertian melody, and the themes are abundantly rich in imagery. Again it is the *andante sostenuto* which is specially beautiful, with its slowly developed melody from the world of romance. Quite original is the last movement, which begins with an alluring call on a high G, conjuring up themes which first are in a lovely gay strain, floating from C minor to B major, and then, rising into a tempest of passion, glide again into a calm *legato*, to end with fiery *élan* in a stormy *presto*.

Of the pianoforte fantasias composed by Schubert, the " Wanderer Fantasia " is, above all, worthy of mention. It is a symphonic composition based on a phrase in the famous song. The first movement begins in a grandiose *crescendo* in C major, and glides with a melodious swing into G major. The charming theme falls, dipping into the deep, to rise ever higher, singing like the lark as it soars into ether. The play of fancy invests the melody with a hundred novel changes till the impassioned rhythm passes into C sharp minor. The wanderer's theme is in the *adagio*, at first *pianissimo*, and then is conducted through various shades of tone, embroidered with effective runs and *tremoli*, till in three-four time the brilliant *presto* hurls itself into a quasi *scherzo* with a dancing trio in waltz form. In the *allegro* of the last movement the theme takes the form of a fugue. All-conquering and triumphant, glowing with tone-painting, it is brought to an effective end in C major.

Besides the " Wanderer Fantasia," we possess in the fantasia in G major (opus 78), a pearl of Schubertian piano composition. It is sonata-like in form, consisting of four movements—*fantasie, andante, menuetto e allegretto*. The first movement is a characteristic Schubert theme, romantic and dreamy with stupendous chords and curious, kaleidoscopic tone-painting.

The touching melody of the second movement sings like a *Volks-lied*, and swells with Schubertian romantic feeling, first in major, then in minor, till it works itself up into a fiery Hungarian theme. Charming and full of smiling grace is the third movement, the *menuetto*, with its genuine Schubertian trio which, in a light Viennese waltz rhythm, floats blissfully away to the stars. The last movement, *allegretto*, might be the music to a country festival, a mixture of gayest song, dance, longing, fragrance of flowers, frolic and dreams.

A speciality in Schubert's music for the piano are his pieces for four hands. In this department of composition he stands above all other musicians. He is the supreme master of the pianoforte duet. The work which Schubert accomplished in this line is extensive and invaluable. It begins with little dances and marches and grows to cyclonic variations, like those of the great sonata "Grand Duo." The period includes the whole of Schubert's creative career, thus from 1810 to 1828. These compositions rank in importance with his chamber music and his solo piano pieces. The poetry of his temperament, his yearning for perfection, his inborn grace, his melancholy, and his delightful gaiety all live, breathe, weep and sing in Schubert's music for four hands.

He finished on May 1st, 1810, his first youthful fantasia-duet, very long and full of detail, and in the course of the same year, with maturer technique and knowledge of tone-painting, enriched his output in this direction with new fantasies, marches and variations.

In the year 1818, while in Zselesz, he composed eight variations for four hands on a French romance in E minor, "Reposez vous, bon chevalier," which Schubert had unearthed from the old store of music in the Esterházy family. In his poetic treatment of the theme the master followed in Beethoven's steps, for when this *opus* was published in the year 1824 it was dedicated to "Beethoven, from his reverer and admirer, Franz Schubert." The year 1824 brought forth specially valuable works, closely connected with his stay at Zselesz. They are the B major sonata (opus 30), the great variations in A flat major (opus 35), the famous sonata in C, the "Grand Duo," and the popular "Divertissement à la Hongroise" (opus 54).

Schubert's most interesting work for four hands is the "Grand Duo." The almost orchestral fullness of sound it extracts from the piano gives it a symphonic character. The first movement is singular, owing to the uniform and inventive compactness of the treatment of the theme. The melody is superabundant and the harmony magnificent. The second movement has three themes more loosely knit, and flows away in a stream of Schubertian melody. Emphatic rhythm marks the *scherzo*, and the themes of the last movement have a Hungarian origin. According to the theory of Schumann, Joachim and others, this splendid duet was really a symphony in disguise.

Essentially Hungarian in character is the composition for four hands of the year 1824, the celebrated "Divertissement à la Hongroise." The master, on his walks in the neighbourhood of Castle Zselesz, must often have heard Hungarian folk and gipsy music, and have absorbed its airs artistically, to use them afterward in his work. There is at least one anecdote to relate concerning this piece. It is said that Schubert once, with the singer, Baron von Schönstein, overheard a dark-eyed girl singing a melancholy Hungarian song as she stood on the hearth in the firelight. On his return to the castle he wrote it down and used it in his "Divertissement." The prevailing tone of the work is melancholy, as is all Hungarian folk music. The tone-painting is naturalistic. Elegiac melodies alternate with strong march motives, fiery national dance rhythm accompanied by syncopated chords. It is a wonderful tone-picture, vibrating with all the sadness and poetry of the Hungarian soul.

To the last year of Schubert's life, 1828, belong also two mighty works of this class for piano, the colossal *allegro* in A minor (opus 144), "Lebensstürme," and the F minor fantasia dedicated to the Countess Karoline Esterházy. The latter is a moving song of longing, which first rises in an ethereal flight to the stars and then sinks in melancholy resignation. Is this Schubert's anthem to his "Unsterbliche Geliebte," and as he composed it did the picture of the lovely young Countess Karoline Esterházy hover before his eyes ? Who can tell ? Anyhow, her name in the master's dedication is eternally associated with this fantasia.

Another speciality of Schubert's compositions for the piano is his dance music. His German dances, Écossaises, Atzenbrugger dances, Ländler (country dances), his Grätzer Gallopps and Waltzes, his minuets, Valses Nobles and Valses Sentimentales, and the Viennese Damenländler, had an enormous influence on Vienna's folk music and dance music. Himself born of the people, he had often in the suburbs listened to the people's music and watched their dancing. These were memories which found an echo in his heart, and brought forth from his genius those wonderful little costly musical pearls in the old-fashioned rhythm of three-four time. They are tender, rocking, laughing children born of the moment; under his light touch on the piano, when he played for his friends at joyous parties, they romped forth with easy, unpremeditated grace. Outside the gates of the city he had picked up these swaying melodies, in old-world lanes and alleys, in blossoming gardens and spacious courtyards, these wild, untamed children of the Viennese Folkmuse, and carried them home and transformed them in his quiet little room into glorified creatures of his sometimes merry, sometimes sentimental, musical spirit. The soul of old Vienna echoes from them, the seething *joie de vivre*, the charm and loveliness, the sentimentality often inclining to melancholy of this fascinating town and its landscape, its green, shady Wienerwald. Schubert's dances are nearly related to the Viennese folks music, they are idylls of gaiety in a major key and of sadness in a minor. They are like the swings hung between the trees of some old Biedermeier garden full of blossom, and where on the wooden tables wine sparkles in the cut glasses and on the green sward and youths and maidens of the people twirl in the giddy dance. Like a poem of Raimund's, like a picture of Danhauser or Fendi, Schubert's dances conjure up a vision of ancient vanished *Wien*.

Let us consider, in conclusion, the religious works with which Schubert's genius endowed the world. The motive for his creations in church music was supplied by the *milieu* in which he passed his boyhood. The great events of his childhood were singing in the choir of the Lichtental Parish Church, where he received his first impressions of church music, and his appointment as a chorister in the Imperial Hofmusikkapelle, where he served for several years. The Court Orchestra gave the most careful attention to the performance of religious works, and his experience here formed the groundwork of his musical education. Undoubtedly it was the magical effect the music of the Catholic Church had on him that awakened his genius and inspired the boy's first compositions. But though his early youth was thus passed in the atmosphere of church music, which exercised the strongest influence on his later artistic creation, the motive which attracted other great masters like Palestrina, Johann Sebastian Bach, Liszt and Anton Bruckner to the composition of sacred music was wanting in Schubert. He had no profound religious feeling. All his life long he was not a religious enthusiast, but much more a simple, naïve, God-fearing child of the world. His *credo* was not Bach's unshakable, rock-like firmness of faith, nor Anton Bruckner's belief that in the adoration of the Divinity through music a loftier plane can be reached in human development; nor was it the Promethean daemonic defiance which filled the soul of Beethoven, who, like Faust, had wrestled and struggled to reach a divine belief. Thus Schubert's religious works, as a rule, have not the monumental and exalted grandeur of a Palestrina, Bach and Bruckner. They lack the heroic uplifting element of Beethoven's masses. In his church music, Schubert, as elsewhere, is for the most part lyrical and romantic. It has its root in the Viennese school, and is chiefly modelled on the works of Haydn and Mozart. As they did, he shows in his religious compositions an orthodox but naïvely humanistic Catholicism, which, confident of the loving-kindness of the Lord, praises God in either jubilant psalms of rejoicing or petitions for the blessings of heaven in gentle, soothing canticles. Like the masters of the old Vienna school, he sends up in the Kyrie the repentant sinner's beseeching prayer for mercy, praises God in His Heaven in the festive jubilation of the Gloria, expresses a pious confidence and firmness of faith in the Credo, revels in the exalted solemnity of the Sanctus, and announces in the Benedictus and Agnus Dei the goodness and loving mercy of God.

Schubert's spiritual works are tone-pictures filled with romantic colour and beautiful harmonies. They paint all the magic and artistic attraction of the Catholic Church from the mystery of the Blessed Sacrament. They accompany in tone-colours the Church ceremonials of the divine service. We see in their music the glow of the altar's candlelight, the waving banners and clouds of incense, we hear the singing of the choir in the festive processions, the chanting of the priests in their gold-embroidered vestments, the chiming of the bells, and the fervid voices of the congregation raised in prayer.

However conservatively Schubert may have clung to the old forms, he made many advances in his later and maturer religious music in his treatment and use of material. In his use of the orchestra and the choir, in a certain sense, he went far beyond the old Vienna school. Brilliant is his conduct of the singing voices, solos as well as choruses, and often full of new ideas is his arrangement of the orchestra. In all the master composed six masses. The first, in F major (for five voices, organ and orchestra), he composed when he was seventeen, in the year 1814, for the hundred years' jubilee celebration of the Lichtental Parish Church, where he had sung in the choir as a boy and where his first teacher, Michael Holzer, was choirmaster. Schubert's method in the handling of the orchestra here is on the lines of the old school. Modest and straightforward, like the heavenly dreams of the Hofkapelle chorister, orchestra and voices accompany the officiating priest. This first performance was a musical idyll in the history of old Vienna. The young tone-poet conducted his own work on Sunday, October 16th, 1814, in the church at Lichtental. The soprano soloist was Therese Grob, the object of his boyish admiration. The whole of Himmelpfortgrund composed the audience : there were honest burghers among it, masters and their apprentices, relations and friends. It was young Schubert's first great success, which made of him the local celebrity of Lichtental. A second performance of the mass in the Augustinen Kirch soon followed.

Another church-music composition also dates from this time, the young master's " Salve Regina " for tenor voice, organ and orchestra. The awakening of Schubert's more original manner is felt in the masses of the year 1815 in G major and B major, especially in the first in the melodious Benedictus, the lovely soprano solo of which was sung by the beloved Therese, and the expressive Agnus Dei. At that time Schubert wrote, too, for his fair friend a little offertorium for soprana (opus 47). Besides, in these days were composed a " Stabat Mater," a graduale, and the offertorium " Tres Sunt." An important step forward in harmonies and melody is shown in the fifth mass, " Missa Solemnis," in A flat major, begun in the year 1816 and finished in 1822. Schubert dreamed then of its being performed by the Imperial Court Orchestra ; at least, the intention of dedicating the mass to the Emperor and Empress seems to point to this. " My mass is finished and will before long be produced," he wrote to his friend Spaun. " I have an idea, as it is good, that I shall dedicate it either to the Emperor or Empress." But neither the dedication nor the performance by the Court Orchestra came off. From the themes of the mass speak the ripened romanticist who revels in melody and paints moods. It is no profound, metaphysical wrestling for the recognition of the divine, but an outpouring of beautiful sentiments ; it is all inner music of the soul. " What has once come from the Godhead by Art must be returned to God," might be the motto of the Mass. The song of the fiddles, the voices of the chorus and the soloists, are like a wreath of spring flowers, woven by the hands of fair maidens, round the picture of the crucified Christ. The Gloria bursts forth with a shout of joy, and the Credo mounts to heaven in pious, jubilant fervour. From the deep shudder of the moving " Crucifixus " rise the powerful-sounding, joyous chorus of the " Resurrexit " ; the solemn Sanctus and winged " Hosannahs " are bathed in Schubert's melody, and in the Benedictus and Agnus Dei the dreams of the worshipping artist dissolve in a flood of heavenly harmonies.

At about the same time that Schubert had begun to occupy himself with his great lyrical masterpiece, the " Winterreise "—the year 1827—he wrote to a German text by a professor at the Technical High School, Johann Neumann, his " Deutsche Messe," a choir composition which, thanks to its wealth of beautiful melodies, has become one of the master's most popular works. Originally composed for chorus with orchestral accompaniment, it was later set by Ignaz von Seyfried for men's voices.

Shortly before his death in 1828, when his soul had already had a glimpse into the darkest depths of life, when he was matured through suffering, Schubert once more turned to the worship of God in that great E flat major mass which is a mighty hymn to the Divinity and the crown of his creations in church music. More boldly than in his other religious works, the harmony in its brilliance and glory develops the tone-painting in the sparkling mixture of light and colour in the orchestra and chorus. The orchestra, consisting of a quintet of strings, two oboes, clarinet, bassoons and horn and three trumpets, is without organ and flutes. The Kyrie begins in *pianissimo* with the whispering melody of the chorus, which, at the call to Christus, is joined in powerful after strains by the wind instruments and the tremulous strings, and rising in an emotional supplication for mercy, the movement dies away in low, tender harmonies. The chorus of voices, praising God in a burst of jubilation, begins the " Gloria in excelsis Deo " ;

the orchestra bursts in like a mighty storm, instruments and voices mingle in the richest tone-painting. The trumpets crash forth, the strings quiver with emotion, and the chorus shouts in gleeful rejoicing the "Domine Deus." Sorrowfully and in bitter repentance the Miserere raises its plaintive petitions; the grand fugue "Cum sanctu spiritu" begins with strength in the basses, and is taken up by other voices, and forms with these a magnificent tone-picture. A tumult of cymbals opens the Credo, the chorus sings in loud steady confidence its formula of faith, the "Et incanatus est," swelling with Schubert melodies, is sung by single voices. The mystery of the "Crucifixus" follows, accompanied by the chorus and the thrill of stirring chords; another clash of cymbals announces the powerfully sounding "Resurrexit." The Amen, which seems as if it could never end, is the mighty close of this wholly artistic and wonderfully built tone-picture.

In the Sanctus, with the famous "Hosannah" fugue, the mass reaches its highest point. Colossally bold is the modulation here and the quick change in tone. Orchestra and voices soar to ever more exalted heights and unite in the fugue-construction of the "Hosannah" in praising God in a hymn of solemnity and beauty. The Benedictus is in a softer tone, first played on the first violin; then the graceful touching melody is sung by four solo voices. The Agnus Dei is melancholy and plaintive, the tone-painting becoming dark in shadow and the rhythm gloomy. It is the gloom of the "Winterreise" which momentarily forces its way to the surface. "Dona nobis pacem" carries the cry of entreaty up to God. Perfect peace relieves life of its pain and glorifies the prayer of the faithful— released and free. The soul flies from the earth into the eternity of everlasting peace.

Thus it was that Schubert praised his God in his music, first with his pure, clear treble in the Lichtentaler Parish Church and in the Imperial Court Chapel; then in his divine imagination he reared temples of sound to the glory of the Creator, and these with the years became greater and grander till in the E flat major mass they grew into that magnificent dome which is the most glorious memorial of Catholic Church music, casting its radiance into the heavens like the spiritual masterpieces of Mozart, Haydn and Bruckner.

It seems to us, when we review the effect of Schubert's spiritual artistry on the history of music, as if a springtime of romanticism, had suddenly burst into blossom. Schubert led Beethoven's world-concept, which was struggling out of the classic ground, into the dream-world of romantic sentiment, and so breathed into the art of music a new soul. It is not the monumental building-up in tones of great human thoughts such as Beethoven's gigantic creativeness achieved; it is rather the jubilation over newly-awakened inner power, a creative ferment of inexhaustible inspiration, an intuitive spontaneous foaming up of musical ideas from the artist's innermost being. And like the only really great of this earth, Schubert was enabled by his genius to see as if in a mystic vision all the brightness and gaiety and all the tragedy and dark side of this mortal life. In his work his range is the whole gamut of the human soul, from tenderest lyrical sentiment to dramatic fury of passion, from naïve lighthearted joyousness to gloomy melancholy, even to the edge of the abyss of death itself.

What in his too short life he gave the world is incalculable. Endless are the far-reaching distances illumined by the light of his genius. Many and many are the decades that must yet pass away before the watchers of the artistic sky will be able to estimate the breadth, fulness and depth of Schubert's works, or to fathom the stream of new music, the flood of musical problems and unlimited possibilities which proceeded from Schubert's creative spirit. A thousand threads connect him with his great successors in the domain of music; they have all nourished themselves on the inexhaustibility and infinite variety of his genius, from Robert Schumann, Cornelius, Franz, Brahms to Liszt, Wagner, Hugo Wolf and Anton Bruckner—a grand but tragic fate. Schubert, regardless of his own health, lavished his gifts carelessly; he poured out his heart's blood and his soul in his work, till the fire of his creative strength, the flames of his genius consumed his young life.

Feminine Influence in Schubert's Life

PRINCE CHARLES DE LIGNE once said about the brilliant days of the Vienna Congress that every man was then a romance, and that love and beauty carried all before them, and in a certain respect the same is equally true of the Biedermeier period. During the time of the Vienna Congress the international type of beauty which François Isabey painted was admired; in the Biedermeier days it was the innate Viennese grace which came triumphantly into the foreground. An air of romance is wafted to us by the charming portraits of youthful beauties painted by Schwind, Kriehuber, Danhauser, Daffinger, Teltscher, Rieder, and sentiment, love and erotics in those days were strongly under romantic influences. It was the time when the German lyric was at its zenith, when the heart of youth was filled with ecstasy by the works of Goethe, Ossian, Hölderlin and Eichendorff, of the romanticists, Tieck, Schlegel, Brentano, Platen, and the young Lenau. Women and girls, youths and men of mature years, all wrote verses, read " Almanack " stories, kept diaries and exchanged romantic letters. The artists, poets, tone-poets were the ideal prototypes for the youth of the day, and influenced by their work the whole trend of thought and feeling in that ecstatic age. Beethoven's susceptibility to love, tinged with romantic yearning, cast many a ray of sunshine into the tragic prison-house of the master's soul, as well as planting there deep scars of suffering. He composed the group of songs, " An die ferne Geliebte," and wrote those letters to the mysterious immortal Beloved so full of fiery passion and wistful pathos. The youthful Grillparzer dedicated beautiful verses to his eternally adored Kathi Fröhlich. Raimund crowned the brow of his beloved Toni Wagner with the flowers of his poetic art; and the elderly, talented *bon viveur*, Friedrich von Gentz, the famous stylist of Biedermeier Vienna, wrote at the age of sixty verses to the beautiful dancer Fanny Elssler, who flitted through the town like a melody of spring, bewitching everyone with her art and grace.

And Franz Schubert, the romanticist—few are the great artists who have given more wonderful expression than he in his music to the sensation of love, from the first awakening to the outburst of passion and the poignancy of pain and tragic resignation. A beautiful memorial to the feelings of his own heart are the " Müller-lieder " in which he has immortalised in song the modest, naïve young miller whose romantic sentiments are so childlike and pure that he delights in every blossom and sunbeam, and asks the flowers and stars whether his love is reciprocated by the *inamorata*. He tastes all the pain and joy of love's longing; and one cannot help thinking that Schubert has drawn himself in the youth who clings to the love of the woman, though she has stabbed his young heart to death, and who, even when dying, hopes that she will not forget him; " *und wenn sie wandelt am Hügel vorbei, und denkt im Herzen der meint es treu! Dann Blümlein alle heraus, heraus.*" It is an outpouring of musical emotion; it is the lover's springs awakening, the glorified apotheosis of the artist's suffering caused by love.

Did Schubert, like his great prototype Beethoven, rave about an immortal beloved whom he never found? Did he who sang so enchantingly of the tender passion go through life loveless because the fiery, never-resting daemon of his artistic creation gave him no time for love-making? Did he enjoy but brief and evanescent flirtations in those excursions into the green country with his friends—those blissful summer evenings as full of allurement as the hearts of women and the scent of roses?

Vain questions—Schubert had no better luck in love than in life. Without a home, dependent on the friendship of his Schubertians, unrecognised and little appreciated by others, his inclination to the tender passion and longings for marital bliss were not likely to be satisfied. But the gods gave him the power of expressing what he suffered, for in himself rested the love which surpasses all earthly bounds. His feelings were interpreted in melody. He sought and found relief in his God-given art, and love and passion were glorified in the exaltation of musical inspiration and in beautiful divine harmonies. Schubert left behind no letters that tell us anything of his relations to the opposite sex. We know nothing of his amorous adventures, though Bauernfeld's words, " Schwind loved, and so did we all, *following Schubert's example*," leave an impression of unrestrained yielding to the lures of love. Yet his heart seems to

Katharina Fröhlich
Crayon drawing by Heinrich
(State Collection, Vienna)

have been capable of the purest and most romantic sentiment, often amounting to ecstasy. The legend is current till this day that his young pupil at Castle Zselesz, Countess Karoline Esterházy, inspired Schubert with an ideal passion. The girl seems never to have understood his deep attachment, and the pain which his love for Karoline caused him was buried in the depths of his heart, and only confided to his music. Only once words that betrayed his feelings escaped' his lips, and this was when the young Countess asked him why he dedicated none of his works to her, and he answered : " Why should I, when everything is dedicated to you ? "

He often played duets with the beloved in the Hungarian castle, and her charming picture accompanied him as his muse through life. Later he dedicated to her the F minor fantasia (opus 105) : " *Fantaisie pour le piano à quartre mains, composée et dediée à Mademoiselle la Contesse Caroline Esterházy de Galantha par François Schubert œuvre* 103." So the dedication runs. In the well-known sepia drawing, " Ein Schubert Abend," Moritz von Schwind drew the portrait of the Countess Karoline von Esterházy on the wall of the room where the Schubertians were assembled listening to Vogl singing the master's *lieder*. Schwind wrote on the subject to the poet Mörike at the time he was setting to work on the famous picture : ". . . A happy chance put me in possession of a portrait of a Countess von Esterházy, whom I never saw, but to whom, as report goes, everything he wrote was dedicated. She had every reason to be satisfied." Also the following words of Bauernfeld's are supposed to allude to the master's romantic feeling towards Countess Karoline : " For poets as well as musicians an unhappy love affair, if it is not too unhappy, is perhaps an advantage, in that it intensifies subjective emotion, and lends the poems and songs it engenders colour, tone, and the most beautiful realism. Productions like the two ' Suleika,' ' Die zürnende Diana,' a great deal of the ' Müllerlieder,' and the ' Winterreise,' are clearly musical confessions, bathed in the glow of a deep and real passion, and transformed into genuine works of art proceeding from the lover's tenderest sentiment."

The lovely girlish figure of the Countess Karoline Esterházy, the Leonore of this musical Tasso, has through his genius taken on immortality.

In his letters from Zselesz, Schubert does not mention his tenderness for the Countess, but during his first visit he praises her piano-playing to his Viennese friends. The words which he wrote six years later to his brother Ferdinand have a melancholy ring : " In case these lines should lead you to believe that I am not well or in merry mood, I hasten to assure you to the contrary. Of course these are no longer those happy times when every object appeared in a halo of youthful glory, but, thank God, I can, by my imagination, try to beautify the fatal recognition of a miserable reality as much as possible. We think that in a place where we have once been happy happiness must exist, when it really exists only in ourselves; thus I was unpleasantly disillusioned. I have renewed an experience already made in Steyr, but now I am more able to find happiness and peace within than I was then."

> " *Verliebt war Schubert ; der Schulerin*
> *galt's : einer der jungen Komtessen,*
> *doch gab er sich einer anderen hin,*
> *um—die andere zu vergessen. . . . "*

> (" Schubert was in love, it is said,
> With one of the pretty young Countesses.
> But he gave himself to another,
> So that he might forget the other.")

Who this other was, of whom Bauernfeld speaks in his verse, is not known. It may have been one of the maids on the Esterházy estate, or Therese Grob, the daughter of the silk merchant, Heinrich Grob, in Lichtental (Haus " Zur heiligen Dreifaltigkeit "). At any rate, Therese played a part in the sentimental life of the young Schubert. The poet had met and learned to love and admire Therese in the choir of the Lichtental Parish Church at the performances of church music, and in his boyhood he was often invited to the musical house of the silk manufacturer. The daughter, if not beautiful, had a magnificent soprano voice, going up to a high D, and in the year 1814 she sang the soprano part in the mass which Schubert composed for the jubilee celebration of the Lichtental Parish Church, and conquered the heart of the young musician. His love for her was not devoid of romance ; it was ardent, full of longing and also of pain. In a letter which has been lost, Schubert confided his love for Therese Grob to his friend Anton Holzapfel. Holzapfel sought in vain to cure the youth of his passion for the girl with the beautiful voice. She was the interpretress of his first songs, which she studied with the young composer in the family circle in Lichtental and sang in public with enthusiasm. She never missed a performance of Schubert's church-music works, which were given on festivals at Grinzing, Heiligenstadt, as well as Lichtental, and added to their beauty by her wonderful singing. Schubert was faithful to her, and contemplated a marriage. In later years, when he was taking a walk in the fields with Anselm Hüttenbrenner, the latter asked him if he had never been seriously in love, and if the fair sex was antipathetic to him. " Oh, no ! " was the answer. " I once dearly loved a girl. She was rather younger than I was, and sang in a mass which I composed the soprano part with wonderful expression. She wasn't pretty, and had smallpox marks on her face, but she was good, with a heart of gold. For three years I thought of marrying her, but I could not find a position with a salary sufficient to provide for us both. She then married, as her parents wished, another, which caused me great sorrow. I love her still, and no one could have suited me as well or better than she." It was on November 21st, 1820, that Therese married the Viennese master-baker, Bergmann. Schubert wrote for her in 1815 an offertorium for soprano voice, orchestra and organ (opus 47).

But though Schubert, whose soul was full of passion, was destined never to enjoy the warmth of a reciprocated *grande passion*, he came in contact with numerous beautiful girls and young married women in the circles in which he moved, and their gracious image seems to have hovered always over his life and work. All his lady friends raved about the genius Schubert, if not the man. When " Schubertiades " were being held in the houses of the music-loving citizens, and the master sat at the piano playing his sonatas, fantasias and impromptus, or accompanied Vogl when he sang his *lieder*, then " Friend Schwammerl " was surrounded by pretty girls and beautiful young matrons. Then from him whom the Goddess of Love had negligently passed over would proceed a stream of love and joy from which they all drank. Many of the fair listeners would feel as if a divine radiance was cast on them from Schubert's music, which made their eyes shine, penetrated to their hearts and gave to their lives a new impetus and exaltation. Quiet and grateful, the women and girls sat, as if lost in a dream of love, in a circle round the genius, listening to his melodies. Who were they, these gracious figures who, in the leading strings of the wild boy Eros, dreamed or laughed, sang and danced, to Schubert's music ?

The name of many among them is to-day forgotten, or only remembered because rays from the sunshine of their youth illumined Schubert's life. Friends and contemporaries of Schubert have perpetuated them in pastels, miniatures, lithographs, oil paintings and engravings. Schwind, Kupelwieser, Daffinger, Kriehuber, Teltscher, Staub, and Brandmüller have depicted them for us in all their loveliness and charm. Here are a few of their names which have been rescued from oblivion. Beautiful Isabel Josefa Bruchmann, later married to Schubert's friend, Ludwig von Streinsberg ; Justine von Bruchmann ; Johanna Lutz, the bride of the painter Kupelwieser ; the sisters Kleyle, of whom Sophie, the well-known friend of the poet Lenau, married Löwenthal ; her sister Rosalie, who married the Schubert singer, Baron von Schön-stein ; Betty Schröder ; Erika Anschütz, the daughter of the Court Theatre actor ; Betty Wanderer, who was a good interpreter of Schubert's songs ; Netty (Schwind's beloved) ; and Therese Hönig, Sophie von Schober, Sophie Hartmann, the matrons Witteczek, Kurzrock, Pompe. Of talented artists there were the pianist Leopoldine Blahetka ; the singers Linhardt and Karoline Unger, later *fiancée* of Lenau ; the pianist Irene von Kiesewetter, the beautiful daughter of the extremely musical Hofrat Raphael Georg von Kiesewetter, who was a patron of Schubert and a colleague of Jenger's. Jenger refers to Irene in a letter to Frau Pachler in Graz as one of the finest piano-players in Vienna. She belonged to Schubert's most intimate inner circle, and played his pieces for four hands with Jenger at the " Schuber-tiades " in her father's house and at the Court actresses's Sophie Müller. Schubert dedicated to her in 1825 the vocal quartet, " Der Tanz." It begins like a parody of Schiller's " Hoffnung " :

> " *Es redet und träumet die jugend so viel*
> *von Tanzen, Galoppen, Gelagen,*
> *auf einmal erreicht sie ein trügliches Ziel ;*
> *da hört man sie seufzen und klagen.*
> *Bald schmerzet der Hals, bald schmerzet die Brust*
> *verschwunden ist alle die himmlische Lust*
> ' *Nur diesmal noch Kahr mir Gesundheit zurcük* '
> *So flehet von Himmel der hoffende Blick !*

Jungst wähnt auch ein Fräulein mit trübem Gefühl,
Schon hätte ihr Stündchen geschlagen,
Doch stand noch das Rädchen der Parze nicht still,
nun schöner die Freuden ihr tagen,
Drum, Freunde, erheben den frohen Gesang,
es lebe die teure Irene noch lang
sie denke zwar oft an das falsche Geschick,
doch trübe sich nimmer ihr heiterer Blick."

" The young people talk and dream
Of nothing but dancing, gallops and waltzes.
One hears them sighing and groaning ;
They have pains in their throat and pains in their heart,
And fear all their pleasure is gone.
' Only let me be well again for this night,'
Is the prayer one reads in their eyes.

Once there was a Fräulein who thought
Her last hour had come.
But the wheels of life still worked
And soon she was lively again.
So friends raise a song,
' May our Irene live long,
And forget all her pain. .
May her bright face never be clouded.' "

And when Irene in 1827 recovered from a second serious illness,
Schubert wrote for the convalescent on December 26th the
cantata " *Alla nostra cara Irene* " :

" *Al par del ruscelletto chiaro*
la tua vita scorra, Irene.
compagne sian le grazie amene,
e l'amistà, virtù e fé.

Il suo rigor, le tu pene serbi
a noi soli 'l fato avaro
e sia per noi ancor più amaro
ond' esser prodigo conte.

Irene dea della pace
conserva in lei tranquillo il cor
del suo filial amor la face
per lungi età, risplenda ancor.

Eviva dunque la bella Irene,
la delizia del nostro amor
Eviva Irene, la bella Irene."

Jenger wrote on January 29th to Frau Pachler :

" . . . The daughter of my chief, Hofrat von Kiesewetter—Irene—whom I think I have mentioned often to you as being one of the leading pianists in Vienna, has lately recovered from a serious illness. Her physician has prescribed change of air, and I have proposed that she shall make a little tour in Styria, as both she and her mother have long wished to visit this land of promise, about which I have told them so much. If this plan comes off, ' Schwammerl ' and I will certainly be engaged as couriers, so, all being well, we may meet in a few months."

Irene married a few years after Schubert's death, on November 25th, 1832, Anton Proskesch, later, *en second noces*, Field-Marshal Count von Osten, a friend of Frau Pachler's youth. The Schubertian Teltscher painted a portrait of Irene, and a lithograph by Josef Kriehuber of Schubert's *Freundin* is preserved in the National Library in Vienna. Both pictures give a good idea of the beauty of this art-loving, refined old Viennese feminine type.

Two stars of the Burgtheater were also connected with Schubert's muse, Sophie Müller and Antoinie Adamberger. The latter was the former fiancée of the poet Körner, and afterwards was Frau von Arneth. She had been connected with Beethoven, having been the first to sing his " Klärchen " songs in " Egmont." She delighted in singing in an intimate circle of artistic friends Schubert's songs, and memorable was the day—it was in October, 1826—when at the Monastery of St. Florian in Upper Austria she sang to a select audience, which numbered Grillparzer among it, songs from the cycle of " Die schöne Müllerin," and from Goethe's " Wilhelm Meister " (the Harper's song), and in the beautiful decorative chapel, accompanied by the organist Kollinger, Schubert's " Ave Maria."

One of the loveliest of the Schubert group of fair women was the Burgtheater actress, Sophie Müller. " She was," as the actor Anschütz wrote of her, " a favourite of Nature, in the creation of whom the generous Alma Mater had showered on her a multitude of gifts and qualities which, as a rule, she only divides in strict fairness between several of her earthly children. Sophie's figure was perfectly formed, striking a happy medium between tall and

Antonie Adamberger

short; in its exquisite proportions and grace it adapted itself to every sort of stage representation. Her face, especially the eyes, beamed with purity and intellect. She was without doubt one of the most charming feminine personalities which have adorned the German stage. Into this beautiful body with the beautiful soul, the Tragic Muse had breathed its consecrating fire and sown the seeds of genius. Sophie Müller belonged to those actresses of genius who, as Ludwig Devrient says, ' involuntarily perform miracles, who never make a false step or exceed the bounds of their exhaustive natural powers. With an almost childlike ingenuousness, they cast their pearls without realising what jewels they are laying at the feet of the world.' "

She loved music and was gifted with a beautiful voice, in which she sang with enthusiasm Schubert's songs. The young master, with Vogl, often came to her house, and there was much music made. Vogl and Sophie sang, Schubert accompanied, and Schubert's friend Jenger often played at her house the master's piano compositions, sometimes the duets with Irene von Kiesewetter. The actress kept a diary in which she conscientiously recorded the musical hours which she passed in the society of Schubert and Vogl:

" Vogl and Schubert dined here to-day," she writes on February 24th, 1825, " for the first time. Afterwards Vogl sang several Schiller poems set by Schubert."

" Vogl and Schubert came," is an entry on March 1st, 1825, " in the afternoon and brought new songs. Vogl sang by heart a scene from ' Tartarus ' of Schiller. Splendid ! "

" After dinner Schubert came," she writes under March 3rd, 1825. " He brought a new song, ' Die junge Nonne ' ; a little later Vogl arrived and I sang it ; it is very beautifully composed. Old Lange called on us as well. We played and sang on till 7 and then the gentlemen departed."

" In the evening we had Déprès, Wedekind, Betty Schröder, Scherer, Ditz, Jenger, Teltscher. We had singing. ' Der Abend,' quartet of Hüttenbrenner, duet by Caraffa, duet by Schubert, " Suleika," " Müllerlieder," till half-past ten. Then I sent Betty home. Teltscher brought Schubert's picture, lithographed."

March 7th, 1825 : " Vogl came before dinner and again at 5 with Schubert ; they brought several new songs. Among others, a scene from Æschylus, ' Ihr Grab,' ' Die Forelle ' and ' der Einsame ' are wonderfully good. At half-past eight they went away."

March 30th, 1825 : " Schubert and Vogl came to-day for the last time. Vogl goes to-morrow to his estate in Steyr."

April 20th, 1825 : " Schubert came to-day. I tried several new songs : ' Der Einsame,' ' böse Farbe,' ' Drang in die Ferne.' "

January 24th, 1826 : " Teltscher, Jenger, Hüttenbrenner came this afternoon. Brought Schubert's picture," etc.

" But genius," continues Anschütz on the subject of Sophie Müller, " had in this case an extraordinary fate. The divine sparks given in such generous measure to this one mortal became liquid fire which flowed through the veins instead of blood, devouring the inner mortal vessel, so that the whole organism withered and fell into dust.

In a few years Sophie Müller had risen to an eminence in her profession which assured her a place in the history of art among the greatest ornaments of the German theatre. Her triumphant career was destined to be short because it was too impetuous. In restless impatience she bore her flying colours into the north : calm, contemplative Berlin, artistic Dresden, worshipped her with fiery enthusiasm. But Sophie became a shadow ; the glory with which her goddess surrounded her consumed her strength. After her last triumphant tour she became hampered with physical suffering ; periodic attacks of hoarseness and coughing began to mar her dramatic efforts. Intolerant of any obstacle, she determined to conquer in spite of physical weakness. She wanted to be strong, and so overtaxed her failing strength. She wanted still to be loved for her amiability, and her temper became tinged with irritability. Her devoted mother, Nature, saw the state of things, and to spare her beloved child a decline, and to prevent the lovely vision of health, beauty and genius which had so dazzled contemporaries being clouded by age and sickness, she took her favourite to herself before time should have left its marks on her. A disease of the chest chained the incomparable artist for fifteen months to a sickroom, and on July 19th, 1830, when all the roses were in bloom in her garden at Hietzing, the most beautiful blossom of them all shed its petals under the cold touch of death.

It was in the spring of 1822, with the first swallows, that this bird of paradise had flown into the world of art. Vienna, enchanted by the magic of her beauty and her genius, threw itself at her feet. Sophie was grateful. She was, of course, clever enough never to release the Viennese from the charm in which she held them spell-bound. She returned love with love, and flung herself into the service of her art, sacrificing her life that her ardent admirers might never be disturbed in their dreams of her or disillusioned by her delightful personality."

Schubert's Vienna circle also included the sisters Fröhlich. Their house was a centre in the Viennese Schubert period of the art-loving society of the town. Here the muses and graces were at home. The best musical and literary people—poets, musicians, painters, singers—went in and out here, sang and played and conversed all day long. Here Viennese beauty, grace and charm united with spiritual gaiety, laughter and jest. The Fröhlichs had once been one of the most prosperous burgher families of Vienna, with their own country house in Döbling. Their considerable income had been derived from the manufacture of a preparation which was used to increase the conserving property of wine barrels. A sharp competition in the improvement of this invention gradually reduced the business and impoverished the family. The great attraction of this household, with its love of art, were the highly talented, intellectual and beautiful daughters, the four sisters Fröhlich. Anna was for years Professor of Singing in the recently-founded Vienna Conservatorium; Josefine was an operatic and concert singer; the pretty, lively Betty (afterwards Frau Bogner), a very gifted painter and assistant of the famous Daffinger; and Katharina, the most charming of the sisters, "Kathi," the typical Vienna citizen's daughter, was "eternally" Grillparzer's bride—but never his wife. Kathi's charm and joyous temperament fascinated everyone. She did the housekeeping, but her heart was entirely in art, especially in music. "As drunkards soak themselves in wine, so she steeps herself in music; when she hears good music she has no longer any control over herself, and is completely carried away," Grillparzer said of her. Her grace captivated the heart of the young poet, and he has immortalised her beauty and her gaiety in many a garland of verse. The two singers, Anna and Josefine, were favourites of the whole concert-going Vienna public. Their co-operation was in great request in musical circles for every sort of entertainment and function. Later Grillparzer lived altogether with the sisters in the Spiegelgasse and died there. Others who were intimately associated with them were Sonnleithner, Gyrowitz, Weigl, Hellmesberger, Hummel and Lachner. Schubert was a frequent guest, and found ready sympathy and hearts opened to him

with enthusiasm. " We learnt to know Schubert," related Anna
Fröhlich, " in the following way. Leopold Sonnleithner (cousin
of Grillparzer's) brought us one day songs by a young man and said
that they ought to be good. Kathi at once sat down to the piano
and tried over the accompaniment. Then suddenly Gimnich, a
clerk who could sing well, stopped and said, ' What is that you are
playing ? Are you improvising ? ' ' No.' ' But that is splendid;
something quite out of the common.' After that we sang the
songs for the rest of the evening. Then a few days later
Sonnleithner brought Schubert and introduced him to us, and from
then onwards he came often to us in the Singerstrasse 18. Sonnleithner asked him why he had not had the songs published, and
when Schubert answered that no publisher would take them and
he hadn't the money to publish them at his own expense, Sonnleithner, Grillparzer, University Professor Schönauer, Baron
Schönstein (who later was the unrivalled Schubert singer), clubbed
together and had the songs published at their own cost. After
next Friday's musical evening at the Kiesewetters', our Sonnleithner
came with a whole packet of printed copies, and after they had been
sung to everyone's admiration, Leopold placed the packet on the
piano and said that if anyone wished to possess these songs he
could buy a copy. There were a hundred copies brought out by
Diabelli."

" Whenever a birthday of Gosmar (later Frau Sonnleithner)
drew near," Anna Fröhlich told Gerhard von Brennung, " I always
went to Grillparzer and begged him to write something for the
occasion. I would say to him, ' Dear Grillparzer, I've nothing to
give them, so you must write a poem for Gosmar's birthday.' He
answered, ' Perhaps I will, if something occurs to me.' A few days
after I had made the request he gave me the serenade ' Leise klop '
ich mit gekrümmten Finger.' And when soon after Schubert came
to us I said, ' Look here, Schubert, you must set this to music.' He
said, ' Very well, give it to me.' Leaning on the piano, he repeated,
as he read it over, ' But this is really beautiful—beautiful.' He went
on looking at the sheet of paper, and then said at last, ' It's done ; I've
got it,' and in three days he brought it to me finished. It was for a
mezzosoprano (for Pepi) and for four men's voices. Then I said,
' No, Schubert, this won't do, because it's to be an ovation for
Gosmar's women friends to sing. You must make the chorus for
women's voices.' I remember so distinctly saying that to him as

Josefine Fröhlich
Crayon drawing by Heinrich
(State Collection, Vienna)

he sat in the window-seat. A little while after he brought it to me written for Pepi and women's voices, as it now is. How little did our dear Schubert worry about his affairs, and how one could never depend, as a rule, on his promise to come at a certain time ; if he met someone on the way he would forget every engagement and go off to a coffee-house or somewhere. I remember how it was when we were to sing his ' Ständchen ' for the first time. I had my pupils in three carriages all ready to drive out to Döbling, where Gosmar then lived, and the piano had been secretly carried under the window outside in the garden, and Schubert invited, but he hadn't come. When I asked him, the next day, why he had not come, he excused himself with, ' Ah ! I quite forgot all about it ! ' Then when I had arranged to produce the ' Ständchen ' publicly in the hall of the Musikverein, and had expressly invited him more than once to be present, he didn't appear. It was time to begin and still no Schubert. Jenger and Hofrat Walcher were present, and when I remarked to them that it would be a thousand pities if to-day he again didn't hear his serenade, as so far he hadn't heard it at all : ' Who knows where he is ? ' Walcher had the happy thought of going to look for him in the ' zur Eiche,' where the beer is good and musicians often go to enjoy it There they found him. He was delighted with the performance and said, ' Really, I had no idea it was so beautiful. . . .' "

" Once I met Schubert," Kathi Fröhlich relates, " near the Maria-hilfe-Linie, and after we had exchanged greetings I gave him a side-long, severe and reproachful glance. He looked embarrassed and almost shy of me. I shall never forget it. He apologised for not having been to see us for so long. Nevertheless, I thought it my duty to lecture him on his conduct, and told him his manner of life was not exactly praiseworthy. He promised me he would make amends, and came soon afterwards and knocked at our door. I was sitting at my window and saw our long-missed Schubert standing there. He opened the door only a few inches and, poking his head through the narrow opening, said, ' Fräulein Kathi, may I come in ? ' I said, ' Since when has our house become so strange to you ? You know it has always been open to you.' He : ' Yes, but I don't feel quite at ease. I haven't forgotten that look you gave me when we met on the Linie. But I had to come to-day because I have something to tell you, for you know that I must always tell you everything that concerns me, whether it is good or bad news. To-day I've had a great pleasure. Someone has given me all Handel's works as a present. And now I see how much I have still to learn. . . .' Soon after he fell ill, and that was his last visit to us."

Another charming woman who played a part in Schubert's life was Maria Leopoldine Pachler, his hostess in Graz. She was the second daughter of the advocate Koschak, a wealthy friend of music in emerald-green Styria, and she had married, on May 12th, 1816, the lawyer, Dr. Karl Pachler, of Graz. Noted for her beauty and many gifts, she was specially distinguished for her musical talent, so that for a long time she had entertained the idea of devoting herself professionally to an artistic career. " I have never found anyone," Beethoven wrote to her, after hearing her play some of his compositions in 1817, " who plays my things as well as you do, not excepting the leading pianists, who are either too mechanical or too affected. You are the true tender nurse for the children of my brain." And Beethoven intended, shortly before his death, to visit the Pachler family in Graz in the company of their friend Jenger, whose splendid piano-playing in Viennese private musical circles had delighted him. But, owing to his decease, this plan was not carried out. The Pachler's house, at the corner of the little " Pfarrgassel," in Graz, was the centre of the artistic life of the Styrian capital. The musical talent and culture of the lady of the house, as well as the genial humour of the host, attracted all the musicians, painters, actors and poets who happened to be passing through Graz, or staying there permanently, to the home of this hospitable family. Thus they numbered among their acquaintance, besides Beethoven and Schubert, the actress Sophie Müller, the actors Löwe and Anschütz, the brothers Anselm and Josef Hüttenbrenner, Jenger, the painter Teltscher, the Styrian poet Gottfried Ritter von Leitner : the Archduke Johann too, the popular prince, associated closely with this delightful family. Frau Pachler, her son tells us, " made her house the centre not only of the (at that time) small town, but musicians and friends of music, actors and theatre-goers from all parts assembled there. Anyone who cultivated music aspired to my mother's recognition and sought her opinion and advice. All the guests, too, were enchanted with my father's witty and humorous company."

Frau Pachler got to know, through the brothers Hüttenbrenner and Jenger, Schubert's compositions, for which her warm, romantic heart was soon enthusiastically opened. Thus she invited the master's friend Jenger on his leave to come to Graz and bring Schubert, an invitation, as we have seen, the two friends gladly accepted in 1827. Those happy days which Schubert spent in the Pachler household at Graz have already been described, and here we merely supplement the description with the letter Schubert wrote on his return to Vienna on September 27th, 1827, to his host:

" DEAR SIR,—

I am now experiencing that I was really too well off in Graz ; for Vienna, though it is a bigger town, seems sadly lacking in real kindness of heart, noble thoughts and talent. There is a great deal of chatter of such a confusing kind that one doesn't know what is clever and what is stupid. Seldom is hearty and unaffected gaiety achieved. It may be that I am myself to blame, being so slow in unbending. In Graz I found it much easier, for there everyone seems natural and easy to get on with, and if I had stayed longer I should have become quite at home. Anyhow, I shall never forget the friendliness of your household and the charming way in which your dear lady, yourself and your little son Faust entertained me. The days I spent with you are among the pleasantest I ever experienced. In the hope that I may be able to show my gratitude some time in the future,

I am, dear sir,

Yours most respectfully,

SCHUBERT."

Several compositions of the master's are associated with Maria Pachler's hospitable house : for instance, the little duet for piano, " Kindermarsch," with trio in G major, which, in October, 1827, he composed for the little son, the above-mentioned Faust Pachler, to present to his father on his birthday. On a sheet of the manuscript which he sent to Frau Maria he wrote the following :

" Herewith I send you, gracious lady, the duet for little Faust ; I fear I shall not win his approbation, as I am not exactly cut out for writing this sort of composition. I trust, dear lady, that you are in better health than I am, for my usual headaches have begun again. I send Dr. Karl every good wish for his birthday, and please tell him that the book of my opera is still with that lazy Hr. Gottdank, who has had it to read and kept it for months.

With all good wishes,

Yours,

FRZ. SCHUBERT."

Friend Jenger, on another sheet, wrote for the boy these lines :

" DEAR LITTLE COMRADE,—

You will see from this enclosure that I have carried out your commission. Study it industriously and on the 4th of the coming month think of Friend Schwammerl and me. Accept every imaginable beautiful wish from us for your dear father's birthday ; we shall be with you in spirit on that day. Write to me again soon. Your letter gave me great pleasure. But I only received it on the 10th of this month through Friend Gometz."

With regard to the songs which Schubert dedicated to Frau Pachler, Jenger, in a letter of April 26th, 1828, thus alludes to them :

" The little volume of songs which our friend Schubert dedicated to you is already in the hands of the printers. It contains the following songs : 1. 'Heimliches Lieben' ; 2. 'Das Weinen' ; 3. 'Vor meiner Wiege' ; 4. Altschottische Ballad. The first and last were composed in your house. When Schubert and I come to you, which, without doubt, will be at the end of August, we will bring you a few copies."

Though Schubert's second visit to the Pachler's in Graz did not come to pass, Jenger's letters contain many references to the never-forgotten days that he and Schubert spent in the artistic household, showing that their thoughts were constantly going back to that happy time. So in a letter of October 26th, 1827, Jenger relates that he has taken part in a " Schubertiade " at the house of the actress Sophie Müller. " I shall deliver your messages to your favourite Sophie Müller and father this evening. There is to be a little service at their house, and a young lady who would so like to know you, because she has heard so much that is nice about you from the Müllers, Friend Schwammerl and me, will play the 'Divertissement à la Hongroise.' This young lady is Irene Kiesewetter, whose signature you will find on the same 'Divertissement' when a copy comes into your hands. This evening we shall speak, as always is the case at the Müllers, much of you, your husband and child. Friend Schwammerl is very fond of the subject, too; so this evening there will certainly be many variations played on this theme. It is a pity, a thousand pities, that you cannot be present to hear for yourself. How heartily we should all welcome you, if you could come, and the great desire of a very dear and very talented pianist, our Irene, would be at last fulfilled."

In the following summer, when Frau Pachler again invited Schubert and his friend Jenger to Graz, the latter wrote on September 6th, 1828:

"Last evening I met Schubert at the Burgtheater. Bauernfeld's comedy was being played for the first time (Der Brautwerber), and now I am able to inform you, dear lady, that Friend Schwammerl expects in a short time an improvement in his finances, and reckons confidently that as soon as this happens he will be able to accept your kind invitation and will appear in Graz with a new operetta. In any case, he or I will let you know for certain 8 days beforehand. He would, of course, like me to come with him, but in the present state of affairs I couldn't get away till after the 24th. If Schubert should stay with you till the end of October, I could get 8 days at least in Graz and see all my dear friends there again and fetch Schwammerl. I look through his diary of a year ago every day and anticipate with delight a repetition of those glorious days.

On the 10th, 11th and 12th I shall think of our delightful excursion to Wildbach and all who took part in it, especially the members of the Wildbach family, and one in particular with much tenderness. . . ."

But the hoped-for improvement in Schubert's finances did not occur. "The journey to Graz must be given up for the present, as both money and weather are unfavourable," runs a letter to Jenger from Schubert dated September 25th, 1828. And scarcely two months later he lay in his coffin. Friend Jenger was brokenhearted, and wrote to Frau Pachler, who was also sorrowing for the young master: "You will understand that I cannot get over the the loss of my friend Schubert; and of how unwell I have been since his death, Baron Grimschitz will tell you. I am very busy arranging the performance of the Requiem by his faithful friend Anselmo (Hüttenbrenner) in the Augustinerkirche, and getting up a subscription for his gravestone. His grave is only divided from Beethoven's by three other graves in the new Währinger Cemetery."

Associated with that memorable stay of Schubert's in green Styria are the six fair, merry daughters of the châtelaine of Castle Wildbach, Frau Anna Massegg, the aunt of Frau Pachler. They were the girl-comrades who accompanied Schubert and his friends, Jenger and Hüttenbrenner, on their wanderings in the forest and on the mountains, who played all sorts of pranks with them, and who, in the evening, were enthralled listeners to the Wildbach " Schubertiades." According to researches made by Otto Erich Deutsch, there is a tradition in the Wildbach family that the eldest daughter, Maria, who was then in her twenty-fourth year, had sung Schubert's songs with so much expression and feeling that the master was moved by her singing to tears. In her old age she often spoke with happy emotion of having had the good fortune as a girl to sing Schubert's songs to the composer himself, and she always alluded to " Der Wanderer " as the most successful. The piano accompaniment was not played by Schubert, but by her music-master, Fuchs, father of the composer, Robert Fuchs. Schubert was delighted, and left Wildbach with the promise to come back again in the following year.

Another sister, Nani, wrote to Frau Pachler, in a letter which has been unearthed by Otto Erich Deutsch in the Graz University Library, on October 25th, 1827: " . . . Never to be forgotten are the days which you and your dear companions spent with us as our guests. I often wish I could call them back, for it will be long before we shall ever have the honour again of entertaining in our house such brilliant company. . . ."

Two artistes have yet to be mentioned before we close this chapter. They are the singer Anna Pauline Milder Hauptmann, to whom Fate assigned a part also in Beethoven's life, and the *prima donna*, Kathi Buchwieser. " Milder's voice is one of the richest and most beautiful," said Reichhardt, conductor of the Prussian Court Orchestra, after a performance of Weigl's opera, " Das Waisen-haus," at the Kärntnertortheater, " that I have ever heard in my life ; it is so pure, full and melodious, and her manner of delivery is extraordinarily correct and beautiful. Not often does a singer please so easily. Her figure, too, is noble, and her face and the play of her features dignified and expressive."

She was the very first impersonator of Leonora, in the year 1808. Beethoven, in writing to thank her for her artistic work in his opera, said: " He can consider himself fortunate when to his lot

Anna Milder-Hauptmann
By Seybold

fall your muse, your genius, your splendid qualities and advantages."
This singer devoted, in passing, her great art to Schubert's songs,
and we have many letters that were exchanged between her and
the composer, and critiques of the concerts at which she sang his
lieder. In all probability it was through the singer Vogl, her friend
and teacher, that her attention was first drawn to Schubert's lyrical
genius.   In a letter dated December 22nd, 1824, from Berlin, where
she was *prima donna* at the Royal Court Opera, to the composer who
had been her enthusiastic admirer since his choir-boy days, she wrote:

"During my stay in Vienna Herr Schick promised me that I
should have the pleasure of making your personal acquaintance.
I waited in vain and was obliged to leave without my wish being
fulfilled.   Allow me to tell you now in writing how enchanted I
am with your songs, and what enthusiasm they excite wherever I
sing them.   This emboldens me to send you a poem which, if you
have time and your muse approves, I should like you to set for me
to music.   You would give me the greatest possible pleasure if you
would do this, as I should wish to sing it at concerts.   I take the
liberty of remarking that it should take into consideration a large
public.   I have been told that you have written several operas, and
I should like to know whether you would not be inclined to give
one of them in Berlin and let me negotiate it with the Intendant.   I
have asked Vogl the same question; but probably our friend is
not in Vienna, as I have had no answer.   If you see him please
greet him heartily from me, and say that I should much like to
have a line from him.   In the hope that I may soon hear from you,
                    I remain,
                Your obedient servant,
                        ANNA MILDER."

Schubert, pleased at this unexpected commission, sent off at once
on the receipt of the letter his troublesome musical child, "Alfonso
und Estrella," the performance of which he had failed to bring off
on any stage; he added, in grateful admiration, "Suleikas Zweiten
Gesang," with a letter in which he announced his wish to dedicate
it to her.   Three months went by, and no answer came from the *diva*
till March 8th, 1825, when she wrote:

"MY MOST HONOURED HERR SCHUBERT,—

I hasten to tell you that your opera "Alfonso und Estrella"
and the second song of Suleika have reached me and given me

intense pleasure. Suleika's Second Song is beautiful and moves me to tears. I thank you with all my heart for your obliging promptness. It is indescribable how you have, as in the 'Ersten Gesang' of 'Suleika,' concentrated all the magic and passionate longing into this melody. It is only to be regretted that one cannot sing the public all these wonderful beauties, for the vast majority only want their ears tickled. Should the 'Nachtschmetterling' not be suitable for giving the singing voice brilliant music, then I would beg you to choose another poem, and, if possible, one by Goethe, which would allow of being sung in a varied *tempo*, so that one could awake thereby a variety of emotions. I leave it to you how this is to be managed, and only make the suggestion that the end shall be extra brilliant.

You can dedicate to me as many songs as you like. I shall be only too charmed and flattered. On the 1st of June I leave here, and if I could have the desired song for my concert tour I should be extremely glad, especially if it contained the suitable passages I have indicated. As to your opera 'Alfonso und Estrella,' I am very sorry indeed to have to remark that the book is not in accordance with the present taste here, where people are used to grand tragic opera or French musical operetta. After what I now tell you of the prevailing taste here, you will see for yourself that 'Alfonso und Estrella' would meet with no success. Should I have the pleasure of appearing in one of your operas the part must, of course, be suited to my individuality—for example, it should be that of a queen, a mother or a peasant woman, and if possible the whole should be in one act, if I may venture to advise, and should be something novel, dealing with an Oriental subject, the soprano being the leading character, something on the lines of Goethe's 'Divan.' A good performance for three characters and chorus, *i.e.*, one soprano, one tenor, one bass, can be relied on here. If you can find the sort of subject, please let me know at once, so that we can arrange matters. The scenario may be left to me. And also kindly tell me what you wish done with 'Alfonso und Estrella.' My heartiest greetings to my friend and teacher. I am indeed sorry that he is not well. Tell him that I have to sing this year in Wiesbaden. It would give me infinite pleasure to have a few lines from him. . . .

Your respectful,

ANNA MILDER."

This letter, especially the part of it relating to the opera " Alfonso und Estrella " must have caused Schubert much disappointment. Nevertheless, acting on the suggestion of the fair singer to compose an opera for Berlin, he set to work and got his friend Bauernfeld to write the text of " Graf von Gleichen." When the libretto was ready, he started with great zeal on the music. But owing to his early death only a sketch was made and the opera' was left unfinished. Even when he lay on his death-bed he discussed with Bauernfeld the continuation of this work. The master had one more letter from the celebrated singer, in which she sent him news of the success with which she had sung his *lieder* at a concert in Berlin :

" DEAR HERR SCHUBERT,—

I cannot refrain from letting you know that I have been singing your songs in public. The ' Erlkönig ' and ' Suleika ' called forth the warmest applause, and I am so glad to be able to send you enclosed newspaper cuttings, and I sincerely wish and hope that they will give you pleasure too. Everyone wishes to buy ' Suleika ' and it will probably soon appear. Trautwein is the most honest music-seller in Berlin, and if you would like to publish ' Suleika ' here I would recommend him strongly.

Have you found anything yet for me in Goethe ? I leave here on the 30th and probably shall not receive anything from you before, for which I am very sorry. In August I shall be in Ems for my health. If you have any opportunity of sending on to me there your latest compositions, or to Paris, where I shall be for two months— September and October—I should be very pleased. How is Vogl ? I hope he is well. Give him a hundred times my love. I still regret so much that when I was in Vienna I was not so fortunate as to see him. Have the kindness to tell him that I am going to Paris. I shall not sing there, though I should have an intelligent public. Goodbye, and don't forget to send me your compositions.

Yours faithfully,

ANNA MILDER."

In the last year of his life Schubert composed yet another song with piano and clarinet accompaniment for the famous singer, " Der Hirt auf dem Felsen," which she only received after the master's death.

The well-known musician and author, Ferdinand Hiller, tells us of the composer's intercourse in the house of the once much-admired singer Buchwieser, and describes his meetings with Beethoven and Schubert when he was in Vienna as a boy.

" . . . I heard the songs of Franz Schubert for the first time at the house of a lady friend of my master, Hummel, the once-famous actress Buchwieser, at that time the wife of a wealthy Hungarian magnate. She invited Hummel and myself two or three times to dine with them. The charming lady still bore traces of her former beauty, but she was a great invalid and scarcely able to walk. Her husband received guests with genial hospitality. Their apartments were stately and spacious, and were pervaded by a genuinely aristocratic atmosphere. No one was invited but Schubert, the favourite and *protégé* of the hostess, and Vogl, the singer of his songs *par excellence*. A little while after we had risen from the dinner table Schubert seated himself at the piano, Vogl standing beside him. The rest of us took comfortable chairs in any part of the great brilliantly lighted salon which suited us best, and then a wonderful concert began. Schubert hadn't much technique and Vogl hadn't much voice, but both were so full of life and feeling, and both were so completely absorbed in their renderings, that it would be impossible to conceive a more glorious interpretation of these wonderful compositions. One thought neither of piano-playing nor of singing; it seemed as if the music needed no material aid, and as if the melodies were spiritual apparitions which revealed themselves to spiritualised ears. I dare not speak of my own enthusiasm and my emotion, but my master, who had half a century of music behind him, was so deeply moved that tears rained down his cheeks. I find that I referred to Schubert in the diary I kept at that time as a ' quiet man '; he hadn't always been so, but it was only with his most intimate friends that he let himself go. When I called on him in his modest dwelling he received me with friendliness, but also with so much respect that I felt terribly shy and embarrassed. He replied to my hesitating and superfluous question if he wrote much (an MS. lay on his desk), ' I compose every morning. When I have finished one thing I begin another.' Obviously he does nothing else, and lives alone for music. . . ."

Schubert and Schwind

AS Vienna's romantic period found its most beautiful musical expression in the works of Schubert, so Schwind, too, in pictures, drawings and sketches, bathed in a dreamy, fantastic atmosphere breathed from the inward soul, like the tone-poet's music, the spirit of Viennese romanticism. What Schumann said of Schubert, " He will always be the favourite of youth, with his overflowing heart, his brave thoughts and stories of knights, fair maids, and adventures," is equally true of Schwind's muse. These two souls were bound together by the most intimate relationship and sympathy; the chain of a spiritual fraternity encircled their creative work; they were not only as men, but as artists, friends and comrades. One can almost say that in a certain respect the songs, ballads, fantasies and symphonies ·composed by Schubert were painted by Schwind. They were psychic landscapes painted in pure ingenuousness with divine artistic *élan*.

Altogether it was scarcely seven years that the two artists lived together in truest friendship, from the beginning of the year 1821 till September, 1827. On September 3rd Schwind moved to Munich. In November, 1828, Schubert died. For the latter those seven years meant the ascent to perfection and mastery in his art; for Schwind the beginning of an ever-increasingly brilliant career as an artist.

When Schwind, at seventeen, became acquainted with Schubert he was, as his portrait by his own hand shows, a slender youth, with great blue eyes and an ecstatic, earnest expression. He met the world with a free and frank air, and only the firmly closed lips demonstrate his serious purpose and strength of will. He had determined to give up scientific studies and devote himself wholly to art. As the painter Führich wrote : " After the urgent *crescendo* and the closing chords of the first movement of Schwind's life-symphony followed a *capriciosa*, a real April-weather period lasting ten years, which contained many fair spring days, with fragrant buds bursting into blossom; then followed storms and snow showers, with an apparent relapse into a petrified winter season, which, however, soon thawed imperceptibly."

It was Schwind's *Sturm und Drang* period. The world was newly discovered. Earth had an extraordinary brilliance ; life was full of a thousand dreams and pictures ; new stars of dazzling radiance rose on the horizon of the boy's ardent soul . . . and then it was that he entered the Schubertian circle. He joined with enthusiasm and an overwhelming sensation of delight the little clique round the already-famous master, at whose shrine he was to worship in the company of the dear friends Schober, Spaun, Kupelwieser, Bruchmann, Mayrhofer, Schnorr von Carolsfeld and Bauernfeld. " His appearance, bearing witness to the healthy soul in the healthy body, his beautiful intelligent eyes, his liveliness and good humour," wrote Spaun in his reminiscences, " prejudiced us strongly in the youth's favour, and we welcomed him as a new member of the circle which had been formed round Schubert by Schober and others." The poet Bauernfeld, who was an old school-fellow of Schwind's, entered in his diary : " His is really a fine, artist's nature—absolutely genuine and pure, full of noble aspirations."

Schubert, instinctively drawn to Schwind, and discerning the genius of his character, responded warmly to the love and worship he offered him. The Schubertians called Schwind " Cherubim," because of his youthful, almost girlish, good looks. Another nick-name was " Giselher." Schubert in joke named him his " Be-loved " on account of his stormy outbursts of feeling towards him-self. For Schwind the friendship was a deep inner experience. An irresistible attraction drew him to Schubert and his circle. In the letters which Schwind in those days addressed to Schubert, Bauern-feld, and especially to Schober, the youth found expression for his overmastering emotions. They did not contain mere phrases of youthful rapture, but were the outpourings in lyrical language of a heart thirsting for love.

On December 12th, 1825, he wrote to Schober :

" DEAR, GOOD FRANZ,—I see more and more that my whole life is a duet with you. I could go on writing for ever and yet would never have written enough. I do so love to sit down of an evening and as one cuts a name dear to one in the bark of a tree, to converse with you in spirit, so that I quite forget to tell you anything of importance. You have embraced so heartily all that lives in me—of course, much more than I know of—that I am almost ashamed to speak to you about it. I see myself reposing on the heart of your love, like an angel which unites us, and I delight in talking to myself, in your arms where all is quiet and peaceful, and I feel as if I had a mirror within me in which you are reflected. You are always communing with yourself, aren't you? And so I sing or speak, too, to myself, and when the notes come easily it is as if you were delighting in my words. But very often I cannot alight on a word, or a song fails me, and then I can somehow only express my feelings by opening wide my arms. . . ."

On April 22nd, 1824, he wrote to Schober :

" I don't want to die, but I am often conscious of the bliss of escaping from the shackles of the body. I long for existence, quiet and self-contained, and I am aflame with yearning and overflowing with love. Where is the heart, where are the arms which will open to soothe and free me ? I don't reproach myself, because I want it all embodied in looks, words and form. I am sure that tenderness is the purest physical emotion. I tremble in my shoes as I write this to you, Schober, beloved one, everlastingly beloved. . . . It does me such infinite good to write to you and to think that all the best of me is imperishably preserved in you. Now, see, it is morning ! To-day and to-morrow I must tilt and slay knights (Schwind was drawing at that time a cycle of illustrations, ' Dit Tuniere der Ritter,' for Trentsenky, in Vienna). I like tournaments and wouldn't mind if my brothers, armed with cardboard shields and wooden swords and helmets made of wire, came and tilted with me ! Now I must go to my work. . . ."

Schwind lived at that time with his brothers in the " Mondschein-hause " on the Wiedau belonging to his grandmother. " This house," the painter Führich writes, " was built on a strong terraced foundation ; its façade looked north, and the second floor was inhabited by the Schwind family. It had a splendid view over the courtyard, which was the scene every week of a horse market, to the Glacis, and beyond the roofs of the town away to the advance-guard of the Alps, Sievering, as far as the Leopoldsberge dipping towards the Danube. This side of the house was occupied by Schwind's mother and three, at that time, unmarried sisters. The south side opened on to a smaller courtyard running from east to west, and abutted on the garden wall belonging to the priest of the Karlskirche. Over this the mighty dome of the church cast its shadow, and one could hear the strains of the organ. This yard was only divided from the small next-door inn, situated in a *cul-de-sac*, by an arbour and espalier of lilac bushes. There were a few flower-beds, and the brothers Schwind had planted some acacias and an elder tree. The whole formed an oasis of unadulterated rusticity in the middle of Vienna such as wealth could not have produced. The " Platzl," as the yard was called, was merely the continuation of a room, and the room served as a protection against the weather. In the arbour the boys drew, studied and watched the stars. On fine nights they brought their mattresses into the open air and slept there. They played at tournaments in the yard, and in winter they built snow fortifications and sphinxes, and had snowball battles, accompanied by recitations of Homeric verse. When the weather drove them to seek the shelter of the room, Cousin Slavik would spout rhymes or play the guitar, Moritz would draw, brother August study, and Franz hammer, and there would be friends dropping in to smoke. . . ."

According to Führich, Schubert's serenade, " Hark, hark the Lark," was written here while he waited till Schwind had finished his drawing before coming for a walk. The other version, of its being written on the back of a menu at an inn one Sunday afternoon, is more interesting if less probable. Schubert and his friends went in and out of the old " Mondschein-hauses " as they liked. It was one of the favourite meeting-places of the Schubertians, and many of Schubert's compositions were first performed here in modest fashion, criticised and greeted with rapture by the intimate little circle. The poets, Schober and Bauernfeld, Kenner and Senn, read aloud the latest fruit of their lyrical and dramatic muses, and raved about the works of the then modern of the moderns, Kleist, Brentano, Tieck, Achim von Arnim, Fouqué, E. T. A. Hoffmann and Heine.

The old German legends and sagas of the North, the heroes of the Nibelungenlied, awoke to new life. The songs of the Trouba-dours, full of brilliant colour, conjured up before the eyes of these youths the splendour of the Middle Ages, its knight errantry, adventures, castles and fortresses. The romantic spirit of the time rang from Schubert's music in enchanting melody. And the young Schwind's artistic imagination was fired as the great kingdom of German romanticism opened before his enchanted gaze. But here, too, they loved, laughed and drank. Dances were got up. They played practical jokes on one another. It was " *Sturm und Drang* " time. "No one who entered the house of that Schwind family (sometimes called "Schwindien") and took part in its revels," wrote Führich many years after, " could ever forget it, and was compelled to admit that the like of it would never be seen again. . . ."

In those days Schwind enjoyed nothing so much as frequenting the society of Schubert and his friends. The relations between the two artists became even still more intimate when Schubert migrated to the Wieden and established himself near the Karlkirche in the Frickwertschen House, where he was a near neighbour of the "Mondschein" house party. From 1825 to 1826 the friends met every day. Visit followed visit ; letters and notes flew backwards and forwards. One confided to the other his most secret thoughts, talked over artistic plans, built castles in the air and golden bridges into the future. Schwind was the first to hear Schubert's newest compositions, and Schubert saw the sketches and pictures of Schwind come into being. Thus they enjoyed in common the ecstacy of artistic creation. They shared their joys, and when Dame Care knocked on the door their troubles and sorrows were divided in brotherly fashion. And all too often they were visited by the grey, pale-faced phantom, for the material position of both artists was at that time far from enviable. In the Schwind house, as well as at Schubert's, finances were often low, so low that orders for New Year's cards and cheap sketches had to be executed in order to wring a few guilders from the publishers. Often the bare necessities of life were lacking, even the very necessary drawing-paper, as a letter from Schwind to his friend Steinhauser testifies : " Send me, I beg of you, three quires of drawing-paper at 30 kreuzer the quire ; for if I can't draw I am a miserable man. But as I am in a position in which I want money rather than am able to spend it, will you be so good as to defray the cost ? " There was a communism of property among Schubert, Bauernfeld and Schwind. " Hats, boots, neckties and coats belonged to all indiscriminately till they were the worse for wear, and then each returned to the articles of clothing which were his undisputed property."

But all this was more advantageous than the reverse, and formed a rare training ground for the development of artistic qualities. How often tobacco—" gold dust " as they called it—was not to be afforded, and how many other things there were of which they were constantly in want. Only the courage of youth never failed them and the ability to accept everything in a poetic, joyous spirit.

It happened sometimes that emissaries from dissatisfied tailors and bootmakers made their appearance. They were disguised under the name " dwarf," and when one " rode into the citadel," he who was sought took flight on the other side.

But these were mere externals. They were young and could afford to wait till fortune and fame strewed their path with abundance. Fantasy was extravagant; she laid firebrands in the heart of the young artists, whose inner riches made them indifferent to outward benefits. They absorbed themselves in their work and their artist's dreams, and the world outside, with its everyday cares, need and suffering, was forgotten.

A collection of Schwind's youthful productions which belong to these years may, at a first glance, be disappointing and give little promise of the later masterly pictures of travel, the " Melusine " and the frescoes in the Vienna Opera House. They are mostly done to order, and have little that is striking in composition and are weak in colour. Among them are New Year cards and valentines—which played a considerable *rôle* in the Vienna of those days—and covers for children's books, sketches of local scenes, picnics and wedding parties done to order for the art dealers, Paterno, Trentsensky, and Schober's Lithograph Institute. Many of them depict the life of the small burgher classes and display a gift of keen observation, combining comic situations with fresh Viennese grace. The work is executed with extreme care and laborious industry. The absolute correctness of costumes and *milieu* render them of historic value. Better known are the six illustrations to " Robinson Crusoe," and the title-page vignettes to the " Arabian Nights," which, thanks to Schober's acting as intermediary, excited the attention of Goethe, who in the sixth volume of " Kunst und Altertum " refers to these drawings in terms of high praise. Schwind all his life was very proud of having won the good opinion of the Weimar prince of poets.

To Schwind's earlier works, which were engraved on stone in Schober's lithographic institute by Kriehuber, belong also the portraits of kings of Hungary, and the costume pictures from Raimund's " Bauer als Millionär," for which the actors themselves stood as models (Raimund as the old Dustman, Therese Krones as Youth, Katherine Ennöckel as Content, etc.). The majority of these drawings and pictures were pot-boilers for publishers, and, as the themes ordered had to be rigidly adhered to, gave little scope for the artist's imagination. Wit and humour could find an outlet certainly in these New Year cards and picnic pictures, and yet

" alongside Schwind's dancing goblin wit," as Führich writes,
" which sometimes wore a black tail-coat, moved a soul which clung
to serious artists like Kupelwieser with childlike reverence. On the
other hand, the shafts of his wit were aimed at friend and foe alike,
and sometimes glanced off himself. This lively artistic temperament
could plunge again so deeply into grave subjects that, for example,
in 1825 no less than sixty tombstones were designed and drawn
by Schwind, and for these his friend Mayrhofer composed short
epitaphs. They indicate with a few strokes of the pen the association
of certain callings and positions in life with thoughts of death.

It was Schubert's music and friendly intercourse with the
Schubertians which awoke in Schwind the romantic ideas which
soon peopled his imagination. In the cycle of illustrations for
Hoffman's poetic story, " Meister Martin und seine Gesellen," and
for Kenner's ballad " Der Liedler," and still more in the " Hochzeitszug," to which Schwind was inspired by witnessing a performance of Mozart's " Figaro," this influence is predominant.
" He was not satisfied with reproducing the stage pictures," writes
Weigmann, " but let many of his favourites from other sources
take part in the procession—four characters from ' Lucinde,' by
Schlegel, followed by his beloved Papageno, the four seasons, with
the afterwards well-known figure of " Herr Winter," and in the
ranks of the guests we meet many a familiar face from the Schubert
circle, with his own portrait added on a separate page."

The brilliant characteristics of his later manner, his elegant, sure
touch and pregnant characterisation, graceful gaiety and poetic
sentiment, are distinctly foreshadowed in these charming works.
On April 2nd, 1825, Schwind wrote to Schubert : " I have just
finished a long wedding procession which contains on thirty sheets
of paper much that is serious as well as merry. The bridal pair are
Figaro and Susanna ; Bartolo and Marceline, the Count and
Countess, follow. Before them march musicians, dancers, soldiers,
servants, pages and such-like people. Behind come guests and
masks ; the four ' Romans ' from Schlegel's ' Lucinde,' the love-
lorn Papageno, the four seasons, then a leaf of various people,
which brings it to an end. Cherubino, the page, and a pretty Bar-
barina are in an arbour together. There are over a hundred figures,
and three or four on a page. The paper is very thin and pens have
caused me a lot of trouble. I am curious to know what you'll
think of it. I believe some of it is really good and the whole
new. . . ."

Schwind wrote to his friend Schubert on July 25th:

"Grillparzer is delighted with the 'Hochzeit,' and says that he is sure in ten years' time he will remember clearly every figure. As we have no Duke of Weimar to be our patron and paymaster, we must make the most of the favourable opinion of celebrated men, so you can imagine that I went home pleased. That he should regard the 'Hochzeit des Figaro' in the same light as myself is for me no small triumph." This, the chief work of Schwind's youth, containing promise of the painter's later remarkable style, Beethoven had by his bed during his last illness. After his death it went back to Schwind and came again into evidence when found among Schwind's artistic remains with the comment made on it by himself, "The first flight of independent and original genius." Quite to the romantic class belong "Ritterliche Liebespaar," "Der Traum des Ritters," and the oil painting, "Kätchen von Heilbronn," depicting the scene where Kätchen rests under the elder tree in a trance and is surprised by the Knight. The picture was exhibited in 1826 at the Viennese Academy. Picture after picture followed in the same romantic vein. It was Schubert, the incarnation in the Vienna of that time of the romantic spirit and Schwind's invaluable prototype, who, through his music, opened up to the young painter the world in which he could make best use of his creative powers, whose art and genius led him onwards to the light, exercising a soothing and taming influence on his friend's wild, stormy and impatient temperament.

The young painter's creative talent, his will to work, increased under the magic spell of Schubert's melodies, his fantasy grew in richness, beauty and depth. And when Schwind, in his little quiet room in the 'Mondschein' house, drew and painted not to order, and with no thought of monetary gain, then the wings of his soul spread, and the youth saw the light dawn in his own inner world— a divine and mild radiance from a miraculous blue heaven. Then arose those first poetic sketches and studies for the famous pictures inspired by the breath of Schubert's music—pictures which for so many years Schwind carried about with him, and not till he had reached a ripe old age, thirty or forty years later, exhibited. Here were the plans for the "Reisebilder," the most beautiful and graceful products of the Schwindian muse, reminiscent of Schubert's *lieder*, lyrical poems in colour—his "unsaleable picture gallery," as he liked to call them. They contained all the inward and outward impressions of his own stormy life, dreams and memories, of joys and sorrows, all that he had learned on his " pilgrimage to his Ideal." There is the " Traum des Ritter," a knight to whom in a dream a princess bewitched by some evil spirit appears. In painting this princess there may have floated before Schwind's eyes the image of his Viennese *fiancée* and love, Netty Hönig, in whose home so many joyous Schubertiades were held. Or the " Waldkapelle," in which one sees a white road leading through a dark pine forest. By the roadside is a chapel, on the steps of which a maiden rests. Two deer bound over the solitary road, winding away into the darkness of the forest. Then there is the poetical " Morgenstunde." A girl who has just risen from her bed opens the window and is greeted by the bright morning breaking through the blue mists of the shimmering mountain peaks. Through a small rift in the other shuttered window a golden sun-ray stretches across the floor of the plain little room. " Abschied im Morgengrauen " shows a young wanderer (Schwind) with a knapsack on his back. Leaving a lonely house and passing out at the garden gate, he strides towards the forest. Then there is " Ein Jüngling mit einem Engel durch die Hallen einer Kirche schwebend " (later called " Dream of Erwin von Steinbach," showing how the great architect as a child saw revealed to him in a dream by an angel his future work, the Cathedral of Strassburg, perfect and complete), a sketch which indicates Schwind's own fate, for he, too, as a young painter, dreamed of his life's work, and in early years conceived pictures and thoughts which took perfected shape only after he had become a mature artist. In the Viennese Schubert period too (beginning of the 'twenties), the first study was made for the great fairy-tale cycle " Aschenbrödel " (Cinderella). As if in anticipation of the picture of the " Zauberflöte," which not till forty years later was seen in the *foyer* of the Vienna Opera House, the young painter wrote in December, 1828, " To end with, I shall paint Tamino and Tamina as they pass through the fire. . . ."

Schwind, like a true Viennese, had received not only a good musical grounding, but possessed an inborn musical talent. He was heart and soul devoted to the sister art. " A mouthful of music is a daily necessity," runs an old proverb. He practised the piano diligently, was a passionate player on the violin and a singer—in short, a musician to his finger-tips. He saw nobler and more perfect beauty in the tone-pictures of Mozart, Beethoven and, above all, in Schubert's, than in the works of contemporary plastic art. What he sought in vain in the latter—depth of feeling, clearness of expression, distinction of form—he found in Schubert's compositions, to which he listened when they were performed in the little circle of devoted friends with rapturous enthusiasm. But he was an intelligent listener, as is to be gathered from his critical comments in his letters on Schubert's work.

" Schubert's quartet," he wrote, referring to the famous quartet in A minor which he had heard given by the violinist Schuppanzigh and his colleagues in March, 1824, " was performed, in my opinion, rather too slowly, but with great purity and tenderness. It is soft throughout, but the melodies are contrived to sound like songs, very pronounced and full of feeling. It was much applauded, especially the minuet, which is extraordinarily natural and sweet. A Chinese sitting near me thought it affected and wanting in style. I should just like to see if Schubert could ever be affected. . . ."

" The day before yesterday," he wrote to Schober on December 22nd, 1825, " they gave at the Theater-an-der-Wien a piece by the incorrigible Frau von Chezy, ' Rosamunde von Cypern,' with music by Schubert. You can picture how we all crowded there. As I hadn't been out the whole day because of my cough, I couldn't get a seat in the *parterre* with the others, and went up to the third gallery. Schubert gave the overture which he wrote for ' Estrella,' as it is too frivolous for ' Estrella ' and he will write another. It was applauded and, to my delight, encored. You can imagine how attentively I watched the stage and the instruments. It seemed to me that the flute, to which the theme is chiefly confided, comes in too soon, but it may have been the fault of the player. Otherwise everything is intelligible and well-balanced. After the first act a piece was inserted that seemed a little inadequate for the place it was meant to fill and too full of repeats. A ballet passed unnoticed, and the second and third *entr'acte*. People are accustomed here to clap directly the act is over, and I can't understand how one could expect from them attention to such serious and lovely things coming after. In the last act there was a chorus of shepherds and huntsmen, so charming and natural. I don't know that I ever heard anything of the kind I liked better. It was clapped and encored, and I believe it will soon be more popular than the chorus out of Weber's ' Euryanthe.' "

In later years, when Schubert's friend Lachner was in Munich, and presented there the master's opera " Die Verschworenen," under the

title of " Der haüsliche Krieg," Schwind wrote : " Schubert's little
opera made me very happy. With what simplicity and innocent
joyousness he made this beautiful music, what wealth of invention
and dramatic instinct it contains. If he had had a little more experience he would not have been far behind Weber. . . ."

The influence of music on Schwind's creative work is demonstrated by the fact that some of his finest creations were directly
inspired by musical subjects. Among others, his *chef d'œuvre*, the
cycle of scenes from famous operas in the Vienna Opera House,
the illustrations to Beethoven's " Fidelio," the merry topical work,
" Die Lachnerrolle," in which he could give rein to his humour,
the " Schubertabend bei Ritter von Spaun," the work of his youth,
" Der Hochzeitszug des Figaro "—and, indeed, the inspiration of
music generally is visible in all his work. It is especially noteworthy
in his last romantic " Die schöne Melusine," which is full of the grace
of Schubertian melodies. In his young days in Vienna he made
use in his art of many of the same themes as inspired his friend
Schubert. Goethe's ballads, " An Schwager Kronos," " Der
Erlkönig " and " Der Schatzgräber," are examples, and it is possible that the idea of his painting, the " Rückkehr des Grafen von
Gleichen," may have originated in the opera-text which Bauernfeld
wrote for Franz Schubert. Schubert's person and that of his
friends, occupied Schwind artistically till the end of his life. The
first work of the painter, for which Schubert and his friends served
as models, was the well-known " Atzenbrugger Fest." Schwind,
it is true, supplied only the figures for this gay Biedermeierish work ;
the landscape was drawn by Schober, and the whole was engraved
by the lithographer Ludwig Mohn, who also belonged to Schubert's circle. It depicts a party of Schubertians amusing themselves
with a game of ball ; one of them plays the fiddle—presumably the
landscape painter Ludwig Kreissle. In the middle sits Schubert
on the grass, smoking a long pipe ; on his right, bareheaded, is
Schwind. In the background the lovely Atzenbrugg rises against
the sky. In the ball-playing group Franz von Schober is visible
on the right, holding his stick and hat in his hand. Several Schubertians were perpetuated by Schwind in portraits in oils and pencil—
Ferdinand Sauter and his zither-playing brother Franz, Netty Hönig,
Frau Therese Hönig, and others.

In the oil painting " Spaziergang vor dem Stadttor " members of
the Schubert circle again appear as accessories in the picture. The

painting dates from 1827, a short time before Schwind's departure for Munich. The ancient town is said to be Tulln, in Lower Austria. On the left Schwind sits studying the map with his hat and luggage beside him ; a girl peeps at him over the garden wall (very likely his Viennese *fiancée*, Netty Hönig, the parting from whom he felt so bitterly). In front of the town gates the whole company are strolling, including Schubert and the singer Vogl. A spirit of sadness pervades the picture, expressive of Schwind's regret at saying " Goodbye " to Vienna and the Schubertians.

Soon after Schwind moved to Munich Schubert died. The young painter was heartbroken at the news of his friend's death, and gave vent to his grief in a pathetic letter to Schober :

" DEAR GOOD SCHOBER,—

I got a letter yesterday from N. telling me Schubert is dead. You know how I loved him, and you can understand how hard I find it to get used to the thought that we have lost him. We have still dear friends left, but none who shared with us from the beginning those unforgettable days which are among our most precious memories. I have mourned for him as if he were my brother, but now I feel it is well that he has died in his greatness and been freed from his troubles. The more I now realise what he was, the more I see what he suffered. But I still have you, and you love me with the same love which bound us both to our beloved dead in those incomparable times. You alone know what the fire of youth means, and how it is still the only thing that can make me happy. All the love I have not buried with him is now yours, and with you to live and share everything is my dearest ambition. His memory will ever be sacred for us, and there will be moments, in spite of all the troubles of this life, when we shall know again what now seems to have totally vanished. . . ."

Schwind clung to memories of the days of his youth in Vienna, of Schubert and the never-to-be-forgotten circle of friends, with faithful affection. Long after, when he had been working and studying for years in Germany, he was constantly attacked with a secret homesickness for Vienna. " I am often homesick for Wien," he wrote on February 23rd, 1845, to Bauernfeld ; " sometimes I hardly know how to bear it, but what is to be done ? In Vienna I can't earn anything." He was always dreaming of going back there, and hoped for commissions from his native city, but in vain.

Moriz von Schwind

Portrait by the Artist

It was not till shortly before his death that he received the order to decorate with frescoes the *foyer* and *loggia* of the Viennese Opera House, and this was one of the greatest joys of his life. His desire to paint a picture for the Belvedere Gallery was never fulfilled. Only after his death was his famous fairy-tale cycle, " Die schöne Melusine," hung in this gallery.

He never gave up regularly corresponding with the Viennese friends of his youth, especially with Bauernfeld, Schober, Kupelwieser, Lachner, Spaun, Feuchtersleben, Grillparzer and Führich. He was in intimate correspondence with Bauernfeld till the day of his death.

Schubert he never forgot. Even in his very last works we come across, over and over again, touches reminiscent of the joyous Viennese Schubert time. Thus, in the picture drawn in 1848 and 1849, and the oil painting painted in 1852, " Die Sinfonie " (in the *Neue Pinakothek* at Munich), we see in the lower part of the picture Schubert on the left; near him Vogl and Schober; the conductor is Franz Lachner. At the piano are Frau von Blittersdorf and Schwind. The singer has the features of Fräulein Hetzenecker, whose love-story is perpetuated in the picture. Schwind, in a letter to Schädel written in November, 1849, thus explains the subject : " For the rehearsal of one of Beethoven's most graceful works, Fantasia for piano, orchestra and chorus, the only work of his written for this combination, so easy to recognize in the picture. The musical guests in a fashionable watering-place are assembled in the gaily-decorated theatre salon. The heroine, by singing a small solo, awakes the interest of a young man. The ingenuous love episode between this pair is developed in three further pictures, which tally with the three movements of a quartet, *andante, scherzo, allegro*. . . . A meeting without speaking—a ball, at which courage is taken to approach the fair one—a happy moment and the honeymoon, when the bride sees the little castle belonging to the happy husband. In harmony with the chorus of Beethoven's composition, which is a song of praise of the joys of Nature, there are woodlands and fresh air in the picture—the fresh air represented by the four winds. . . ."

We meet Schubert's likeness over and over again in the humourously drawn " Lachnerrolle," executed in the year 1862 to commemorate Franz Lachner's twenty-five years' service as conductor —" Lachner, Schwind, Bauernfeld and Schubert serenading," " Lachner, Schubert and Bauernfeld at Grinzing," and so on.

In 1868, in a pen-and-ink drawing for a Schubert fountain designed by Schwind, is a bust of the master, with two muses, Grave and Gay, on either side.

We find Schubert's portrait again among friends in the medallions for the architectural setting of the " Sieben Raben." To Schubert's music he dedicated, in the years 1865 and 1866 the " Lünette," in the *foyer*, of the Vienna Opera and in the famous frescoes in the centre picture is a scene from " Der Laüslicher Krieg," and figures of the " Wanderer," the " Zürnende Diana," the " Erlkönig " and " Der Fischer." In the evening of his days (the later 'sixties) Schwind created his most memorable souvenir of the Viennese Schubert era in " Ein Schubertabend bei Josef Ritter von Spaun." He had meditated for years the idea of immortalising in a great painting Schubert and his circle of friends, and had dreamed of creating his own Schubert Hall, the walls of which should be adorned with nothing but frescoes inspired by Schubert's life and works. He mentioned this plan in a letter from Rome in the year 1835. He hoped that the funds might be forthcoming from the enthusiastic Schubertian Witteczek. " I have done ' Die Arbeiter im Weinberg des Herrn ' in water-colours and have had praise and eulogies enough. Also I've designed a room in which Schubert's songs are to be sung. The Mayrhofer wall is well advanced, too, and can be sent next year for exhibition with Goethe's. Couldn't Witteczek order something of the kind ? All has been done for a few thousand guldens. ' Urania ' and ' Einsamkeit' as arabesques are ready in colour. But I'll have a look round in Pompei. ' Antigone und Œdip,' the ' Zürnende Diana ' and ' Memnon ' are composed. . . ." He is always coming back to this pet idea. So he writes in a letter in 1851 to Bauernfeld : " . . . You say nothing about the Schubert Hall. The more convinced I am that this will never come off, all the more I dream of it, and ' perhapses ' run through my brain, and their frustration pains me. . . ."

" When Liszt tries a piano at a count's," he wrote once ironically, " it is painted and valued as a relic. But our dear Schubert, who delighted us a thousand times improvising on the piano, and to what a circle of genuine artists he played. . . . We have to beg guldens for that ! "

On May 30th, 1862, in a letter to Bauernfeld, he refers again to his plan : " . . . Secondly, I received yesterday from the sculptor Schönthaler a letter asking if I would paint in the dining-room of a house belonging to a Herr Todeseo a series of remembrances of the ' Baumannshöhle,' but I haven't any ! Just say if it would not be a grand solution of the problem to suggest to this man that he should dedicate his walls to the memory of Schubert. I am full of it. The space would just do."

In May, 1865, he wrote to the poet Mörike that he had begun a picture of Schubert: "I feel I owe the intelligent part of Germany this perpetuation of my admirable friend Schubert at the piano playing to a gathering of friends and acquaintances. I know the people all by heart, and a happy chance put me in possession of a portrait of a Countess Esterházy, whom I've never seen, but to whom he used to say he had dedicated everything. She had every reason to be satisfied."

On October 29th, 1868, he wrote to Bauernfeld : ". . . I have done something which in a certain way would do to illustrate your ' Letters of an old Viennese.' It had, in my anxious days, quite gone out of my head, and I had put it with its face to the wall *nonum prematur in annum.* It was ' Schubert am Klavier,' with old Vogl singing and the whole Vienna society of that day listening— all the little ladies and gentlemen of the *haute-monde.*"

In December, 1868, he writes : ". . . ' Melusine ' is getting on pretty well. It required a lot of thinking out. It is now all in order and divided up, and the two or three pieces I've finished are quite good. Whatever comes of it, I find it an agreeable occupation. There are enough pictures in the world, so what does it matter if one here and there fails. A ' Schubertiade ' is also ready, but I've hung it on the wall ; perhaps it will improve by keeping. . . ."

This refers to the celebrated "Ein Schubertabend bei Ritter von Spaun," a large beautiful sepia drawing which, after many wanderings, came into the possession of the Vienna Schubert Museum. Many striking portraits of men of the time—Grillparzer, Schubert, Vogl, Schober—were evolved out of studies for this picture. In the first row of the sitting figures (from left to right) are Kapellmeister Ignaz Lachner, Fräulein Eleonore Stohl, Marie Pintericz. At the piano, singer Vogl, Schubert, Josef Spaun, Franz Hartmann, Frau Vogl, Josef Kenner, Frau von Ottenwald, Netty Hönig, Therese Puffer, Schober, Justine Bruchmann, Bauernfeld, Castelli. In the second row (left to right), Hofrat Franz Witteczek, Kapellmeister Franz Lachner. In the background by the door, the Munich friends, the married couple Dietz and Karoline Hetzenecker ; further, there are Baron Schönstein, the superb amateur Schubert singer, Ferdinand Mayerhofer von Grünbühel, Anton Freiherr von Doblhoff, and on the wall the portrait of Schubert's lovely pupil, Countess Esterházy.

Schwind also took a lively interest in the erection of the Schubert Memorial Statue in the State Park of Vienna. Thus he sketched, probably at the end of the 'sixties, in the studio of the sculptor Kundmann, who was working on the statue of Schubert, the famous portrait sketch of his friend that one sees everywhere. It was drawn in pencil on a piece of clay.

A touching proof of the love and reverence in which Schwind held the genius of Schubert was expressed in his own words when he was a mature artist. Once when Schubert wanted to compose something quickly and had no music-paper at his disposal, Schwind took a pen and ruler and on a sheet of paper ruled lines which, before they were dry, were immortalised by Schubert's melodies. In his old age Schwind declared that these hastily ruled lines were the most valuable that his hand had ever drawn.

In conclusion, a few letters of Schwind to his friends Schubert and Schober, written in the days of their youthful friendship, when their life was full of artistic dreams and garlanded with roses, are given here.:

SCHWIND TO SCHOBER

" The Bruchmann girls wish very much to keep the vigil of their mother's birthday on November 10th with a ' Schubertiade ' so as to dispel, as much as possible, the sad thoughts which occur on this festive day of the departed Sybille. Be sure you don't forget to come."

SCHWIND TO SCHOBER

" WIEN, *November* 9, 1825.

" The day before yesterday Kupelwieser started for Rome. Two or three days before we had a kind of Bacchanalian feast at the ' Krone ' ; we all dined there except Schubert, who that day was in bed, poor fellow. Schaeffer and Bernard, who visited him, say he is on the way to recovery, and talk of his being quite well again in perhaps four weeks' time. The table was fuller than usual and all went merrily as a marriage bell. After dinner we had two fiddles and a guitar, and after the music an excellent ' rum punch,' which increased our jollity considerably. Bruchmann drank our health in all brotherliness, and then a general *Schmollieren* began, ending in a bitter bombardment of glasses. Schubert's health, Senn's and Professor Dedl's were drunk with special enthusiasm."

SCHWIND TO SCHOBER
" Dec. 26, 1825.

" Schubert is better; his illness won't last much longer, and then he will again be able to wear his own hair, which, because of the rash, had to be shorn. He has a very comfortable peruque. He is very often with Vogl and Leidesdorf. The doctor in attendance, too, goes out with him a great deal. The doctor is thinking of a musical academy or a public ' Schubertiade.' If anything comes of this I will let you know."

SCHWIND TO SCHOBER
" January 2nd, 1824.

" Our New Year's Eve festivities came off happily. We were at Mohn's. Bruchmann and Doblhoff came back on the stroke of 12 from the town, where they had been looking for Schubert. Your health, Senn's, Kupelwieser's and everybody's sweethearts, were drunk with the congratulations of the season. Then Schubert and Dr. Bernard announced their advent by a little fusilade on the window pane. Schubert's arm had effect and the injured pane caused an uproar. I boxed with the doctor, which was good for my muscles. At half-past five we went home. The whole affair was rather rough and vulgar, but better than we could have expected."

SCHWIND TO SCHOBER
" January 19*th,* 1824.

" This evening we had a sort of Schubertiade at Mohn's ; the first this winter was at Bruchmann's."

SCHWIND TO SCHOBER
" February 2nd, 1824.

" Justine read out parts of your letter . . . the part about myself. That was on Schubert's birthday. We had a supper at the ' Krone ' and were all a bit screwed ; but for your sake I wish you could have been there and seen Schubert's joy. I was never too far gone to notice what the others were about. All were more or less silly.

Schubert went to sleep. Bruchmann, alone, although he declares now he knew nothing about it, seemed like one inspired. He embraced me passionately. Julien's health he drank with me alone and with Schubert. . . . Schubert is now undergoing a fortnight's faſt and is ſtaying indoors. He looks much better, and is very lively and comically hungry. He is composing quartets, " Deutsche " and variations without end."

Schwind to Schober

" Vienna, *February 22nd,* 1824.

" Schubert is very well. He has given up wearing his wig and has a soft, natural moleskin head of hair. He has again turned out a whole crowd of the lovelieſt " Deutsche " dances. And the firſt volume of the ' Müllerlieder ' has come out."

Schwind to Schober

" *April 14th,* 1824.

" Schubert isn't very well. He has a pain in his left arm which prevents his playing the piano, otherwise he is in good case."

Schwind to Schober

" *Auguſt 20th,* 1824.

" Schubert has written. He is very well and busy. So much I know ; he is working at a symphony. I have an opportunity, to my joy, of hearing other things by Schubert at a certain Herr Pintericz', whose acquaintance I've made at Vogl's. He is a ſteady and placid fellow, full of love for old German art curios."

Schwind to Schober

" *September 10th,* 1824.

" I am sending you of Schubertian songs the ' Müllerlieder.' . . . He will send you the others himself, as he can get them for nothing."

Schwind to Schober

" *November 20th,* 1824.

" I have lately had a talkwith Doblhof. I am bored when I speak with anyone who isn't Schubert, or the dear comrades, about you. Other people respeſt you, but that is all. D. was very reticent on the subjeſt, but warmed up about Schubert and myself."

SCHWIND TO SCHOBER

"VIENNA, *Christmas Eve*, 1824.

"Schubert may be coming this evening. This morning he was here with Spaun, who is in Vienna for a few weeks on leave."

SCHWIND TO SCHOBER

"*January 7th*, 1825.

"As a rule I paint the whole day and go out very little. Only bound off now and then to Schubert or Hönig. If you could but see Schubert and me on these occasions, when I go to him early in the Rosau, or when we take a Sunday afternoon outing together. It is as funny as anything in the world! A week ago he came with me to Hönig's, after he had accepted the invitation ten times and ten times not come! We met at six, but waited till seven o'clock before going, because the mother goes out at that hour. What should we do meanwhile was the question. He wouldn't come to any coffee-house but to Lenkay's, where he is always going with Senn. We had half a bottle of Tokay, and after we had drunk half it was advisable not to risk the danger of drinking the rest, so we filled with it a little bottle and took it away. As there was no one near to relieve us of it I brought it to the Hönigs, where, amid much laughter, it was produced and emptied. Schubert enjoyed himself immensely and intends going again soon. He likes Netty very much, and she is certainly a darling."

SCHWIND TO SCHOBER

"*April 2nd*, 1825.

"To-morrow I am going to show it ('Die Hochzeit des Figaro') to Netty Hönig, who is much concerned with it. I meant to write yesterday, but Schubert and Bauernfeld came with a very lively stranger. They played the devil and 'Figaro' was hidden. A pity to spoil such cheap amusement with serious stuff, thought I. I expected Schubert the whole afternoon, but he kept me waiting. First I slept, then I smoked, then waited again, and now I've nothing to do but chew the prospect of a bad Easter. . . . I visit Schubert always early in the morning; the rest of the day everyone looks in on him. He is often with his brothers; I am often with Bauernfeld, but generally at home. Poor, dear Láscny is so ill no one may go to see her because she is forbidden to speak. I am so very sorry for her, and she is very sorry for us, as, of course, I don't let her speak a word. I used to go and see her often and always understood her, even when she was not allowed to talk. Let us hope that she will soon be better. She is a strong character, and in the whirl of temptations, in a lax environment always retained her honesty and self-respect. God preserve for me you, the good Schubert, and this pious woman friend."

SCHWIND TO SCHUBERT

"*July 2nd*, 1825.

MY DEAR SCHUBERT,—

"I almost fancy that my last letter contained something that you didn't like.

I will be frank and confess to you that I am still a little hurt. You remember, of course, the last time that you didn't come to the Hönigs. I should be very foolish to let it annoy me if you do what you like and don't trouble yourself about what I should like you to do. But if you had thought of how much love awaited you there you would have come. It won't prevent my being and doing what till now you have liked, though I almost fear to indulge in this pleasure, when I see how little my year-long endeavours to have you loved and understood weigh against your mistrust and shyness. Silly jokes that I can't suppress, though they hurt me myself, may have something to do with it. That infernal chaff! Why should I not be frank? Ever since I've known you and Schober I've been used to being completely understood. But then others come and mock and get hold of a fragment of what we've been saying and thinking, generally at the wrong end of the stick; at first we tolerate the foolery, then we do it ourselves, and, as men are not made of diamonds, much that is of value in our intercourse is sacrificed to emulative nonsense. If I am now too bitter on the subject; I have often been too kind. I beg you will answer me in the same strain of brutal sincerity, for anything is better than these tormenting thoughts which I can't get rid of.

I hear that you are expecting me at once, but unfortunately I can't come. I cannot neglect giving up my whole soul at present to painting, and a whole summer is the least I need to gain any sureness. Also I am expecting Schober, and can't run away directly he comes; he will be sorry enough that you aren't here. Meanwhile I go regularly to Grinzing and find an antidote there to many a week of overwork. I wanted to write something else, but I fancy

I hear you mocking me, though you know better than anyone how good it is to be understood in intercourse with one's friends. Netty sends you the enclosed newspaper cutting. You will see how she has tried to annihilate your friendship with Tietze. . . . Everyone wishes to be remembered to you, and there is no end to the memories of your visit.

Did I tell you that I had seen Grillparzer ? He was delighted with my ' Hochzeit,' and declared that in ten years' time he would remember vividly every figure in it. . . . He was very friendly and conversational. . . . Nothing will come of his opera, for he is not his own master and can't do all he would like. But he knows the Director of the Königstädter Theater in Berlin and thinks he might get you an opera book in that quarter. Bauernfeld is studying and sends you his love. Many compliments to Herr von Vogl, and tell him not to forget to filch those two drawings, if possible, from the most lovely Frl. Amalie when she is not looking, as I want them badly. Write soon, tell me how you are and what you are doing, and if you find everything as I told you. Have you heard nothing of Fritz Dornfeld or from Linz and Florian ?

Your SCHWIND."

SCHWIND TO SCHUBERT
" August 1st, 1825.

DEAREST SCHUBERT

" I must have written rubbish, as your allusion to ' fragments ' and ' diamonds ' prove. But let that be. I have found out something which didn't occur to me when I was asleep, i.e., that someone offended you at Hönig's. I don't believe it can have been Netty, and if it was any of the others I should be much surprised. If you had told me at once, the affair would have worn another aspect, or I shouldn't have proposed, for a moment, that you should come. You must believe that I would not frequent such society. Meanwhile, in the Devil's name, I'll turn the house upside down in search of something that will bear out your accusation. But I swear by all the saints I haven't a notion what it is."

SCHWIND TO SCHUBERT
" August 6th.

I have asked Netty, and she is sure that even if she had not known how fond I am of you she would not have behaved so curiously, much less would she have said anything with a *double entendre*. I hope that when you come back you'll think no more about it. Schober is here and sends you a thousand greetings. He is quite his old self, but more lively and fresh. A letter has come to-day from Kuppl. at Padua. In three weeks he is due here. ' Die junge Nonne ' has come out. I have so much to do that I don't know when I shall get away, but I hope for certain to see you. Now, goodbye and write soon. Bauernfeld is doing examinations and society verses at the same time, and we are as happy together as we can be without you. If you see Rosi Clodi, give her my love. I should like to see her again. Remember me to Herr von Vogl and tell him not to forget the two drawings which Mali had. Pintericz, Doblhof and all send greetings.

Your SCHWIND.

I nearly forgot the most important news : Schober has spoken to Tieck, who has been made theatre Hofrat in Dresden, about your opera ' Alfonso.' You must write at once to Dresden, as Tieck is waiting to hear from you. No time for more. Farewell."

SCHWIND TO SCHUBERT

" *Aug.* 14*th*, 1825.

"I don't know where you are, but this letter will be sent on to you. You will have learnt from my last, if you have received it, that Schober is here. And now Kuppl has arrived. He wasn't expected for another three weeks. He looked splendid and has a perfect head of hair which, when he had fever, he was obliged to sacrifice. All we want now is *you !* Schober and Kuppl are putting up together. Your landlord wants to know for certain whether you will be keeping on your quarters for this winter ? Write what you intend doing and I will tell him.

If certain negotiations turn out as I wish, I am resolved to live alone, probably somewhere on the Wieden. Rieder has got a post with 6,000 florins salary at the Engineering Academy. If only you would seriously apply for the place as Court Organist you might be as well off. There seems now nothing to hope for from the theatre, at least not opera, and as in winter there is no music at Wasserburger's we can only whistle. With what joy I look forward to the first Schubertiade ! We can build great hopes on your symphony. Old Hönig is Dean of the Juristic Faculty, and will have in that capacity an academy, and so we can reckon on an opportunity in that quarter of getting a performance."

"*Sept.* 1*st.*

"I was a little depressed, but now I am quite fit again. So long as one has courage to be sincere all comes right in the end. I am still too busy to get away. But in case you should think that I am prevented by certain people, I let you know that I go out sometimes to Merkenstein and to Atzenbrugg, where Schober is now, to enjoy country life. Kuppl is very industrious, and Schober appears to make serious attempts to be the same, but happy as this state of things is we have no real enjoyment without you. Netty Hönig, the only one of us you are doubtful about, shows such a boundless attachment for you and love and interest in your concerns, so naturally and spontaneously that, if you can believe me, there is no one, I affirm, who more thoroughly appreciates you and listens to your songs with more intense pleasure.

Worschizek is on his last legs and the Court Organistship will soon be vacant. It is only a matter, I am told, of improvising a Gregorian on a given theme to be a made man. In Gmunden you'll find an organ at your disposal to practise on.

In conclusion, my best respects to Vogl, and thereby a reminder to move heaven and earth to procure the two drawings and to carry them off and bring them here like a conqueror's booty. I hope that he will value me and my art in this matter more than the lady, who may be as amiable as she likes apart from it, and I wish him all luck in winning her favours and friendship, and will, if necessary, do my utmost to help him. I want to paint those things and will hold him who helps me thereto a friend, and he who doesn't the contrary. I remain yours so long as I live, and wish for myself and all those who love you your speedy return or answer.

Your SCHWIND.

Wherever I go my letters will be sent on to me from this house. Many charming messages are sent you by Pintericz, Doblhoff, Randhartinger ; and on my word of honour the heartiest from the ' little person.' "

Schubert's Friends

SCHUBERTIADE " has become a winged word which brings before us that enchanting picture of an ingenuous, pleasure-loving society in old-world Vienna during the Biedermeier period, where ordinary everyday life was transformed and deepened by the magic of music and clothed in a mantle of beauty and grace. The circle which gathered round the genius of Schubert was all exaltation, enthusiasm and sentiment; it bound the hearts of his friends together with shackles of gold. It was the triumph of youth, with roses in its hair and the shining sceptre in its hand, over the barrenness of existence, which it converted into a kingdom of dreams and of joy.

The genius of Schubert was the centre of this circle given up to harmless enjoyment of life. " Through him we were all brothers and friends," Spaun relates. The simple schoolmaster's son from Lichtental exercised a magnetic attraction on his surroundings. At first it was only one or two friends belonging to the Konvikt days; then soon these were joined in common admiration for Schubert's muse by young artists, poets, composers, music-friends and distinguished amateurs. The circle widened, and soon it was a little community composed of the *élite* of Vienna's youth, who did homage to the genius of Schubert, who held loyally to the master, and exerted themselves increasingly to further his fame in the musical world. Mutual endeavour, intellectual pursuits and merry social intercourse kept the friends of Schubert together in close intimacy. One inspired the other, but love for Schubert animated them all. Poesie, the fine arts, above all, music exemplified by Schubert's genius, forged the magic bond which held their young hearts fettered to each other.

Let us enter the circle of Schubert's friends and consider some of its most striking personalities more nearly. First, there is Franz von Schober, a brilliant combination in one person of intellect and man of the world, a gifted amateur in every department of art, in painting, music, the theatre and poetry. He was born of an Austrian mother at Schloss Torup, near Malmo, in Sweden. He had led, as Bauernfeld tells us in his diary, " a somewhat adventurous life ; was for a time actor *à la* Wilhelm Meister. He is five or six years older than we are, a sort of man of the world ; possesses great dialectic ability and persuasive eloquence ; is very popular with women, in spite of his slightly bandy legs. We came together in very agreeable circumstances. Klementine Russ called him the god Mahadö. She did not, however, want him to lift her in the air with fiery arms. Moriz (Schwind), too, idolises him. I find him human but interesting."

Schober, who was the best-off of the Schubertians, took over in January, 1817, the lithographic institute founded by Count Pötting in Vienna, where many of the youthful works of Schwind and Danhauser were produced. Full of enthusiasm for art himself, he took the liveliest interest in the two great artists Schubert and Schwind, shared their joys and sorrows, and gave them the most valuable advice and unselfish encouragement. If it was Schubert and Schwind who had the overflowing creative souls, it was Schober who was the stimulating and leading spirit of the circle. He also, as a creative artist himself, was active. He drew in partnership with Schwind the well-known " Atzenbrugger Fest," and designed the gravestone of Schubert in the Währinger Cemetery. As poet he wrote the text for Schubert's unlucky opera, " Alfonso und Estrella." Many of his poems were published at that time in papers and almanacks. Schubert's genius crowned some of them with exquisite tones, the hymn, for instance, " An die Musik " :

> " *Du holde Kunst in wie viel grauen Stunden,*
> *Wo mich des Lebens wilder Kreis umstrickt,*
> *Hast du mein Herz zu warmer Lieb' entzunden,*
> *Hast mich in eine bessre Welt entrückt.*
>
> *Oft hat ein Seufzer deiner Harf' entflossen,*
> *Ein susser, heiliger Akkord von dir*
> *Den Himmel bessrer Zeiten mir erschlossen.*
> *Du holde Kunst, ich danke dir dafür !* "

" Thou gentle Art, in how many hours gray,
When life's wild struggle held me fast,
Hast thou my heart to warm love inflamed,
And my spirit into a better world has passed.

Often a sigh that from thy harp has flown,
A chord so sweet and sacred.
A heaven of better things to me has shown,
Thou gentle Art for this I thank thee."

The lasting friendship which Schwind, with a heart thirsting for love, entered into with Schober has received a noble memorial in the " Correspondence between Schwind and Schober," published soon after Schwind's death by Professor Hyacinth Holland, of Munich.

We have already described in detail the part Schober played in Schubert's life, and shown how it was he who freed him from the profession of a schoolmaster, to him deadening to the spirit ; who lent him his rooms to dwell in ; who, through material assistance, made propaganda for him in Viennese society, and succeeded in interesting the great singer Vogl in his friend's compositions. Here we need only indicate how attached Schubert was to Schober, how closely knit the two were in the bonds of friendship, how much they loved and valued one another.

Thus we read in a letter of Schubert's to his friend of November 30th, 1825 : " . . . Vogl is here and has sung once at Bruchmann's and once at Witteczek's. He sings hardly anything now but my songs. Copies the singing part and is entirely taken up with them. He is, in consequence, very affable and gracious. And now let me hear how you are ? Have you made your appearance yet in the eyes of the world ? I pray you to let me know soon how things are going with you, and to satisfy the longing I have to be told everything that concerns you. . . . I have composed nothing since the opera except a few " Müllerlieder." The latter are to appear in four copybooks with vignettes by Schwind. I am hoping meanwhile to regain my health, which will help to forget many things, but you, dear Schober, I shall never, never forget, for what you have been to me no one else can ever be. And now farewell and never forget

Your everlastingly loving friend,

FRANZ SCHUBERT."

And the same intense feeling of noble friendship breathes through the answer which Schober sent to a letter of Schubert's written from Zselesz.

" DEAREST AND BELOVED SCHUBERT,—

You will not have been able to make much out of my last letter to you in Zselesz, because it was written in the most uncomfortable circumstances. My good, eternally dear friend, my affection for you never wanes. You have loved me for myself alone, like my Schwind; and dear Kupelwieser, too, will always be true. And haven't we lived our whole lives in art, while others only find entertainment in it? We understand its innermost kernel, as only Germans can. I felt that a crowd of superfluous things and people were distracting me and wasting my time, and that it was necessary to wrench myself from my environment and to compel myself to work. Now this has partly happened, and the rest will soon be a *fait accompli*, and I can look forward to a better condition of things confidently. But if all should come to nothing, I can still at least return to your arms as full of love as ever, for you are everything to me. I have a remote hope of seeing you this winter—a curious but beautiful dream, isn't it? Now as to your affairs. How about the operas? Is the Castelli one disposed of and the Kupelwieser? Have you heard nothing from C. M. Weber? Write to him, and if the reply is not satisfactory, ask for it back. I have a means of getting into touch with Spontini. Would you like me to make an effort to prevail on him to give a performance? He is said to be a difficult person to deal with. So the matter with Leidesdorf is going badly, and your ' Müllerlieder ' have not made a sensation? The fools have no initiative or capacity for judging for themselves, and blindly follow the multitude and listen only to the noisy plaudits of foreign opinion. Now, if you could get a few reviewers and critics to beat your drum and to rave in all the newspapers about you without ceasing you would be made. I know of quite insignificant people who by this method have become famous and popular. Why shouldn't you make use of it, you who deserve such *réclame* in the highest degree? Castelli writes for a few foreign papers, and you've set an opera book of his—why shouldn't he open his mouth? Moriz has sent us the ' Müllerlieder.' Send me anything else that's come out. How glad I am that you are quite well again. I hope I shall soon be able to say the same of myself. I thank you a thousand times for the poem; it is so sincere and full of feeling. It has made a great impression on me. Farewell and love me always. We are sure to come together once more. . . ."

Schober, long after Schubert's death, remained in closest friendship with Schwind. Only in later life the two comrades who in youth had been so much to each other fell asunder. Long years of separation, the entirely different development of their lives, together with regrettable misunderstandings, may have led to the cooling in their friendship and finally to its rupture. Schober, who with Schubert had been for many years the best and most sacred on earth to Schwind, was, nevertheless, true to him till death. When Schober came later to Weimar, where he made friends with Liszt, whom he accompanied on his tours, he recommended Schwind to the Grand Duke of Weimar as the best painter to execute the Wartburg Frescoes, which were then being talked of. Afterwards Schober became the Duke's Chamberlain and Legation Secretary.

A very intimate friend of Schubert from his early Konvikt days was Josef von Spaun. Born in Linz, he came to Vienna in 1806 to study law. Schubert, who was then boarding in the Konvikt as a Court chorister, became at once deeply attached to Spaun, and their friendship lasted without a cloud till the death of the composer. Spaun made propaganda for the struggling young artist everywhere in the Viennese society circles which he frequented, and sought the patronage of influential people for the work of his friend, whose genius he believed in with unshaken steadfastness. He organised in his mother's house many musical parties at which Schubert's songs were sung to a select audience. It was one of these parties which Schwind immortalised in his picture " A Schubert Evening at Spaun's." A touching proof of genuine friendship remains in the letter which Spaun wrote in vain to Goethe on April 17th, 1815, with the object of awakening his interest in the publication of Schubert's first collection of songs.

In 1813 Spaun was director of the Lottery Company, and remained in its service for several years. In reference to this he wrote : " It was a curious fate which put me, who had always been opposed to this gambling concern and had never drawn a prize in a lottery or even bought a ticket, at its head." In 1818 he was Court Advocate, in 1821 bank manager in Linz, and was in a like capacity at Lemburg. In the following year he came to Vienna again as lottery director and Court Advocate, and was one of the many Viennese Hofrats who, during the Biedermeier time, were zealous patrons of art.

Spaun wrote and bequeathed to posterity valuable remembrances of Schubert. It was he who made Schubert acquainted with his

Josef von Spaun
By Leopold Kupelwieser

friend, Witticzek, who was also a true, enthusiastic Schubertian, and possessed a complete collection of Schubert's compositions, which he bequeathed on his death to Spaun on condition that when Spaun died he should leave these to the Society of Music Friends in Vienna. He obeyed these instructions, and the Society is to-day in happy possession of these extraordinarily valuable music treasures. Of Schubert's friendship with " Pepi " Spaun, the correspondence between them gives many proofs. Here, for example, is a letter of Schubert's to the, at that time, bank director in Linz, dated December 7th, 1822 :

" I hope that the dedication to you of these three songs will give you a little pleasure. But you deserve a great deal more, and I would like *ex officio* to compose if I only could something tremendous for you. Anyhow, you'll be pleased with the choice because I've chosen your favourites. Besides this number there is to appear in a short time two more, one of which is already in print, and I have ordered a copy for you. The first of these contains, as you know, the three Harper's songs (from Wilhelm Meister), of which the second, ' Wer nie sein Brot mit Thränen ass,' is new, and dedicated to the Bishop of St. Pölten ; the other contains ' Suleika ' and ' Geheimniss,' and is dedicated to Schober. Besides these, I have composed a solo pianoforte fantasia, which is appearing in print and is dedicated to a wealthy magnate. I've also composed some new Goethe songs, ' Die Musensohn,' ' An die Entfernte,' 'Am Flusse ' and ' Willkommen und Abschied.' There is nothing to be done with my opera in Vienna, and I have demanded and got it back ; and Vogl really now has little to do with the theatre. I shall be sending it either to Dresden shortly, from where I have had a letter from Weber full of promises, or to Berlin. My mass is finished and will before long be produced. I still hanker after the old idea of dedicating it to the Kaiser and Kaiserin, because I think it is a success. Now I've told you all the news there is to tell about myself and my music ; about somebody else's, ' Libussa,' a grand opera by C. Kreutzer, has been given and was liked, especially the second act. But I only heard the first and it left me cold. And now, how are you ? I ask this late in the day because I hope and believe that you are well. How are the rest of your family ? What is Streinsberg doing ? Write me all particulars soon. I should be pretty well if the opera disgrace did not hurt me so horribly. I am now again hand-in-glove with Vogl, as he has nothing more to do with the theatre. . . . Our life in Vienna is at present very agreeable. We have at Schober's readings three times a week and a Schubertiade, at which Bruchmann puts in an appearance. And now, dear Spaun, farewell. Write to me soon and at length, so as to fill the blank which your absence always causes. Greet all your brothers, your wife and sisters, and Ottenwald, also Streinsberg and everybody.

Your true friend,

FRANZ SCHUBERT."

A sincere friendship lasting over many years also bound Spaun to Schwind, who made a sepia drawing of Spaun's grave in Traunkirchen.

When speaking of Schubert and the Schubertians, the name of the singer Michael Vogl should not be omitted, as it was his art which had the greatest influence on the song composer's development and helped to make his work well known in society circles. In his diary the singer wrote the following memorable words : " Nothing could demonstrate more clearly the need for a practical school of singing than Schubert's *Lieder*. Who can conceive the enormous effect all over the world where the German language is known of these truly divine inspirations and products of musical clairvoyance ? How many have only understood for the first time on hearing them what language, poetry in tones, harmony in words and thoughts clothed in music mean ? They have learnt how the most beautiful words of our greatest poets can be not only translated into music, but even exalted and made more beautiful in the process. One can cite examples without end : ' Erlkönig,' ' Gretchen am Spinnrad,' ' Schwager Kronos,' Mignon's und Harfner's Lieder, Schiller's ' Sehnsucht,' ' Der Pilgrim ' and ' Die Burgschaft.' "

Another of Schubert's valuable acquaintances was the Censor official, Johann Mayrhofer. A great friend of music himself, he was enthusiastic about Schubert's, and his poems gave rise to a famous series of Schubert's compositions. He was born in Steyr, and if he had followed his father's wishes would have been a priest. After he had completed his studies in Linz, he was three years a novice in the Monastery of St. Florian. On giving up the study of theology he turned to jurisprudence. Mayrhofer, when he entered the service of the State in Vienna and got an appointment in the Censor's office, was twenty-seven years of age ; Schubert, with whom he then became acquainted, was eighteen. Quickly a very close spiritual relationship was formed between them. Mayrhofer, who was extremely literary and cultivated, had in 1817 and 1818 edited, with the assistance of Krül, Kenner, Ottenwald and Spaun, a periodical, *Beiträge zur Bildung für Jünglinge*, and for many years was Schubert's literary adviser. His was an eccentric nature. He advocated hotly freedom of the Press, yet, though he detested the Metternich censorship system, he performed his duties as Censor with the utmost conscientiousness. Mayrhofer's several years' housekeeping with Schubert was on very simple lines ; according to the testimony of Feuchtersleben, in moderation and self-denial Mayrhofer was a Stoic. His furniture consisted of a few books, a guitar and a pipe. He was abrupt in manner, often ailing, and embittered by his employment being in direct opposition to his personal convictions. He avoided society, and was only sometimes attracted to a social gathering when Schubert's songs were to be sung there. He became transfigured when he listened to them. Bauernfeld, in one of his verses, hit off his queer, contradictory character :

> " . . . Gay society he abhorred.
> He only cared for study.
> In the evening he played whist,
> Very curious his look and stony.
> Never did he smile or joke.
> Filled us lax folk with awe . . .
> Little did he speak—what he said
> Was weighty. All that was light,
> Whether women or *belles lettres*,
>   He disapproved.
> Only music could sometimes
> Thaw his stiff frigidity.
> And when it was Schubert's songs
> Then his whole being was changed. . . ."

Grillparzer said of Mayrhofer's poems, which were ethically severe, full of depth of feeling for Nature and enthusiasm for antiquity : " They are always like the text for a melody—either they anticipate being set to a melody by a composer or they recall a melody from another poem which has been unconsciously absorbed and reproduced." His contemporary, Feuchtersleben, criticised

them more favourably: " . . . A sense of sublimity and love
of Nature pervades them. They were reflective with the reflection
without which he couldn't think or be what he was. Finally, conciliatory wisdom on a background of melancholy, idealism based
on a foundation of reality, strength and clearness, melodious form,
were the qualities of his poetry."

Many of them were ennobled through Schubert's music ; many,
crowned by the eternally fresh melodies of the master's genius, have
become immortal. The reminiscences which he wrote in 1829, a
year after Schubert's death, have already been referred to. They
are of extreme value as they throw light on the spiritual relationship between the two men. " While we lived together," he says,
" we couldn't fail to discover each other's peculiarities . . . for
we were both in this respect amply endowed and couldn't help
revealing it. We teased each other on the point, and derived much
amusement and satisfaction from so doing. His joyous, good-
natured disposition and my reserved, silent character often came
into collision, but we laughed it off by pretending that we were
playing certain *rôles*. Unfortunately, I always played my own.

For me Franz Schubert was a genius whose melodies accompanied me in everything I did every day of my life. Among his
most lovable characteristics were unpretentiousness, kindness in
udging other people's performances (he carried this rather to
excess from the point of view of cleverness) and candour.

Social intercourse was for him, when the day's work was finished,
a necessity ; no banquet, no brilliant conversation, had any value
for him if his own particular friends were not there to share it."

The early death of his friend moved Mayrhofer to the depths of
his being, and after he had been present at the Requiem held for
Schubert he went again to the house in Wipplingerstrasse where
they had lived together, and gave vent to his emotion in the poems
" Geheimnis und Nachgefühl an Franz Schubert " (November 19th,
1828). A collected edition of Mayrhofer's poems was issued by
Feuchtersleben in the year 1845. Here is to be found the cycle of
poems full of love and friendship for Schubert, " An Franz," which
begins with the lines—

> " Du liebst mich !   Tief hab' ich's empfunden
> Du treuer Junge zart und gut."

After Schubert's death the conflict in Mayrhofer between idealism and life became sharper. On February 8th, 1836, he came as usual, early in the morning, to his office in Laurenzerbergl and began, as Bauernfeld relates, " to write; then he stood up, restlessness preventing his settling to his work. He left the room, strode through the twilight of the corridors, and, rigid and slowly, as if in a trance, without returning his colleagues' greeting, ascended to the upstair rooms, stood still and stared out through the open window. Spring zephyrs fanned his face, but to the gloomily brooding man they were a breath from the grave. The sun poured its rays through the open window, making the dust shine like golden rain, but the man lay in the street with shattered limbs. . . ."

Another intimate friend of Schubert's was this poet Bauernfeld. " In the winter of 1824, when I was a lawyer in my fourth year," he says in his reminiscences, " Aus Alt-und Neu-Wien," I was up to my ears in my own work as well as on the Viennese edition of Shakespeare. A whole heap of plays, comedies and tragedies lay piled up before me, with which the practical theatre would have nothing to do. Still I worked on unceasingly, and spent at that time all my evenings alone in my small room.

" So I was sitting, one evening in February, 1825, in my den when my youthful friend Schwind, already become famous, brought the less well-known Schubert to see me. We were soon on good terms. At Schwind's request I had to recite some of my mad verses belonging to my salad days; then we opened the piano, Schubert sang or we played duets, and then went on to an inn till late in the night. Thus the friendship was sealed. We three comrades from that day were almost inseparable. We often wandered about the town till three in the morning, and accompanied each other home—as we were sometimes not in a condition to part, one or other of us not seldom slept the rest of the night in each other's rooms. We weren't very particular about comfort in those days. Friend Moriz threw himself, wrapped only in a leather cover, on the bare floor, and once carved me a pipe, which article I had forgotten, out of Schubert's spectacle case. Who happened to be flush of cash paid the piper for all. Sometimes, however, it happened that two of us had no money and the third none. Of course it was Schubert who played the Crœsus among us generally; he swam in silver coins when he had sold a few *Lieder* or when Artaria had paid him five hundred guldens for songs out of Sir Walter Scott. . . . Then we spent right and left and lived for the first few days like fighting-cocks, but before long had to economise again. Such was the ebb and flow of our fortunes.

I owed it to a ' flow ' that I heard Paganini. The five guldens that this concert corsair wanted were for me unobtainable ; needless to say, Schubert had heard him, but he refused to go and hear him again without me. He got seriously angry when I wouldn't take the ticket from him. ' Don't be stupid,' he exclaimed, ' I've heard him once and was annoyed that you weren't with me. He's a devil of a player, I tell you, and there'll never be another like him. I've got money from Häckerlings, so come along,' and he carried me off. . . . We heard the most infernally sublime fiddler in existence, and we were not less delighted with his perfect *adagio* than amazed at his devilish antics on the strings, and amused by his incredibly scarecrow dæmonic figure, which resembles nothing so much as a black skeleton doll stretched on wires. After the concert I was entertained, free of cost, too, at the inn, and a bottle extra, at the cost of our enthusiasm, was set before us.

That was certainly the ' flowing time ' ! And another time I went soon after the dinner hour to the coffee-house near Kärntnertor-Theater, indulged in a *mélange* and devoured half-a-dozen *Kipfel* (rolls). Soon Schubert joined me and did the same. We congratulated ourselves mutually on the good appetite which we both had acquired in such a short time after dinner. ' The fact is, I had nothing for dinner,' my friend confided to me shamefacedly. ' Neither had I,' said I, laughing."

Bauernfeld, who was very musical, and had taken piano lessons from Beethoven's teacher, Johann Schenk, the composer of the "Dorfbarbier," erects in his diaries kept during that joyous " Sturm und Drang " period a lasting memorial to the Schubertians, and casts illuminating and critical sidelights on his friends' temperaments :

" Schober is our superior in mind," he writes under March 8th, 1826, " that is, in talk ! But there's a great deal about him that's artificial; his best powers threaten to end in nothing. Schwind is a splendid, pure nature, which is always in process of germinating afresh and threatens to devour itself. Schubert has the right mixture of idealism and realism : the earth is all beauty to him. Mayrhofer is simple and natural ; Schober maintains that he is a sort of good-natured *intrigant*. And I ? Who knows himself ? Till I've done something decent I am nobody."

Among the most faithful of Schubertians was, besides, the

Imperial War Office Secretary, Dr. Johann Jenger. He was an enthusiastic musician, a first-rate accompanist of Schubert's *Lieder*, and learnt to know the composer personally in 1817 and was soon bound to him in bonds of sincerest friendship. Jenger associated with all the best people in the musical society of Vienna, and used to accompany at the Schubertiades the magnificent singer of Schubert's songs, Karl Freiherr von Schönstein. In the year 1818 he was transferred to Graz, where he remained till July, 1825. There he played in the newly founded Styrian Music Society, in which as Secretary he took an active part, and it was to his influence that Schubert owed the honour of being elected an honorary member. Jenger was indefatigable in his efforts to make propaganda for Schubert's works. He had known Beethoven, and, as we have seen, took Schubert to see the great master shortly before he died. In every musical quart r where he was *persona grata* he brought Schubert to the notice of persons likely to be of assistance to him. He introduced him to the Court actress Sophie Müller, the Hofrat Kiesewetter, the Pachler family in Graz, the homeopathic surgeon, Dr. Menz, and others. The expedition to Graz which Schubert made in Jenger's company was one of the happiest and most delightful events in his life.

An original Biedermeier figure who stood for a short time in intimacy with the Schubert-Schwind circle was the poet Ferdinand Sauter, whose portrait by Schwind was one of the most successful works of the latter's youth. Sauter came from Salzburg to Vienna in 1825, where he for many years had a position in a paper business, and made friends with Schwind and his circle. His first poetical efforts belong to this period. An unhappy passion for his brother's *fiancée*, with whom he carried on a clandestine correspondence, had a disastrous effect on his character. Disappointed with life, he sank alternately into melancholy and frivolity, and became in his outward behaviour an eccentric. In later years his Bohemian nature brought him into the company of boon companions in the suburban beer-gardens of Vienna, and there he wrote his " Gstanzln," which dazzles with the originality of its wit and humour. By day he was a clerk in an office; at night he squandered his paltry earnings in wine-cellars and coffee-houses. His wild life brought him down lower and lower in the social scale. He neglected his clothes and appearance, and applauded by an audience of wine-bibbers, drank and sang, making fun of himself:

> *Die Stiefel sen z'rissen,*
> *Der Strumpf hat a Loch,*
> *Und da Kommt ein'm der Schuster*
> *Jetzte nomal so hoch !*
> *'Gwand, dos is schleisslig,*
> *Was liegt denn da dran*
> *Wann m'r heim Geschwander*
> *Nur eintreten kann !* "

In his later years he frequented mostly, of an evening, the inn in Larchenberg called " Die blaue Flasche," where Mozart often used to go and where Sauter gave rein to his genial humour and composed Biedermeier verses, but his burlesque and cynical eccentricities were more appreciated than his serious efforts. Still, there were some among the worthier members of his audiences who honestly esteemed him and protected him from the assaults of ribald, careless youths, who hurt his easily-wounded feelings with their jeers. Often these affronts drew bitter tears from his eyes, all the more bitter because he felt conscious that it was his own manner of life that was to blame. In this way, though he oftener now exchanged the " Blaue Flasche " for the shady garden of the old Monastery courtyard, where he held communion in solitude with his muse, Sauter lived on. Once when a young physician rallied him with the prophecy that he wouldn't escape the cholera then prevalent in Vienna and would be the victim of his dissecting knife, he replied vehemently, with tears in his eyes, " You shall not touch my body ; I'll see you don't get it ! "

Soon after he fell ill coming from the funeral of the author Ebersberg in the Hernalser Cemetery, and died of dropsy. He had said of this God's acre once : " A pleasant place to rest in ; there the Gallitzinberg, on the right the Kahlenberg, here flowers and trees. This is where I would like to be buried." When someone remarked that the Währinger Friedhof was much more beautiful, he answered, " Schubert and Beethoven are there, it is true, but for me it is too aristocratic. Too many tombstones and monuments." His friends erected over his grave a simple stone with a lyre carved thereon and some lines of his own as epitaph.

> " Much he suffered, much enjoyed ;
>   Had only medium luck,
>   Felt much, earned nothing ;
>   Lived gaily and died easily,

Don't ask the number of his years,
There is no calendar in the grave.
And a man in his shroud
Is a closed book.
So wanderer pause not here,
For putrefacation is unpleasing."

Of native poets who lived their *Sturm und Drang* period in the Schubert and Schwind circle was the Tyrolese Johann Michael Senn, a friend of Schubert's at the Konvikt Town School. Senn studied law at the Vienna University, and Schubert set some of his poems to music—" Selige Welt " and " Schwanengesang." Senn often met his friends at an inn or coffee-house, where the young people's harmless discussions excited the attention of the Metternich secret police, who, in their zeal to find documents of an incriminating description, scented treason everywhere. When one day the young artists and students noticed that there was a spy amongst them, they forestalled his meditated exit by throwing him out at the door. Out of revenge, the ejected one made haste to accuse them all publicly of treasonable conspiring. Now the hands of the police were full. In the night Senn's colleagues and friends were hauled out of their beds and marched off to prison. Only Senn, who happened not to be at home, remained unmolested, but encountered a worse fate. His friends, so soon as their case had been heard and the authorities convinced of the groundlessness of the suspicion, were discharged. But on their arrest papers had been found, and among these was a diary kept by a friend of Senn's in which occurred the passage, " Senn is the only man, I believe, who is capable of dying for an idea." Senn was instantly arrested, and the next day he raised the question of whether the police had the right to arrest him. That was sufficient to damn him as a dangerous character. He was obliged to languish in prison for several months. The police commissioner, as the Tyrolese writer Pichler states, wound up the inquiry with the opinion that Senn was a genius. But this good opinion brought him further trouble. He was banished to his own country. Schwind, who visited him in Innsbrück in 1830, wrote : " I was greatly astonished at his fiery and striking manner of speaking, but ten times more charmed with the play of heavenly emotion which reflected his innermost soul on his features ; his expression was wonderfully attractive." Of Senn's numerous writings, which are distinguished by originality of thought as well as thorough conciseness of language, the " Tiroler Adler " spread from mouth to mouth and became a popular national song.

The young Grillparzer, too, sometimes associated with Schubertians, and was connected with Schubert especially through the musical family of Sonnleithner and the sisters Fröhlich. Grillparzer's " Serenade " was set to music by Schubert. One of his most beautiful poems, " Als sie, zuhörend, am Klavier sass," in which the poet described Kathi Fröhlich as she sat listening to Schubert's music, was said to have been written after a " Schubertiade " at the house of the brothers Spaun.

" There she sat still, of all, the loveliest,
    Listening, giving neither praise nor blame,
The dusky shawl had fallen from her breast,
    Beneath her scarf her gentle breathing came,
Her head was sunk, her body forward bent,
As if to seek the fleeting tones she went.

Beautiful is she ?   Beauty's picture seeks
    To paint itself and for itself has meaning,
But something higher from these features speaks,
    It is a script whose substance we are gleaning.
Each letter in itself a simple sign,
But through their inmost meaning made divine.

So she sat there—only her cheeks were moving,
    With their most tender muscles never at rest,
Her lashes quivered, of sweet eyes the roofing,
    Her lips were like a crimson treasure-chest,
Its treasures of pure pearl hiding, revealing,
With no word said, her mien betrayed her feeling.

And, as the tones in wild confusion straining,
    In constant battle, but half-reconciled,
Fell low, like lost and homing doves complaining,
    Or stormed like furious tempests, roaring, wild.
So pain and pleasure gave each other place,
I saw each sound reflected in her face.

In sympathy I fain would cry : Musician !
   Oh, stay thy hand, torment the maid no more,
But then the music reached its last position,
   And pleasure rang where pain had been before.
Like Neptune, before whom the storms are fleeing,
The triple chord rose from the waves of being.

And as the sun may rise, its rays divining
   Their path through stormy weather's darkest night,
So rose her eyes, still with salt waters shining,
   So, like a sun, she shone in heavenly light.
From her sweet lips there breathed a gentle sound,
And seeking sympathy, she looked around.

I started up : now I would let her know
   What so long had moved me ; but she looked around :
A warning finger on her lip, to show
   I should not mar the wizardry of sound.
And then I saw her listen and bend once more
And I must sit in silence as before." *

   The musicians who belonged to the Schubertian circle, besides
the singers Vogl and Baron Schönstein, were Anselm and Josef
Hüttenbrenner, Ignaz Assmayer, Benedikt Randhartinger and
Franz Lachner. The Styrian Anselm Hüttenbrenner first became
acquainted with Schubert at Salieri's, where they were both taking
lessons. He enjoyed a certain reputation as a composer, and Schubert, among others, appreciated his talent. He wrote a good many
quartets for men's voices, several operas, symphonies, masses and
requiems (one of these in C minor was performed after Salieri's and
Beethoven's deaths in Graz, and after Schubert's death in the
Augustinerkirche in Vienna), and quartets for strings, but his works
to-day are forgotten. He was a friend of Beethoven's, whose death-
bed he visited, and a firm friend of Schubert's. His reminiscences,
like those of Spaun, Mayrhofer and Bauernfeld, are of the greatest
value in helping us to reconstruct the Schubertian era. We learn
from them how the friends shared together poverty, pleasures and
pain, joys and sorrows, how they entered into each other's artistic
plans and work, and how their lives were ennobled through art, and
transformed and made lovely by their ideal relationship. When

(* *Translated by Ethel Talbot Scheffauer*).

Hüttenbrenner first saw Schubert the latter was a little stiff towards him. " He thought that I only wished to become superficially acquainted with him, to make use of him and then turn my back ; but when he saw, in time, that I hit on the very passages in his songs to praise that he himself regarded as the best he began to trust me, and we were the best of friends. Schubert, Assmayer, Mozatti and I every Thursday met to sing a quartet for men's voices which we had composed during the week. We met at the hospitable Mozatti's. Once Schubert came without a quartet, but on a little reprimand from us wrote one on the spot in our presence. He regarded such occasional compositions as of little worth, and not more than six have survived. We sang on these Thursdays, too, the very popular men's quartet of Weber's, and some of Konradin Kreutzer's, of whose work Schubert thought highly."

Schubert often visited Hüttenbrenner at his lodgings. They made music together and played duets. They had a great love for the scores of Handel's oratorios—Handel, that giant spirit, Schubert, like Beethoven, held in highest admiration. Hüttenbrenner took the bass while Schubert played the treble. " Ah ! what grand and bold modulations ! " Schubert would exclaim while playing Handel sometimes. " Nothing like them has ever occurred to anyone else, even in a dream." These two friends laid artistic plans, built castles in the air together, drank wine and smoked their pipes. It was in Hüttenbrenner's den that Schubert wrote " Die Forelle."

" One evening I invited Schubert to come to me, as I had been presented with half a dozen bottles of red wine from an aristrocratic cellar in return for playing the owner's accompaniments. After we had drained the noble nectar to the last drop, he sat down at my desk and composed that wonderful song ' Die Forelle,' which I still possess in the original. When he had nearly finished it he was already getting sleepy and took the ink instead of the sand to dry it with, so that several bars were rendered unreadable." He wrote in the margin, for Anselm's brother, Josef Hüttenbrenner, the following remark : " Dearest Friend ! I am uncommonly delighted that you like my *Lieder*. As a proof of my sincere friendship, I send you herewith another which I have just composed at Anselm Hüttenbrenner's after 12 o'clock at night, and wish that I could have you here to drink to our friendship in a glass of good punch. Just as I was going in a hurry to sprinkle sand on the paper I caught hold of the ink bottle by mistake (I was half-asleep) and poured it over the end. What a misfortune! It happened on the twenty-first of February, 1818, after midnight!"

Through Anselm Hüttenbrenner, who lived permanently in Graz after 1821, and his brothers Josef and Heinrich, all zealous Schubertians, Schubert was brought in touch with Graz and became first known outside Vienna.

Josef Hüttenbrenner, who had come into public notice as the composer of dance pieces, became, when he settled in Vienna, Schubert's faithful *famulus*, undertaking his business affairs, arranging terms with publishers and theatre directors, and, being an accomplished musician himself, he prepared his pianoforte works for the press. Schubert, for whose creations he worked with the utmost energy, once wrote to Josef:

"DEAR HÜTTENBRENNER—I am and always shall be your affectionate friend. I am uncommonly glad that you have finished the symphony. Bring it to me this evening at 5 o'clock. I live now in the Wipplingerstrasse with Mayrhofer."

It was Josef Hüttenbrenner, too, who preserved the works of Schubert with loving care, knowing that the composer himself cared little what became of them. To him is due thanks for saving many from perishing in oblivion. "For Schubert," Anselm Hüttenbrenner says in his memoirs, "was extremely careless about his numerous manuscripts. Constantly friends to whom he sang new songs were so charmed with them that they begged to be allowed to borrow them, and carried off copies which they promised to return, but very seldom kept their word. Often Schubert couldn't remember to whom he had lent a song and did not know where it had gone. Thus my brother Josef resolved to collect all the scattered copies, which he succeeded in a great measure in doing after long and laborious inquiries and research. I found one day that my brother had more than a hundred *Lieder* of Schubert's carefully sorted and catalogued in a drawer."

Benedikt Randhartinger had been, like Schubert, a Court chorister. He had a specially lovely voice, and the Imperial Kapellmeister Eybler once composed for him an offertorium. He was in the Konvikt a comrade of Schubert, who, owing to his voice having cracked, left in 1812. But, for the sake of the music there, Schubert continued to come, often bringing with him his compositions, which Randhartinger generally sang and Schubert accompanied on the piano. The "Erlkönig" was one of these. As Randhartinger possessed unusual musical talent, Salieri gave him lessons in composition for nothing. It was to this friend that Schubert owed the inspiration to his famous "Müllerlieder." One day Schubert visited Randhartinger, who was then private secretary to Count Ludwig Széchény. "Hardly had he come into the room," relates Heinrich von Kreissle, "when the secretary was summoned to the Count. He hurried away, telling the composer that he would be back in a few minutes. Schubert came to the writing-table and found lying on it a volume of poems, one or two of which he read at a glance. He then put the book in his pocket and went away without waiting for Randhartinger's return. The latter missed the book from his table, and the next day went to Schubert to recover it. Schubert's excuse for his conduct was that the poems had so greatly interested him he could not resist the temptation of carrying them away. As a proof that the borrowing of the book had not been without results, he presented the astonished secretary with the composition of the first 'Müllerlied,' which he had finished in the night."

Randhartinger was later singer and Hofkapellmeister of the Court Orchestra, and as a composer, too, his activity bore fruit.

The composer Franz Lachner, by birth a Bavarian, came to Vienna in the twenties of last century to study composition under the Abbé Stadler and Simon Sechter. In 1824 he was organist at the Evangelical Church in Vienna, and from 1826 onwards for many years conductor at the Kärntnertortheater. He made friends with Schubert and Schwind, and soon was one of the most intimate members of the circle. Schwind, in the celebrated "Lachnerrolle," has commemorated delightfully the friendly relations between Lachner, Schubert, Bauernfeld and Schober. Lachner afterwards was Court Conductor and Music Director in Munich, and remained after the death of Schubert in friendly correspondence with Bauernfeld and Schwind.

"When Schubert's statue was unveiled in the Vienna Public Park on May 1st, 1872," wrote Bauernfeld, "I found myself present with Franz Lachner—alas! not Schwind—at the ceremony. 'Do you remember,' Lachner reminded me, 'how you played with Schubert his new fantasia for four hands for the first time?' and then followed a recapitulation of our youthful memories."

Many young painters were numbered among the friends of Schubert and Schwind, and for this reason there is no other musician of old Vienna of whom we have so many excellent portraits as of Schubert. As Schwind drew and painted Schubert at all ages, either by himself or with his friends, so other young painters, lithographists and pastel-portraitists living in Vienna at the time repeatedly chose Schubert as a subject for their artistic skill. Schubertians were the painters Leopold Kupelwieser, A. W. Rieder, Josef Teltscher, Ludwig Schnorr von Carolsfeld, Daffinger, and the lithographer Kriehuber ; also the painter Führich, who was closely associated with Schwind, and Danhauser were sometimes seen in convivial intercourse with the Schubertians.

Especially dear to Schubert was the painter Leopold Kupelwieser. He was for a short time Schwind's teacher, and studied at the Viennese Academy. In several of his drawings and aquarelles he has depicted the life and habits of the Schubertians. His aquarelles belonging to the years 1820 and 1821 are famous. These are the " Picnic of Schubertians at Atzenbrugg (Charade : Der Sündenfall), as well as the portrait of Schubert and a pencil drawing belonging to the year 1821."

The first-named aquarelle shows us the friends with their lady companions, in all eighteen people, at a picnic. The majority of the party are driving in a vehicle called a " Wurst," and one of the friends has lost his hat, which the wheels have crushed. Two men run in front of the carriage, and behind are two young gentlemen, one of whom is Schubert.

The second aquarelle shows Schubert *en profile* in a corner at the piano, turning to the right with a baton in his hand.

Kupelwieser soon left the Schubert circle and travelled to Italy for the sake of his studies. How deeply attached the tone-poet was to this friend is shown by the characteristic letter (already quoted at length in these pages) addressed to " *M. Signor Leopoldo Kupelwieser pittore tedesco, recapito at Caffé Greco, Roma.*" Letters exchanged between Kupelwieser when he was in Italy and his *fiancée* Johanna Lutz, are also full of memories of Schubert and his circle :

" Before dinner," wrote Johanna Lutz on December 9th, 1825, " when I am alone, I generally play Schubert's songs. They are so beautiful. Quite wonderful is the ' Schatzgräber ' and ' Das Lob der Thränen,' and—but it's impossible to say which is the loveliest."

On April 7th she wrote to Kupelwieser : " The day before yesterday my father brought me two books of the ' Müllerlieder,'

which have just come out. They have delighted me. I can't tell
you how wonderfully beautiful they are. There are several that
you don't know. If only you could hear them, too, that would give
me double delight."

" What gives me great pleasure here," wrote Kupelwieser to
Johanna Lutz in September, 1824, from Palermo, " is that I have
in Palermo a friend who comes from Vienna and whom I used to
meet at the Schubertiades, and always liked because of his admiration for Schubert's songs. He is Austrian Consul here, and in
talks with him I go back to those times when Schubert's glorious
songs made such a new and wonderful impression on me."

On March 7th, 1825, Kupelwieser's *fiancée* wrote to him at
Naples :

" I am very curious to know what Franz von Bruchmann will
write to you about Schober. When I saw them all so merry I could
not help feeling sad on your account. Alas ! all partings and
separations are too painful to bear philosophically. But there is a
bright side to it. For when you and Schober were gone the whole
society was altered in character and not for the better, and so was
dissolved. But the better part of it came together again inevitably ;
so not much harm is done. I can only tell you what I have heard
about the *contretemps* between the Bruchmann faction and Schwind's,
and the conclusion to be drawn from it. Rieder, Dietrich, Schubert
and Schwind are on as good and friendly terms as ever, but quite
different from Bruchmann. Rieder and Bruchmann are not hostile
to each other, but don't look each other up. Schubert and Schwind,
on the other hand, make no disguise of their feud with Bruchmann.
They seem to me like children, and they express their antipathy in
a childish way. They don't come together, cut each other when
they meet in the street, and altogether are enemies. It is true that
Justin has been weak and vacillating and F. rude to Schober. Of
course it was easier to see the worst side of Schober than the good.
They can do as they like about not loving him ; but their behaviour
is childish. The love and loyalty of the others to Schober is
splendid. Schubert is now very busy and well, of which I am glad.
The Bruchmann faction now are only a small party. Smetana and
Eichholzer are often there. The latter is making great progress in
art. The hatred between Eichholzer and Schwind is babyish on
both sides. I cannot understand it. And the two girls, who used
to say the happiest day of their lives was when they first got to know

the circle, now seem not to have vestige of gratitude left for all the love and kindness they received. They just try to excuse themselves by saying it's all the fault of the others.

I don't know to which side Mohn belongs. . . . Doblhoff and Hönig go their own way. When you come back you'll find it difficult to choose, for naturally both sides will be all right with you. . . ."

A. W. Rieder, who was later curator of the Imperial Picture Gallery, did one of the best portraits of Schubert in the year 1825. The picture owed its existence to a heavy shower of rain, from which Rieder sought shelter at Schubert's, and, to employ the time till the rain stopped, made a sketch of him. Schubert afterwards gave him several sittings. Rieder painted it later in oils, and the engraving by Johann Passini has made it one of the best known of the composer's portraits.

Josef Teltscher was busy in Vienna as a portraitist in Schubert's day. He was introduced to the Schubertian circle by the Graz friends, Jenger and Hüttenbrenner. He drew Beethoven on his death-bed, and his lithographed likeness of Schubert is also one of the most successful pictures of the composer. He immortalised Schubert, too, with his Graz friends, Jenger and Hüttenbrenner, in a delicate pencil sketch. After Schubert's death he moved to Graz, became intimate with the Pachler family, and was a favourite pastel and miniature portraitist. He was drowned in the year 1857 in the sea near Athens in saving the life of an official in the Austrian Embassy.

Josef Kriehuber, the celebrated sculptor of Viennese society at that date, made interesting lithograph portraits of both Schwind and Schubert. He engraved on stone the well-known costume-group from Raimund's " Bauer als Millionär." It was at Kriehuber's wedding, at which many of the Schubertians were present, that Schubert played for the dancers. Besides the above-named artists and musicians, Schubert's circle numbered various officials in Government departments, authors, amateurs in art, students and men of letters. Josef Kenner, Albert Stadler, Anton Holzapfel, Franz Bruchmann, the son of a wealthy merchant—all these, like Spaun, were faithful comrades from Konvikt schooldays. Then there were Ludwig Mohn, Franz von Schlechta, and the barrister Josef von Gahy, the distinguished accompanist of Schubert's songs and his favourite partner in playing duets. " . . . The now soft, now brilliant rippling runs and perfect touch of Schubert, who played the treble part," records Gahy, " made of our hours of playing together a memorable delight." There were also the connoisseur Josef Witteczek; Karl Pintericz—a music-loving Government clerk who had known Beethoven, steadfast in devotion to Schubert, made a collection with conscientious pertinacity of all his songs. He studied in his office each song as it appeared, varying the monotonous sorting of dusty documents with worship of the muse's creations : a real Biedermeier idealist ; Anton Dietrich ; the army officer, Ferdinand Mayerhofer von Grünbühel ; the brothers Fritz and Franz Hartmann ; Romeo Seligmann ; Max Clodi, and others too numerous to mention.

The Schubertians first met at Schober's rooms and at the lithographist Mohn ; later at the house of the rich tradesman Johann von Bruchmann, and at the brothers Spaun, at Enderes, and outside the town on the Wieden at Pintericz's, or in the old Mondschein house of the brothers Schwind. They called their gatherings " Schubertiades." They played, danced and made music. Dramas, each taking an allotted part, were read aloud, and recitations from the literature of the world were given—Schober and the younger Bruchmann generally officiated as reciters. Those were hours of youthful, spontaneous enjoyment, of intellectual stimulus and sheer careless gaiety. Mayrhofer, Bauernfeld, Schober and Senn declaimed their newest verses ; Schubert played duets with Gahy or accompanied the singer Vogl or the elegant Baron Schönstein as they sang his songs. The friends called themselves by names from the Nibelungenlied. Thus Schubert was " Volker der Fiedler," Schwind, the youngest of the Schubertians, " Giselher das Kind," Kupelwieser " Rüdiger." Schubert found in this society enthusiastic love and appreciation. The youths felt instinctively that Schubert was a master by the grace of God, and association with his friends was the bright spot in his sad existence as an impoverished musician. At these meetings the generally melancholy artist became the gayest of the gay and joined wholeheartedly in all the merry antics of his intellectual young friends. He often good-naturedly played for his friends to dance, and the happy couples would whirl in the waltz till dawn ; their young hearts would melt and overflow in an ecstasy of joy and tenderness. Schwind and Kupelwieser and the poets Schober, Bauernfeld and Mayrhofer commemorated in their drawings and verse and parodies the friends' merry doings. For New Year's Eve, 1825, Schober composed a particularly happy and characteristic description in rhyme of the " Schubertiades," that has come down to us with many a charming sketch and clever picture from the skilled hand of young Schubertian artists. It ends thus :

> " Dann lasst uns auf die Hingeschwund'ne blicken,
> Die mit der milden Rede von uns schied,
> Es wird uns ihr Gedächtniss suss erquicken
> Und heilen des zerrissine Gemüt.
> Der liebe Kreis wird wieder uns umschweben,
> Die alten Freuden werden jung und neu,
> Und jeder wird mit voller Seele streben,
> Dass der Vergangenheit er würdig sei."

And in the circles of the Viennese *bourgeoisie*, where artistic and literary tastes were displayed in the serious cultivation of music by Mozart, Haydn and Beethoven, Schubert's art gradually gained ground. It was not the musical clique and the critics of reputation who were the first to recognise the value of Schubert's genius, but that attractive Viennese amateurism which at that time reached an unusually high standard of excellence. The cultured middle-class families of Sonnleithner, Fröhlich, Hönig, Sophie Müller, Bruchmann, Anschütz, Kieserwetter, and the Pachler household in Graz, played a similar *rôle* in Schubert's career as did the aristocratic salons of Lichnowsky, Browne, Erdödy, Van Swieten, Rasumofsky and Brunswick in that of Beethoven. Here Schubert won his first triumphs ; here Vogl, Baron Schönstein and Jenger were the faithful and accurate interpreters of his art ; here he met with stimulating enthusiasm and affection. The entry into these houses Schubert owed to the indefatigable efforts of his devoted friends, above all to Vogl, Spaun, Schober and Jenger, who were unremitting in their determination to bring his genius to the notice of the most influential people in Vienna.

Thus Spaun negotiated Schubert's intercourse with the æsthetic house of Matthäus Collin, who, when he had once heard with admiration Schubert's songs, was prevailed upon by Spaun to invite Schubert and Vogl to a party at his house, where the leading friends of art in Vienna would have an opportunity of making further acquaintance with the works of Schubert. There Schubert met all the most influential men and women in Viennese society. Schubert played Vogl's accompaniments to his songs. " That evening," wrote Hüttenbrenner, " he both played and sang his ' Wanderer ' for the first time and enraptured the authoress, Karoline Pichler, who was present. She gave him most encouraging praise and appeared to be quite carried away by his music."

At Christmas, 1821, Schubert was invited to the house of the actor Heinrich Anschütz. " This Christmas was for me," records Anschütz in his " Recollections," " of more than usual interest because Schubert was brought to my house for the first time. Franz Schubert was one of the most conspicuous members of that once notorious, merry, skylarking society. My brother for years had associated with him in it on a most intimate footing. His second visit to me occurred on a very exciting evening, as it happened. I had invited a party of friends and Schubert, and we had a number of young ladies and young men. My wife was very young at the time, and my brother Gustav a passionate dancer, and soon conversation gave place to dancing. Schubert, who had already played a few pieces in masterly fashion on the piano, sat down at the instrument again in the liveliest spirits and played for the dancers, and the whole company were soon whirling and twirling. There was much laughter and wine flowed. Suddenly I was summoned to speak to a stranger downstairs. He was a commissioner of police, who demanded the cessation of the dance because we were fasting. When I entered the salon and introduced the police officer, in feigned horror everyone sprang apart. ' He has done this to spite me,' remarked Schubert, laughing, ' because he knows how fond I am of composing dance music.' Schubert often came to my house after that. I found him a thoroughly sincere and honest artist. whom it was impossible not to love. His eyes, which through short sight were dim, flashed fire when he was playing or when he spoke of music. He was very fond of talking about music, but generally denounced the bad taste of the public and the Italian ' Dudelei.' "

Ten years later, in 1831, the Schubertian friends assembled again on Christmas Eve at the house of Heinrich Anschütz, when the singer Cremolini sang some of Schubert's songs " with much soul." The dead master was remembered with sadness and affectionate regret. All present recalled how much beauty and sunshine he had brought into their lives, and it seemed as if his invisible presence hovered still among the mortals he had left behind, with the diadem of genius shining on his brow.

According to the statement of the judge, Johann Karl Ritter von Umlauf, in his work, " Leben und Wirken eines Österreichischen Justizbeamten," Schubert and his friends for a long time frequented once a week the house of Frau von André, where music went on till late in the night. The string instruments were played by the violinist Karl Gross and his viola-playing brother Friedrich and by the 'cellist Linke, the piano by the celebrated pianist Karl Czerny, and the songs were sung by the tenors Barth and Binder and the baritone of the Kärntnertortheater.

One of the houses in which Schubert was made at home was that of the advocate Franz Hönig in the Schulestrasse. He was indebted to Bauernfeld, who was a schoolfellow of the son of the Hönig family, for his *entré* into this circle. Here, too, there was a great deal of music. Schubert played duets with the daughter, Netty, and a young student with a beautiful voice, Friedrich Dratschmied, sang Schubert's songs. Here, too, there was dancing, flirting and fun. Young Schwind's first love was Netty Hönig. " Schwind," wrote Bauernfeld in his reminiscences, " won the heart of Netty in a ragged frock-coat. All the girl's kith and kin were summoned to the betrothal with drum and trumpet, a collection of cousins, aunts, uncles and old Hofrats, and such-like relations, coffee and whist besides and bridal guests. Friend Moriz at first didn't want to be present, for he hadn't a decent coat, only his painting smock, but a friend came to the rescue and lent him his, but in the first half hour he almost tore it off. His *fiancée* had the greatest difficulty in keeping him there till ten. I awaited with Schubert the happy future bridegroom at a coffee-house. He arrived quite distracted and desperate, and began wittily making game of the Philistine company. Schubert was so delighted he couldn't stop giggling."

In spite of Schwind's passionate adoration for Netty, it never came to a marriage between them. " A fitting position could not be found. The relatives shook their Hofratish heads." Netty became later the wife of the officer Ferdinand Mayerhofer von Grünbühel.

Schubert often met his friends in old Vienna inns and coffee-houses; the " Ungarische Krone " on the Seilerstätte was their most frequent haunt between 1819 and 1826, and other favourite resorts were the " Grünen Anker," in Beisel, " Zu den Gänsen predigenden Wolf " (" The Wolf preaching to the Geese "), " Der Schwarze Katze," the " Schnecke," the Gasthof " Zum Römischen Kaiser," and the " Goldene Rebhuhn." All the Schubertians would crowd into the small, stuffy guest- and coffee-rooms: Schwind, Schober, Spaun, Kupelwieser, Bauernfeld, Senn, the brothers Hüttenbrenner, Teltscher, Gahy, Schnorr von Carolsfeld, Witteczek, Franz von Bruchmann, and later Franz Lachner and sometimes Mayrhofer and others. If a stranger was introduced into this brilliant gathering, Schubert used to ask his neighbour " Kann er was ? " (" Can he do anything ? "). Thus one of his nicknames was " Canevas " ; as well as this and " Schwammerl," he was sometimes called " Bertl " by his friends. " When the faithful music-brethren," relates Anselm Hüttenbrenner, " sat together, sometimes nine or ten of them, each addressed the other by his special Schubertian name. Schubert was called ' Schwammerl.' "

In Bauernfeld's diaries, and those of the student brothers Franz and Fritz Hartmann, of Linz, we get delightful glimpses of the joyous "Schubertiades," and can conjure up a picture of these meetings of extraordinary charm in which music—Schubert's music—played the all-important part.

" Schubert evenings," writes Bauernfeld, " so-called ' Schubertiades,' were of frequent occurrence. The company was always fresh and gay, wine flowed in streams, the excellent Vogl at his very best sang all the splendid songs, and poor Schubert Franz was obliged to accompany till his short, stout fingers nearly failed him. He fared even worse at our house entertainments—Würstelbälle (Sausage Balls, so-called because the ladies during the dance regaled the gentlemen with those slender little dainties of the sausage tribe : the times were simple !), but, all the same, elegant ladies and charming young girls attended these parties. Then our ' Bertl,' as we called him sometimes in a flattering mood, would play and play again his newest waltzes till they developed into an endless cotillion, and the dear little corpulent man, pouring with perspiration, only recovered his equilibrium at the supper table."

Here are extracts for March and April, 1825 from Bauernfeld's dairies :

" Have been much with Schwind and Schubert. He sang his *Lieder* at my rooms. Finally we slept at his. He wants an opera text from me, and proposed the ' Bezauberte Rose,' and I told him that a ' Graf von Gleichen ' was in my head. . . . We visited singer Vogl. Marvellous old bachelor ! He reads Epictetus and is a perfect pink of refined dandyism. Moriz behaved rather badly to him. Schubert is always the same, always natural and un-affected."

" At Weintridt in Rötz with Moriz (Schwind), who painted us

on the signboard of a carriage-builder. After, great Schubertiade with friends, musicians and painters—the small barrel of ' Rötzir ' that we brought back with us the reason."

" Slept at Moriz's. Important conversation which lasted half the night; went home at 6 in the morning." (Bauernfeld's diaries, Whitsunday, 1825.)

" With Schober and Schwind at Atzenbruck. Billeted at the Mill. We all three slept together in one big bed." (Bauernfeld's diaries, September, 1825.)

" Schubert is back; a coffee-housing life with friends often till two or three in the morning—

> *Wirtshaus, wir schämen uns,*
> *Hast uns ergözt ;*
> *Faulheit wir grämen uns*
> *Hast uns geletzt.*

Schober is the worst offender. Of course he has nothing to do and does nothing, which Moriz is always throwing up at him." (Bauernfeld's Diaries, October, 1825.)

" Sunday with Schubert in Redoutensaal. The D Symphony and ' Egmont.' Then we ate with him. After to Schuppanzigh. Quartet of Haydn's and Beethoven; quartet of Mozart's—all heavenly. Grillparzer there too."

" Farewell meal with Schwind, Schober, Schubert, Feuchtersleben and other friends—on the 15th—a glorious spring morning. The trip into the Blue undertaken. Chief people with their wives, young officers, soldiers, a cavalcade of carriages, comfortable and uncomfortable *calèches*, carts and waggons. Trees in blossom, cockchafers, warm spring sunshine. (Bauernfeld's Diaries, May 2nd, 1826.)

" To Gastein by the Mallnitzer Tauern. Mayrhofer accompanied me to Salzburg, then I him to Gölling. He went on further for his work. I to Hallein to Eduard Feuchtersleben, who received me very hospitably. Stayed with him a few days. Sent on my heavy luggage to Gmunden, where I hoped to meet Schubert. With my knapsack on my back to Ischl." (Bauernfeld's Diaries, July 10th, 1826.)

" When we got to Nussdorf in the evening we ran against Schwind and Schubert in the coffee-house. Great glee ! ' Where is the opera ? ' asked Schubert. Here I handed him solemnly the ' Graf von Gleichen.' Went to Schober at Währing. According to old custom, we all spent the night together. Now the poesie is over—the prose of life begins anew." (Bauernfeld's Diaries, July, 1826.)

" Schubert is very pleased with the opera, but we have fears about the Censor. Called on Schreyvogel. He was exceedingly affable. Have been much at the theatre. Wonderful voice—Wilhelmine Schröder. The opera somewhat Philistine, but two or three songs capital. Maurer and Schlosser not bad. Light wares. Schober and Schwind were together. Poor Moriz is suffering from his love affair (with Netty Hönig) and is getting little encouragement in his art. Schubert has no money, nor have any of us." (Bauernfeld's Diaries, August, 1826.)

" The day before yesterday, party at Josef Spaun's. Vogl sang Schubert songs . . . but not without pedantry. Adamberger there, also Grillparzer, to whom I was introduced. He was very pleasant, but I am not sure that he took to me." (Bauernfeld's Diaries, December 17th, 1826.)

From the diaries of the Linz students, Franz and Fritz Hartmann, we take the following passages :

Franz von Hartmann writes on April 27th, 1827 : " At 7 o'clock we are going to Spaun's with Maurus, Mayrhofer, Enk and Haas. There is to be a ' Schubertiade ' there and a crowd of people. The programme is ' Grenzen der Menscheit,' ' Das Abendbrot,' ' Der Wanderer ' and ' Der Mond,' ' Wer wagt's,' ' Romanze aus Ivanhoe,' ' Romanze aus Walter Scott,' ' Fragment aus dem Æschylus.' "

About this " Schubertiade," Fritz von Hartmann recorded in his diary the next day :

" Vogl sang splendidly most of Schubert's newest songs. When the music was over we had refreshments, and everyone joined in the brilliant conversation and there was great fun. We stayed till 12.30, then several of us—that is, Schober, Schwind, Schubert, Mayrhofer, Enk, Hönig, Franz and I—went on to the Café Bogner, where we quietly discussed together all the delightful things we had seen and heard. At 1 o'clock we went to bed."

On the subject of a " Würstelball " (" Sausage Ball ") at Schober's, Fritz von Hartmann writes in February, 1827 : " At 7 I went with Franz to Schober's, who had invited us a long time beforehand, and Spaun repeated the invitation for Schober this morning. I met there Spaun, Gahy, Enderes, Schubert, Schwind and his brother,

Bauernfeld, and ladies with whom we were not acquainted, among others Netty Hönig, Frl. Puffer, Leopoldine Blahetka, Frl. Grünwedel, and so on. Most of these ladies are very beautiful, and the room was a pretty picture. The music was glorious, consisting mainly of Schubert's waltzes, which either he or Gahy played. We stayed at Schober's till 2 o'clock. . . . Afterwards I walked with the Schwind brothers as far as the Karolinentor."

From an entry in Franz von Hartmann's diary of December 30th, 1826, we learn how very lively the " Schubertiades " often were :

" We went to the ' Anker ' where we met Schubert, Schwind, Schober, Bauernfeld and Derffel. Spaun came later. . . . The talk was of knights, tournaments, adventures of Konvikt days, etc. When we came out of the ' Anker ' it had snowed and all was white. We started snowballing at the place where the Grünangerstrasse runs into the Singerstrasse. Spaun took my side and Fritz and Schober were on Schwind's. Schober always hit me, and pretty hard, but I paid him and Schwind back. Spaun shielded himself finely with an open umbrella. Schubert and Haas didn't take part in the battle. . . ."

In summer the scene of the " Schubertiades " was often outside Vienna. They were held in the open air, for it was not only the arts which had such a strong fascination for these enthusiastic young men—the beauties of Nature also filled their hearts with rapture. Beyond the gates of the city the Wienerwald whispered ; the green hills and valleys seemed to smile a welcome and the sunny vineyards too. The Schubertians would take a two-horse carriage, standing ready for them at the Linie, and would gallop out laughing and singing to Weinhaus, Pötzleinsdorf, Dornbach, Währing, Grinzing, or Hütteldorf, where the Bruchmann family had a country house, Nussdorf, Perchtoldsdorf, Mödling, Heiligenkreuz. They would wander through the woods and climb the mountains, sing and play round games, and when the sun went down behind the blue hills the god Bacchus drew them back to the valley. They would troop singing into some little wine village, where the latticed windows of the little houses with pointed gables, standing in gardens full of lavender bushes and vines, seemed to beckon to them. There they sat in the green arbours with Viennese Folk music entrancing their ears in the soft light of swinging lanterns, and they joked and laughed and sang and drank the golden

juice of the grape, which soothed and lulled their boisterous spirits.
And late at night—perhaps not till morning dawned—the Schubertians started on their pilgrimage back to the town, and their joyous
songs echoed under the clear, starless sky.

A specially popular place for excursions was Atzenbrugg, a
charming landscape, part of the property belonging to the Monastery of Klosterneuburg.   Schober's uncle was steward of the estate,
and every year he sent out invitations to a great festival which
was held there, lasting three days.   Schober, Schubert, Schwind,
Jenger, Kupelwieser, Bauernfeld, and the rest all took part in
the proceedings.   Pastel sketches by Kupelwieser, drawings
by Schober and the lovely dances "Atzenbrugger Deutschen"
which Schubert's genius supplied for the occasion, as he played
for his friends to dance, tell us of the happy days spent in
Atzenbrugg.

About an expedition to the Wienerwald, Franz von Hartmann, in
his diary, gives the following account :

" Sunday, December, 1826.   At Spaun's, where Gahy played
Schubert's brand new Deutsche (with the title "Hommages aux belles
Viennoises," at which title Schubert is very angry).   Next, breakfast ; then in two carriages, as guests of the Wandrerischen, we drove
off to Nussdorf.   In the first carriage Pepi Spaun, Schubert, Derffel
and Fritz ; in the second Enderes, Spax, Gahy and I.   We had a
magnificent dinner at the very nice and pretty Wandrerischen. . . .
After the meal there arrives the Kurzrock pair and the three
adorers of Frau Kurzrock—Schober, Schwind, Bauernfeld.   The
last two played and sang Schubert's songs deplorably.   Before that
we had danced, and Betty had made herself very charming.   But I
never fall in love.   ' Ich bin nemmer verliebt.'   When all these
afternoon guests had cleared off, we were all very comfortable
again.   Schubert sang splendidly.   I liked especially ' Einsame '
and ' Dürre Blumen ' from the ' Müllerlieder.'   Betty, too, sang
three Müller songs very prettily.   Then Schubert played again and
Gahy.   A great treat.   Then we had all sorts of gymnastics and
drop-the-handkerchief games, and then at last took our leave very
unwillingly.   We drove back in the same order as we came, only
Derffel and Gahy changed places.   At Spaun's we chatted for a
while and went from there two-and-two to the ' Anker,' Fritz and
Max at the head, then Enderes and Gahy, then Schubert and
Pepi Spaun, and, finally, Derffel and I.   Derffel said ' Goodbye ' at

the ' Anker,' but Schober joined us there. I got back my old hat and we passed the rest of the evening in telling stories and anecdotes. At 11.30 all separated in the best of humours and went home to bed."

And we have seen how, in the provincial towns of St. Pölten, Steyr, Linz, Gmunden, Salzburg and Graz, Schubertian communities were formed with which the Viennese friends were in constant intercourse. We remember how Schubert made that Salzburg tour with the great singer Vogl, and paid those happy visits first to the Bishop of St. Pölten's and then under the ægis of his friend Jenger to the Pachler family in Graz. We know how much he was admired and appreciated in these circles of musical enthusiasts; how they sang, danced and flirted round the little great master—in Linz at the house of Spaun's family and Anton Ottenwalt's, and at Gmunden in Traweger's house. We have gathered from his own letters and those of his friends what bright and joyous times those were and what solace they brought to his melancholy spirit.

So the days and years passed quickly away and the gay Schubertians became older, maturer and more staid. Farewell from joyous youth had to be taken. Serious love caught them in its net. One friend after the other, as has been told in another chapter, drifted into the haven of matrimony. Kupelwieser married his Johanna, Spaun, the young assessor, made a home for Franziska Römer, and the ageing Vogl found late in the day domestic bliss with his pupil, Kunigunde Rosa. The last merry farewell " Schubertiades " were held at the wedding festivities of his friends, when the master played while the guests danced. Then came a sudden calm, or rather blank, in the composer's life. The friends were scattered. Schwind went to Munich; Mayrhofer and Sauter became eccentrics, haunted by hallucinations, and withdrew from society; other friends were promoted and became steady officials and secretaries about the Court. Only Schubert remained, the poor musician, without money and unblessed by love, but with his head still teeming with divine melodies. Now were poured forth the " Winterreise," the great C major Symphony, the E flat major Mass, the three last sonatas, and his swan song, the famous settings to the words of Rellstab, Heine, and Seidl.

Then the master fell sick and laid himself on his bed, from which he never rose again.

A dull, rainy November day came. The " Wienerwald " sylphs, to whose voices Schubert in his lonely wanderings had often listened, fled across moor and heath, weeping for their favourite. The last dry, yellow leaves fell from the boughs, and raindrops like tears dripped from the branches of the bare trees. The great, quiet, deserted Wienerwald mourned, and below in the streets of the city the faithful Schubertians followed their adored genius to the grave.

Once more the friends came together and Schober read to them, in a voice moved to emotion, his poem of farewell to the master :

"Peace be with thee, O angel soul and bright,
    In the fresh bloom of all thy youthful breath
    Thou hast been stricken by the dart of death,
That he might mate thee with the purest light,
The light that was a very part of thee,
The spirit, hymned in sacred melody,
That wakened, led thee, set thy soul aflame,
From God alone it came.

Transfigured friend, look down on these my tears,
    The human heart is weak, forgive the pain,
    Ours is the loss, we robbed ones, thine the gain.
From all set free, thou wing'st to other spheres.
Full many a rose thou gav'st the world to guard,
And hast received but sharp thorns in reward.
Long suffering years, a grave beneath the clay ;
There the chains fell away.

And that which thou hast given us to keep,
    The warm love in thy works with pure power mated,
    The holy truth, great and still uncreated,
We'll shut it in our souls, secure and deep.
And what thou wast to Art, who was thy lord,
It is revealed in many a heavenly chord.
And if we follow after that sweet strain,
We shall find thee again."

(*Translated by Ethel Talbot Scheffauer.*)

It was the last " Schubertiade " held in the circle of youthful friends. The blossoms of Vienna's spiritual spring's awakening, the Viennese romanticism, shed their petals and fell asunder. The sun of its genius had set and there were to be no more beautiful and intimate music meetings. The joyous social " Schubertiades " were over for ever. That wonderfully refined soul of old Vienna, with all its gaiety and grace and melancholy charm, was buried in the grave with Schubert.

DATE DUE